David Hume

David Hume

A Skeptic for Conservative Evangelicals

ROBERT CASE

WIPF & STOCK · Eugene, Oregon

DAVID HUME
A Skeptic for Conservative Evangelicals

Copyright © 2021 Robert Case. All rights reserved. Except for brief quotations in critical publications or reviews, no part of this book may be reproduced in any manner without prior written permission from the publisher. Write: Permissions, Wipf and Stock Publishers, 199 W. 8th Ave., Suite 3, Eugene, OR 97401.

Wipf & Stock
An Imprint of Wipf and Stock Publishers
199 W. 8th Ave., Suite 3
Eugene, OR 97401

www.wipfandstock.com

PAPERBACK ISBN: 978-1-6667-0640-6
HARDCOVER ISBN: 978-1-6667-0641-3
EBOOK ISBN: 978-1-6667-0642-0

08/26/21

Scripture quotations are from The Holy Bible, English Standard Version (ESV) copyright ©2001 by Crossway Bibles, a publishing ministry of Good News Publishers. Used by permission. All rights reserved.

Dedicated to the late Peter Manning Burkholder of Central Washington University who, while disagreeing with some of my points, encouraged me to press ahead. Besides being an astonishingly well-read scholar, he was the best department chairman a colleague could have.

Contents

Abbreviations | ix
Preface: A Skeptic for Conservative Evangelicals | xi
Acknowledgments | xix

    Introduction: Meet David Hume | 1
1. Preliminary Considerations about David Hume | 16
2. David Hume's True Philosophy | 42
3. David Hume's Learned Philosophy | 64
4. David Hume's Conversible Philosophy | 93
5. David Hume for Conservative Evangelicals | 128
    A Concluding Observation | 162

Bibliography | 165
Index of Scripture | 177
Index of Names | 181

Abbreviations

T/TM

A Treatise of Human Nature (T), edited by L. A. Selby-Bigge, with an analytical index. Since the Selby-Bigge edition is difficult to obtain, I have also referenced the readily available Penguin edition of the *Treatise* (TM), edited by Ernest C. Mossner.

EU/EM/OC/P

Enquiries Concerning Human Understanding, and Concerning the Principles of Morals (two titles in one volume, but referred to as EU and EM, respectively), edited by L. A. Selby-Bigge and revised by P. H. Nidditch. Since the Selby-Bigge edition is difficult to obtain, I also have referenced the readily available Open Court edition of *An Enquiry Concerning the Principles of Morals* (OC), edited by John B. Stewart, and the readily available Prometheus edition of *An Enquiry Concerning Human Understanding* (P).

WOR

David Hume: Writings on Religion, edited by Antony Flew.

H

The History of England, with the author's last corrections and improvements. 6 vols.

E/LF

Essays, Moral, Political, and Literary (E). I have noted the title of the essay in a footnote. Since the Clarendon volume is out of print, I have also referenced the Liberty Fund (LF) edition of the *Essays,* edited by Eugene F. Miller.

B

Life and Correspondence of David Hume, vol. 1 (B1), by John Hill Burton. "My Own Life" (B2), by David Hume, in *The Life of David Hume,* by Ernest Campbell Mossner. Numerical notations accompany these abbreviations in footnotes and intratextual citations refer to page number.

Preface

A Skeptic for Conservative Evangelicals

"David Hume is the greatest of British philosophers, and his greatness, it is now believed, reveals itself most strikingly . . . when he was twenty-four and [twenty-five]."[1]

DAVID HUME SWAM IN the eighteenth-century philosophic waters created by and dominated by Scottish Presbyterian thought and politics.[2] Hume was a child of Calvinist theology at home, and his Reformed heritage was expressed, however inchoately, in much of what he wrote. Hume's eighteenth-century views on experience, customs, and common life provide a viable social and political framework for American contemporary life. If the New Testament writer Jude marinated his theological thoughts in the midst of the prevailing Jewish culture of his day in order to arrive at the inspired narrative of his little book, and if the American founding fathers can be said to have established a Christian nation, however that is defined, David Hume can be said to have been greatly influenced by the political and theological pieties of John Knox (1513–1572), Samuel Rutherford (1600–1661), and their successors. Indeed, one of the controlling convictions of this book is that the King James Bible of Knox and Rutherford provided an unappreciated philosophic background to much of Hume's political, economic, and social views—thus, the unique extensive footnoting of scriptural passages.[3]

American culture is now in a post-Christian phase in which Judeo-Christian convictions are considered at least irrelevant, if not offensive, in

---

1. Mossner, opening sentence of "Introduction," in Hume, *Treatise of Human Nature*, 7.

2. See Anderson, *Defense of the Church-Government*.

3. Both Knox and Rutherford used a Hebrew/Latin edition, but Rutherford was familiar with the King James English 1611 translation.

the daily discourse of public affairs. Into this secular culture, David Hume (1711–1776) comes as one who ought to receive more study and appreciation from evangelical Christians, for he offers a non-religious-based society as an alternative for securing stable, secure, and satisfying social relationships and structures.

Gertrude Himmelfarb opines that David Hume's ideas do not enjoy the reputation or stature of most of the classical philosophers for good reason.

> [His] works are surely wanting in the profundity and gravity of great philosophy. And the social virtues he esteemed—sympathy, compassion, benevolence—lack the grandeur of the classical virtues: heroism, courage, wisdom. Yet his moral philosophy is deserving of serious consideration and respect.[4]

It is just such soft or social virtues that our post-Christian (or, probably more correctly, post-religion, per Edmund Fawcett) culture needs.

By post-Christian, I mean that ours is a society that has relegated supernatural (revealed, orthodox, biblical) Christianity to the margins of consideration in public and private decision-making.[5] For one to find traditional Christianity a living, vital, dominant influence in one's life is to find oneself out of the mainstream of culture and social life. To the extent that David Hume considered revealed Christianity to be irrelevant to life's decisions and only valuable as a social pacifier, Hume was the first authentic post-Christian philosopher. In a revealing 1761 letter that Hume wrote to the Scottish Enlightenment[6] leader Rev. Dr. Hugh Blair (1718–1800), Hume set forth his terms of conversations with members of the clergy: stay away from the topic of Christianity.[7]

---

4. Himmelfarb, *Roads to Modernity*, 231.

5. In a study of prime-time television programming undertaken by University of Dayton communication professors Thomas Skill and James D. Robinson, it was stated that "Christian leaders were depicted mostly as useless and irrelevant. They aren't portrayed as rogues, and they aren't ridiculed or demeaned, as is sometimes claimed. But their significance is minimized. They're presented as shallow, marginal figures with little influence in life." Skill is quoted as stating that from the way TV portrays religion, "the conclusion would be that religion, religious leaders and their activities are unimportant in society." The report states that religious leaders "are important to their communities and make important contributions to society" (Cornell, "Study Finds TV's Pastor Portrayal").

6. The term Scottish Enlightenment was first coined in 1900 by William Robert Scott to describe the Scottish philosophers, including David Hume, Adam Smith, Thomas Reid, among others.

7. "Whenever I have had the pleasure to be in your company, if the discourse turned upon any common subject of literature, or reasoning, I always parted from you both entertained and instructed. But when the conversation was diverted by you from this

Orthodox Christianity has become a subculture and, increasingly, a counterculture. Alan Gilbert writes that Western society has become "a society where to be irreligious is to be normal, where to think and act in secular terms is to be conventional, where neither status nor respectability depends upon the practice or profession of religious faith."[8] More on our post-Christian culture later.

Garry Wills, in his fine study *Explaining America*, suggests that the ideas contained in Hume's essay "Idea of a Perfect Commonwealth" can be found throughout the writings of the Founding Fathers.[9]

In the *Treatise,* Hume presciently stated, "Generally Speaking, the errors in religion are dangerous; those in philosophy only ridiculous."[10] Given the wars of religion convulsing the world in the 2020s, Hume couldn't have been more right if he were a Presbyterian cleric, which he despised.

My principal objective is to show how Hume's ambassadorial task of straddling the world of the academy and the world of the Main Street is relevant for today's American post-Christian conservative philosophical mindset. David Hume's notion of the power of custom can lead the way to a more secure and stable society. And through it all, Hume was consistently well-mannered and charming, a *bon vivant,* a hail-fellow-well-met. Even when fighting against the prevailing Calvinist culture of his day, Hume was generous in words, thoughtful in attitude, and gracious in action. We conservative evangelicals can take a cue from our Scottish critic.[11]

> I am an American in my Principles and wish we would let them alone to govern or misgovern themselves as they think proper.[12]

---

channel towards the subject of your profession [Christianity]; though I doubt not but your intentions were very friendly towards me, I own I never received the same satisfaction: I was apt to be tired, and you to be angry. I would therefore wish, for the future, wherever my good fortune throws me in your way, that these topics should be forborne between us. I have long since done with all inquiries on such subjects, and am become incapable of instruction" (B2, 117). There is an interesting corollary passage in Hume's *Dialogues Concerning Natural Religion* in which the pietistic Demea, offended by the philosophic betrayal of Philo and tired of the constant debating, decides to leave the group (OC, 276).

8. Gilbert, *Making of Post-Christian Britain*, ix.

9. Wills, *Explaining America*, 256.

10. T, 319. All the more pungent if Stephen Hawking is correct, that "philosophy is dead."

11. Edmund Fawcett, in his mammoth opus on conservatism, wrongly criticizes the great American Calvinist scholar Charles Hodge as being "pessimistic," "strict," bleak," and "impatient."

12. B2, 117.

With these politically incorrect words to the English ear, written in the turmoil of 1775, the Scotsman David Hume became forever an honorary American citizen and should become the "Sage of Ninewells" for all American evangelicals.[13]

Hume wrote reflectively, systematically, and widely, and therefore left a body of substantial work that effectively does combat with the age of rationalism from a secular vantage point. One can find in Hume three basic secular conservative philosophic tenets: 1) subordination of idealist reason to the conserving tonic of experience and sentiment, 2) emphasis on the role of custom in human affairs, and 3) reticence to change existing social conventions. Herein lies the significance for Christians in a post-Christian culture—the value of custom and human tradition over rationalistic utopian governmental schemes. The biblical doctrine of common grace teaches us that the Holy Spirit moves over the nations to work his will and favor in history. Thus, he uses custom, tradition, and habits to stabilize human flourishing. Of course, governmental legislation[14] is needed from time to time to curb human sin, but custom is more lasting and less disruptive.[15]

Hume is as worthy of American evangelical conservative esteem as is Edmund Burke (1729–1797), the godfather of modern conservatives, given the current state of our post-Christian culture in America—perhaps even more so, since Burke thought that American servitude to England could last longer, if negotiated properly.[16] Furthermore, Hume can be of service to religious conservatives, even though he had no use for religious fundamentalists as defined by the secular culture.[17] We evangelicals should dig the man from Ninewells, the Scottish family estate, as a cogent, non-sectarian answer to the liberal, rationalistic, and intrusive government philosophy that if we can think of it, we can implement it. The bedrock of Humean/Burkean conservatism is tradition as it is expressed in the rule of law, which

---

13. See the fine discussion of Hume's American sentiments in Harris's *Hume*, 434ff.

14. Acts 16:37; 19:39; 22:25ff.; 25:11ff.; Gen 47:26; Esth 8:8ff.; Ps 94:20; Dan 6:8, 12, 15.

15. Indeed, to push the argument a bit further, the Princeton Seminary divines of the mid-nineteenth century jumped over their guy, Thomas Reid (1710–1796), to use Humean ideas of custom and social incrementalism to argue against rapid emancipation of slaves until the Civil War. And while William Barker has criticized the deficient theology in the Princetonian approach (Barker, "Social Views of Charles Hodge"), Hume's articulated view of history and tradition is writ large in the Nassau Hall views.

16. 1775 speech to parliament, "Conciliation with the Colonies."

17. Andrew Hoffecker, in his foreword to James Anderson's *David Hume*, writes that "reformed readers . . . will agree that Hume made several valuable contributions" (xv). Hoffecker is referencing certain aspects of Hume's epistemology, but I suggest other aspects are worthy of consideration as well.

recognizes human limitations and imperfections. Hume implicitly understood the fall of Adam. I have sprinkled biblical references throughout the examination of Hume to show the confluence of thought.

The great nineteenth-century Scottish Presbyterian theologian James Orr (1844–1913) and originator of *The Fundamentals*[18] wrote in 1903 that Hume is "far from being obsolete and how imperative is the need of recurrence to his drastic, but at least consistent logic."[19]

Here's to the recurrence of Hume's drasticity.

A word needs to be said about Hume's skepticism concerning both Protestant and Roman Catholic Christianity and the church. While we evangelical conservatives rightly reject Hume's theological epistemology of skepticism, we could make a Humean defense for the church's role in establishing a stable society with rules and beneficial customs. The church confers a certain sacredness on social life in general, but it also acts as a check on the power of the rationalistic state. Hume's focus on experience also played a huge part in his conception of a stable government. Humean conservatives decry the application to society and politics of a mode of thought which is overly abstract, rationalistic, and utterly removed from common experience. Modern political liberals depend on a systematic, universalistic, and reductivist form of reasoning, which fails to account for the complexity and peculiarity of human nature and the institutions they want to transform.[20]

While disagreeing with much of what he had to say, the contemporary French conservative Roman Catholic theocrats[21] would wholeheartedly agree. Indeed, the Irishman Edmund Burke[22] argued for an established church for these very reasons. With an established church, religion becomes

---

18. *The Fundamentals: A Testimony to the Truth* is a twelve-volume set of essays outlining orthodox Christian doctrine from 1910 to 1916. The books contain ninety essays, many by recognized Christian scholars of the day. The essays were written by a wide range of authors, mostly theologians with higher degrees. Many of the authors' names are still recognized for their foundational influences.

19. Orr, *David Hume and his Influence*, 12. Interestingly, Orr's book on Hume, which is 246 pages and is part of the Christian biographical series World Epoch Makers, edited by Oliphant Smeaton, contains no interaction with Scripture.

20. Cf. Muller, *Conservatism*, 14.

21. Louis de Bonald (1754–1840), François-René de Chateaubriand (1768–1848), Joseph de Maistre (1753–1821).

22. While a practicing Protestant thinker, Burke was not theocratic in his political ideas but rather a utilitarian: "The practical consequences of any political tenet go a great way in deciding upon its value. Political problems do not primarily concern truth or falsehood. They relate to good or evil. What in the result is likely to produce evil, is politically false; that which is productive of good, politically is true . . . Nothing universal can be rationally affirmed on any moral or any political subject. Metaphysics cannot live without definition; but prudence is cautious how she defines" (Appeal, 102).

a civil affair, and the British conservative could argue that all societies then have a common essence of value that manifests itself in civil/religious holidays.

But we don't need to argue for an established church. The neo-orthodox New Testament Swiss scholar (but conservative political thinker) Emil Brunner (1889–1966) argued:

> Two things will always distinguish the Christian from a secular revolutionary. First, structural changes will never be given first place because of their ambiguity and ambivalence. Second, the Christian will not be in favour of outward changes before the situation is "ripe" for them.[23]

Many of today's leading secular conservatives share Hume's distrust of Christians who rely on divine revelation for guidance, since such enthusiasts inject personal religious convictions into the public policy debate.[24] Hume dramatically broke with the theocratic political scientists and argued his conservative theory based on the utility of historically developed institutions. There are good reasons to obey government based on historical precedent and not on any divine origins or design (unlike Maistre, who saw God's design in everything). This reliance on divinity is an ill-founded fear, but it does point out Hume's relevance to today's post-Christian conservative political theory.

But more than just criticize, evangelical conservatives should be the most socially, culturally, and politically active of all citizens, since we believe in the unique efficacy of evolving social institutions and conventions to protect the individual and his associations, thus promoting a beneficent society.[25] And as we get involved in our various voluntary factions, society will change and adapt to the majority interest in a democracy. It is at this point that evangelical voters will bring their point of view to the national conversation.

David Hume is enormously relevant, because without resorting to revelation, he prudentially stresses human historical experience as it accrues through individual involvement and development, leading to custom, habit, and convention. It is evident to Hume that only through experience can we receive information about the world, and not through "abstract reasoning

---

23. Brunner, *Christianity and Civilization*, 40. "The principle of tradition is deeply rooted in the Christian conception of life . . . all mankind is bound together with solidarity in creation and sin. In the Christian message history is of capital importance. It is not surprising, then, that tradition is the very essence of the Christian Church" (30–31).

24. Will, *Conservative Sensibility*, 2019.

25. Cf. the Old Testament book of Esther and Jeremiah 29.

or reflection."[26] In short, we evangelicals should have no religious litmus test for our politicians, only an experiential litmus test, which is: Do our politicians respect the beneficial social institutions we have voluntarily created and not work to undo them?

David Hume was part of a massive brain trust in the English-speaking world during the eighteenth century that thought through what a democratic society should look like. Democracy had not been seen in Western civilization for many centuries before the American experiment. Even as the American colonists were laying the groundwork for a new country, their philosophical brethren across the ocean were thinking through the governance of a modern state. Hume can help American evangelical conservatives maintain a stable and free society in which we can flourish, even in our changing world, and thus honor Ceasar and our Lord at the same time.

---

26. T, 69; TM, 117

Acknowledgments

I THANK MY STUDENTS at Central Washington University for enduring my affection for David Hume as I taught classes on empiricism, humanities, and general philosophy to patient young philosophers. Many of these young philosophers were in my required classes under protest, so I endeavored to make the stuff interesting. During my time at Central, I had the benefit of colleagues who encouraged me, but none more so than Rae Heimbeck and Peter Burkholder. Both these men are no longer with us, but their memory is sharp in my mind. Thank you, scholarly endorsers, for cleaning up and sharpening the text.

Introduction
Meet David Hume[1]

HERE IS WHAT THEY said about David Hume. He was:

- the "Socrates of Edinburgh,"[2]
- the "last great English philosopher,"[3]
- the "greatest of all British philosophers,"[4]
- the "most authentic voice of the Enlightenment,"[5]
- the "author of all our subsequent philosophy,"[6]
- and the "model of amiability."[7]

"Davey is a well-meanin' critter, but uncommon[ly] weak-minded." So said Davey's mother when he was just a pre-teen. As it turned out, his mother was a poor judge of her son, for he was to become the strongest

---

1. Critical volumes for Hume's biographical history are the older yet indispensable Ernest Mossner's *Life of David Hume* and the newer work by James A. Harris, *Hume: An Intellectual Biography* (2015).

2. Mossner, *Life of David Hume*, 403.

3. Thomas Hill Green, Introduction to *Treatise of Human Nature*, in Hume, *Philosophic Works*, 1:2.

4. Ayer, *Hume*, 1. "By fairly general consent David Hume is accounted the greatest British philosopher" (Tsanoff, *Great Philosophers*, 375).

5. Mossner, *Life of David Hume*, 4.

6. In 1839, William Hamilton wrote that "Hume . . . is author, in a sort, of all our subsequent philosophy." A. J. Ayer records how the Vienna Circle, in its manifesto of 1929, officially included Hume as a founder: "Those who stand closest to the Vienna Circle in their general outlook are Hume and Mach." Both cited in Livingston and King, eds., *Hume*, 2–3. For confirmation of Ayer's assessment, see Wittgenstein, *Philosophical Investigations*, 113n355.

7. By the amiable conservative atheist, George Will, *Conservative Sensibility*, 479.

intellect in the history of British philosophy, not what you would call weak-minded. And as for being a "well-meanin' critter," her son Davey, while being generally even-tempered, was the most mercilessly destructive of all the British empiricists. He took delight in demolishing the claims of philosophy, theology, and science and destroying the Enlightenment belief in human progress.

Mom should have known better. The Hume (or Home, then) family tradition was steeped in serious, devout Presbyterianism. Mother (Katherine) Home was a pious woman who, at the age of thirty, raised three children after her husband Joseph died in 1713 when David was only two. David Hume's grandfather, Alexander Home of Kennetsidehead, had been hanged at Edinburgh in 1682 as a Covenanter.[8] The Scottish turncoat spy John Macky travelled through Scotland in 1720–1721 in order to report to the English, and he published a diary (*Journey Through Scotland*) in 1723 in which he mentioned the Sabbatarianism of the Scottish Presbyterians:

> Certainly no Nation on Earth observes the Sabbath with that Strictness of Devotion and Resignation to the Will of God: They all pray in their Families before they go to Church, and between Sermons they fast; after Sermon every Body retires to his own Home, and reads some Book of devotion till Supper (which is generally very good on Sundays); after which they sing Psalms till they go to Bed.

Hume's early life was relatively uneventful. He was born in Edinburgh, Scotland, in 1711. He grew up in genteel poverty at the Hume family estate called Ninewells in the Scottish Lowlands, a few miles from the English border. Ninewells is described by a recent biographer of Hume as "the pleasantest place imaginable," situated on a bluff overlooking the rushing waters of the White-Adder River in a breathtaking and storybook landscape of distant mountains, thatched-roof cottages, and sheep and cattle grazing on the surrounding hills.

---

8. The name comes from the Scottish National Covenant of 1638, which bound the signers to keep the Church of Scotland Presbyterian. At the Restoration of the Stuart monarchy in 1660, episcopacy and royal supremacy over the church were re-established, and non-episcopal minsters were fired. A large part of the people in the name of the Covenant refused to attend these church services and attended open air preaching from the deprived Scottish ministers. English King Charles II enforced church attendance by committing cruelties. The Covenanters rebelled and armed themselves. At the decisive battle of Bothwell Bridge in 1672, the Covenanters were defeated by the royal forces. After the defeat, some Covenanters compromised, but others did not and maintained their implacable resistance. The resisters were savagely persecuted by Charles II and James II, especially in the Killing Times of 1684–1688. At the Revolution of 1689, Presbyterianism was restored in the Church of Scotland.

As a young boy, Hume tells us in his biography that he took his family's Calvinism seriously and was prone to soul searching. In fact, he read, digested, and copied the religious practice outlined in Richard Allestree's (1621–1681) famous Calvinistic devotional book *The Whole Duty of Man* (1658), of listing sins in his battle with self and the devil. He was tutored by an uncle, Rev. George Home of Broadhaugh (d. 1755), so he had formal training in the doctrine of the Church of Scotland. Clearly, while young earnest Hume would later reject Christian piety, he did not reject the notion of moral living.

Hume attended the University of Edinburgh for three or four years, leaving before he was sixteen years old without earning a degree. At first he tried to do what his family wished him to do, which was to become a lawyer. But he tells us in his autobiography that while his family thought he was reading law books, he was secretly devouring philosophy.

After three years, during which he was working out his philosophical views while at the same time struggling to keep up with his law studies, he reports that "there opened up to me a new Scene of Thought," which was so exciting that it made him want to give up everything else and devote himself entirely to it. Legal briefs now appeared nauseous to him, and as a result, he promptly abandoned the study of law and the prospects of financial security. For six months, he worked on this "new Scene of Thought" with a sense of discovery and feelings of great jubilation. What was this new scene that filled him with such enthusiasm?

David Hume had discovered the works of Francis Hutcheson (1694–1746), a Scottish moral philosopher at the University of Glasgow, who had argued that moral principles, or our moral beliefs, are not based upon divine revelation, as Christianity claims, nor are they based upon reason, as continental Enlightenment thinkers had said, but only on our feelings, our sentiments of approval or disapproval.[9]

Why not extend this view—that moral beliefs are neither divine nor rational but only expressive of our feelings—to all our beliefs? What if all scientific knowledge is not knowledge at all and has no certainty, has no way of being shown to be certain, but is based only upon the feelings that what the senses give us is true? Then, all the achievements of the great new sciences of astronomy, physics, chemistry, and physiology, all these marvels of the Age of Enlightenment, bite the dust. They are nothing but sentiments or feelings that what we perceive over and over again in orderly fashion is true.

Is it any wonder that after the first flush of excitement, the first gratification of feeling that he was the young David slaying the Goliath of all

---

9. See Haakonssen, "Structure of Hume's Political Theory," 350ff.

science, philosophy, and theology with his slingshot of empiricism that he panicked, overcome by anxiety? In the fall of 1729, when he was only eighteen years old, he had a severe nervous breakdown that lasted for the next five years, manifested in physical symptoms and in feelings of depression and weakness.

Hume wrote in one of his letters, "My disease was a cruel encumbrance to me." His physician told him he had the "disease of the learned": depression, lowness of spirits, the vapors, as it was called at the time. We might say he was in the pits. Hume struggled to read, to write, to think, but he said he was "not able to follow out any train of thought." He complained, "I had no hopes of delivering my opinions with such elegance and neatness as to draw to me the attention of the world." After five years of being in the slough of despond, as John Bunyan would say, Hume decided to give up the life of the mind. He decided that the life of action might be the cure, so he left home and went to La Fleche, a village 150 miles southeast of Paris, the location of Descartes's old Jesuit college (a fact that Hume pointedly ignored). There Hume holed up in a small apartment on a country estate and made use of the college library.

At the end of three years of intensive writing at La Fleche, his first book, the *Treatise of Human Nature,* was almost completed in 1737. He returned to London, edited the manuscript, and arranged for the *Treatise* to be published. He expected the *Treatise* to be hailed immediately as a philosophic masterpiece, but he was bitterly disappointed. The reviews were unfavorable. Few people seemed to have read it; fewer still seemed to have understood it. Hume famously said of the book that "it fell dead-born from the press."

Hume next tried to get a professorship at the University of Edinburgh but was turned down on religious grounds because of his skepticism and his atheistic contempt for Christianity, as well as the coordinated opposition from others who wanted this plum job. Some years later, the University of Glasgow turned him down for the same reasons. Hume was never to become a university professor. In 1748 he published his next major work, *Enquiry Concerning Human Understanding.* In 1762 he finished his massive six-volume *The History of England.*

He supported himself first as a tutor and later as secretary to various wealthy and influential persons, including the British ambassador to France in 1763. By the time Hume went back to France in 1763 as secretary to this ambassador, he was a huge success, feted in Paris as Britain's most brilliant, witty, exciting man of letters. He had fulfilled what he said was his "ruling passion—the love of literary fame." He had at last accomplished what in the depths of his early depression and nervous breakdown he thought he would never be able to do—"draw to himself the attention of the world." But, in his lifetime, his fame came more from his writing his great multi-volume history of Great Britain than from his philosophy.

In 1767 he was appointed by British Prime Minister William Pitt as Under Secretary of State in the Northern Department. Nevertheless, Hume was not happy as a politician and wrote that he was a "Philosopher who degenerated into a Petty Statesman."

As a mature man Hume was described in this way:

> His face was broad and fat, his mouth wide, and without any other expression than that of imbecility. His eyes vacant and spiritless and the corpulence of his whole person was far better fitted to communicate the idea of a turtle-eating alderman than of a refined philosopher. His speech in English was rendered ridiculous by the broadest Scotch accent, and his French was, if possible, still more laughable, so that wisdom never before disguised herself in so uncouth a garb.[10]

English historian Edward Gibbon (1737–1794), lampooned Hume as "the fattest pig in the sty." Despite these unflattering descriptions, Hume became a celebrity, a well-established literary figure as an historian and philosopher.

By the summer of 1776, Hume knew that he was dying, as he had been for some time suffering from the same disease which had killed his mother. Yet he appeared calm and serene, still the witty and urbane conversationalist to all visitors who came to the handsome house that in 1770, at the peak of his fame, he had built in a new section of Edinburgh, on a street which was soon called, in his honor, St. David Street.

Just months before he died, while very sick (like Ulysses S. Grant in 1885), Hume hurriedly wrote a biography, *My Own Life,* in 1775.

Among the distinguished visitors he received was James Boswell (1740–1795), who later became famous as a diarist and as the biographer of Samuel Johnson (1709–1784), the most distinguished literary figure of his time. Boswell was fearful of damnation in hell, subject to periodic attacks of deep depression, and inclined toward religious piety. Boswell had for a long time been repelled and fascinated by Hume's bold attacks upon religious belief and churchgoers. Boswell could not resist the temptation to go to see Hume, the God-denier, on his deathbed, to ask him if he had repented of his blasphemy or if he had changed his mind, perhaps, about denying the immortality of the soul.

Boswell asked Hume, "Don't you believe that there is life after death, that your soul will live on after you are dead?" In apparent ease, with the

---

10. By seventeen-year old James Caulfeild in 1748, who became Lord Charlemont.

humor and irony that had made Hume a celebrity, he replied: "Yes, it is possible that the soul is immortal. It's also possible that if I toss this piece of coal into the flames of that fire, it will not burn. Possible, but there is no basis for believing it—not by reason, and not by sense perception, not by our experience."

On the afternoon of Sunday, August 25, 1776, sixty-five-year-old David Hume died at his home on St. David Street, perhaps of stomach or colon cancer or perhaps of "chronic ulcerative colitis following an acute dysentery" (Mossner).[11]

Always committed to ancient ways and historical precedents, Hume, in his will, left money to repair a lovely and charming old bridge by his ancestral home Ninewells, in a way that did not disturb the old stone quarry that he found so interesting and memorable.

For years after his death, Hume was not allowed to rest in peace because British evangelicals took out their anger with his ideas in public.

Bishop George Horne (1730–1792), president of Magdalen College, Oxford, wrote a public letter to Hume's good friend Adam Smith in 1777 in which he excoriated Hume:

> You talk much, Sir, of our philosopher's [Hume] gentleness of manners, good nature, compassion, generosity, charity. Alas, Sir, whither were they all fled, when he so often sat down calmly and deliberately to obliterate from the hearts of the human species every trace of the knowledge of God and his dispensations; all faith in his kind providence, and fatherly protection; all hope of enjoying his grace and favour, here, or hereafter; all love of him, and of their brethren for his sake; all the patience under tribulation, all the comforts, in time of sorrow, derived from these fruitful and perennial sources? Did a good man think himself able, by the force of metaphysic incantation, in a moment, to blot the sun out of heaven, and dry up every fountain upon earth, would he attempt to do it? Would we know the baneful and pestilential influences of false philosophy on the human heart? We need only contemplate them in this most deplorable influence of Mr. Hume.[12]

---

11. Mossner, *Life of David Hume*, 596. Interestingly, neither Ernest Mossner nor James Harris has much to say about Hume's influence on the contemporaneous thoughts of America's founding fathers. Mossner has only one phrase mentioning James Madison and Hume: "and later influenced the Federalists, especially James Madison, in formulating the guiding philosophy of the American constitution" (269).

12. Horne, *Letter to Adam Smith*.

John Wesley (1703–1791), in a 1790 sermon entitled "The Deceitfulness of the Human Heart," thundered, "Did ever a book so well deserve to be burned by the common hangman, as [Lord Chesterfield's] letters? Did Mr. David Hume, lower, if possible, than either of the former, know the heart of man? No more than a worm or beetle does." Not content with slapping around Hume, Wesley also took Hume's intellectual mentor, Francis Hutcheson, behind the woodshed in the same sermon.

William Agutter (1758–1835), the popular Methodist preacher, in a 1786 sermon entitled "On the Difference between the Deaths of the Righteous and the Wicked, Illustrated in the Instance of Dr. Samuel Johnson and David Hume, Esq.," referred to the widespread report that Hume died unrepentant and arrogantly. He skeptically compared Hume to a criminal about to be punished.[13]

∼

David Hume's multi-volume history of England, published in the late 1750s, was the standard history for a century until Macaulay's multi-volume *History* appeared in the mid-1800s. Scottish Presbyterian theologian James Orr (1844–1913) commented, "It was the first really great *History* of which our language could boast, and there are critics who doubt whether, in certain respects it is not the best still" (1903).[14]

---

13. "The philosophic deist and avowed sceptic and infidel either professes his total ignorance on the subject of futurity, or, if his fears be alarmed or his opinions shaken, he has recourse to the subterfuge of doubts. Irregular passions will make it the interest of reason to question or to deny the reality of another world, and nothing is more easy than to continue ignorant, where we are unwilling to learn, but that conduct which results from voluntary ignorance may be perverse infatuation, but never can be valued as true courage. He who has rushed forward in the dark may stand on the brink of a precipice without feeling emotions of terror and without meriting any tribute of applause. . . . [The situation of] the deist laughing may be illustrated by a criminal who from an habitual course of guilt has attained that total want of reflection which induces him to deride the decision of justice and to undergo his sentence with that stupid indifference which superficial observers may mistake for fortitude. . . . The ostentatious bravery of them so unseasonably displayed may justly be imputed to the delusions of vanity, or the obstinacy of pride."

14. Orr, *David Hume and His Influence*, 227. The Marquis de Sade, when imprisoned in the Bastille by King Louis XVI, brought into his prison cell, among other books, the complete historical works of Hume (Schama, *Citizens*, 391). British Prime Minister William Gladstone (1809–1898) preferred Hume's histories to Gibbon's: "Finish Gibbon, Elegant and acute as he is, he seems to me not so clear, so able, nor so attractive as Hume: does not impress my mind so much." It is a "delightful history, barring the religious principles." Gladstone was a serious and devout Christian and believed that Hume's view of stable government was critical to the spread of Christianity. H. C. G. Matthew writes, "The function of the British constitution was to permit the living of

Hume is credited with awakening from his "dogmatic slumbers" the arguably greatest of the modern philosophers, Immanuel Kant.[15]

"David Hume justly takes rank as the most distinguished member of that brilliant circle of literary men whose names gave such a lustre to the second half of the 18th century in Scotland."[16]

There was more:

- "David Hume is empiricism's 'most brilliant exponent'"—Presbyterian theologian Greg Bahnsen[17]
- "Hume takes his place alongside [Emmanuel] Kant as a major representative of a new direction in Western intellectual culture."—Presbyterian theologian Diogenes Allen[18]
- "Hume was a 'conqueror' of Enlightenment rationalism."—liberal theologian Paul Tillich[19]
- "Hume is regarded as their master by the most advanced physicists of the modern scientific school, so far as their general principles and method of philosophizing are concerned."—Presbyterian theologian Charles Hodge[20]

---

a Christian life; it had no other legitimacy and certainly no natural rights inherent in it. Property, in Gladstone's view, had duties but no absolute rights. Its tenure was a convenient and on the whole beneficial social arrangement which could be changed (Matthew, *Gladstone*, 15, 26). Interestingly, Edmund Burke had been engaged to write a history of England in 1757, but Hume's history was so resoundingly popular that Burke backed away from the project. Burke was "very well acquainted" with Hume, but he was not enthusiastic about the Scotsman.

15. "I openly confess my recollection of David Hume was that very thing which many years ago first interrupted my dogmatic slumber and gave my investigations in the field of speculative philosophy a quite new direction" (Kant, *Prolegomena*, 8).

16. Orr, *David Hume and His Influence*, 1. Harris notes, "Hume's sense of the inferiority of English letters to Scottish caused him to tell Edward Gibbon [in a 1776 letter] that he was surprised that the *Decline and Fall of the Roman Empire* had been written by an Englishman" (Harris, *Hume*, 440).

17. Bahnsen, *Van Til's Apologetics*, 335.

18. Allen, *Philosophy for Understanding Theology*, 202.

19. Tillich, *History of Christian Thought*, 353.

20. Hodge, *Systematic Theology*, 1:253. Charles Hodge is not usually included in any discussion of American political conservatism, but Edmund Fawcett's recent study *Conservatism* (2020) has more on Hodge than on Hume! Fawcett slanders Hodge to make a political point: "A holder of slaves, Hodge took the institution [of slavery] as being biblically justified." In fact, Paul Gutjahr, historian and author of the most current biography of Hodge, *Charles Hodge*, states that Hodge employed one slave laborer (Henrietta) in 1828 and a few years later acquired an enslaved woman, Lena (perhaps

- "Hume has been called the father of modern agnosticism"—Reformed theologian Louis Berkhof[21]
- "The only way to escape David Hume's religious skepticism is to presuppose Christianity as one's worldview"—Presbyterian Cornelius Van Til[22]
- "I don't think it has been sufficiently appreciated that [Nobel-winning economist and darling of conservative free marketers] Milton Friedman is the heir to Hume,"[23] and yet "the greatest of the modern conservative thinkers, Edmund Burke ... detested" Hume—Russell Kirk[24]
- "The writings of David Hume are a watershed in the history of philosophy and theology."—Presbyterian philosopher Ronald Nash[25]

Thelma Z. Lavine (1915–2011), in her widely watched PBS television series (1979) and widely read book (1984), *From Socrates to Sartre: The Philosophic Quest*, states, "In turning to David Hume we are about to encounter the excitement of the most destructive force in the history of Western philosophy."[26]

His dear friend Adam Smith wrote that he "approached as nearly to the idea of a perfectly wise and virtuous man, as perhaps the nature of human frailty will permit."[27] Smith, because of his close friendship with the great skeptic, was appointed, over his objections, to be his literary executor, charged with publishing the *Dialogues*. Smith refused, and ultimately Hume's nephew, David, published the controversial writing. Smith's tribute was his way of easing his conscience. Interestingly for our time of the vitriolic cancel culture by the political and cultural left, Smith would later write

---

as an inheritance from his mother's estate). During the 1830s, Hodge had two other African-American servants, John and Cato, both of which were probably free black wage earners. Thus, there is no evidence that Dr. Hodge engaged in slavery. As time went on, the New Jersey-born and -raised Hodge became a vociferous opponent of slavery.

21. Berkhof, *Systematic Theology*, 31.
22. Van Til's seminary syllabus, chapter 2, noted in Bahnsen's *Van Til's Apologetics*, 78.
23. Kristol, *Neo-Conservatism*, 102.
24. Kirk, *Conservative Mind*, 1, 44. See *The Imaginative Conservative* for more Kirk.
25. Nash, *Faith and Reason*, 226.
26. Lavine, *From Socrates to Sartre*, 130.
27. Letter from Adam Smith to William Strahan, as cited in Hume, *Essays* (Miller), xlix.

that his eulogy "brought upon me ten times more abuse than the very violent attack I had made upon the whole commercial system of Great Britain."[28]

The English Episcopalian Colin Brown, in his indispensable multi-volume *Christianity and Western Thought*, began his chapter on Hume with "Of all the British philosophers, none has been more discussed than David Hume. Certainly, no British philosopher has been more controversial."[29] And from an earlier book, Brown argued that Hume's "historical significance is as a patriarch of modern scepticism."[30]

Hume counted as friend or admirer every great thinker in Great Britain and Continental Europe of his age.

And yet, in his own day his essays were self-censored;[31] he prudently postponed publishing some of his works in his own name (some were not published for almost a century after his death). Because of some of his writings, he could not get a job teaching in his beloved Scotland. He published his first writing after the publishing death of his *Treatise* in 1741 as a collection of essays, which had become the preferred form of literary composition (after magazine publishers Joseph Addison, 1672–1719, and Richard Steele, 1672–1729, made the form popular). Rev. Isaac Watts (1674–1748) was not impressed with the short and shallow essay form that Hume would perfect:

> Now we deal much in Essays, and most unreasonably despise systematic Learning, whereas our Fathers had a just Value for Regularity and Systems; then Folio's and Quarto's were the fashionable Sizes, as Volumes in Octavo are now.[32]

Hume described himself in his own obituary as a "man of mild disposition, of command of temper, of open, social, and cheerful humour, little

---

28. Ross, *Life of Adam Smith*, 339–40.
29. Brown, *From the Ancient World*, 235.
30. Brown, *Philosophy and the Christian Faith*, 73.
31. Mossner notes that Anglican bishop Joseph Butler (1692–1752), author of *Analogy of Religion* (1736), was the one living theologian for whom Hume had intellectual respect. Butler is considered by many to be England's greatest moralist and a preeminent eighteenth century apologist: "Your thoughts and mine agree with respect to Dr. Butler, and I would be glad to be introduced to him. I am at present castrating my work, that is, cutting off its nobler parts; that is, endeavoring it shall give as little offense as possible, before which, I could not pretend to put it into the Doctor's hands. This is a piece of cowardice, for which I blame myself, though I believe none of my friends will blame me. But I was resolved not to be an enthusiast in philosophy, while I was blaming other enthusiasms." Letter to Henry Home, 1737 (B1, 64). Butler equated enthusiasm with fanaticism and told John Wesley (1703–1791) that "enthusiasm is a very horrid thing." Hume would continually equate Protestantism with enthusiasm.
32. Watts, *Logick: Or the Right Use of Reason in the Enquiry after Truth* (1729), 219, as cited in Mossner, *Life of David Hume*, 140.

susceptible of enmity, and of great moderation in all my passions," yet he engaged in an epistolary brawl with the Swiss/French philosopher Jean Jacques Rousseau, which did not adorn his reputation. Hume admired Rousseau's literary skill but detested his ideas.[33] To be fair to Hume, Rousseau was admittedly mentally ill in his later years.[34] Hume said, perhaps ironically, that books of modern philosophy, rooted in rationalism, ought to be burned.[35]

Hume was raised in a Calvinist environment, yet he allowed that orthodox Christianity could be called pernicious, and religious people in general were "monkeys in human shape."[36]

At the same time, he could be warmly gracious in his personal criticism, as witnessed in his essay on Sir Robert Walpole.[37]

---

33. Mossner notes a Hume letter to Mme de Boufflers in which he wrote about Rousseau's writing skills: "All the writings of that author [Rousseau] appear to me admirable, particularly on the head of eloquence; and if I be not much mistaken, he gives to the French tongue an energy, which it scarce seems to have reached in any other hands" (Mossner, *Life of David Hume*, 508). Later, in a letter to Rev. Hugh Blair, Hume wrote of Rousseau, "As he writes and speaks and acts from the Impulse of Genius, more than from the Use of his ordinary Faculties, it is very likely that he forgets its Force, whenever it is laid asleep" (512).

34. Blanchard details Rousseau's relationship with Hume and states, "This letter alone [of eighteen folio pages to Hume in 1776 in which he 'gave vent to all the ruminations of his paranoid ideation and exposed in full the circumstantiality of this thought'], without any supporting testimony, clearly indicates that Rousseau was mentally ill" (Blanchard, *Rousseau*, 209). Other references in this book speak of Rousseau's "delusional system" (221), "diagnosis of paranoia" (227), "sadism and masochism" (227).

35. "If we take in our hand any volume; of divinity or school metaphysics, for instance; let us ask, *Does it contain any abstract reasoning concerning quantity or number?* No. *Does it contain any experimental reasoning concerning matter of fact and existence?* No. Commit it then to the flames: for it can contain nothing but sophistry and illusion" (EU, 165; P, 149).

36. "Examine the religious principles, which have, in fact, prevailed in the world. You will scarcely be persuaded, that they are anything but sick men's dreams: Or perhaps will regard them more as the playsome whimsies of monkeys in human shape" ("Natural History of Religion," in WOR, 181). In his essay "Of Parties in General," Hume referred to the "impudent zeal and bigotry of the first propagators of that sect" (E, 60n; LF, 62n). In his *History*, Hume called Oliver Cromwell a "fanatical hypocrite" (H, 5:58). In a letter to his publisher, Andrew Miller (1755), Hume wrote that he "shall give no farther umbrage to the godly" in publishing considerations (B1, 416).

37. "A Character of Sir Robert Walpole." If only contemporary political discourse were written with his style: "His ministry has been more advantageous to his family than to the public, better for this age than for posterity, and more pernicious by bad precedents than by real grievances. During his time trade has flourished, liberty declined, and learning gone to ruin. As I am a man, I love him; as I am a scholar, I hate him; as I am a BRITON, I calmly wish his fall. As were I a member of either house, I would give my vote for removing him from ST. JAMES'S; but should be glad to see him retire to HOUGHTON-HALL, to pass the remainder of his days in ease and pleasure"

While he loved companionship and fine conversation, he was a cautious bachelor[38] and solitary man.[39]

He loved the Scottish, admired the French,[40] disliked the English, and wanted to be an American.[41] He thought the common individual simpleminded in reasoning ability, rude in manners, and tasteless in artistic

---

(E, 576; LF, 576).

38. In a letter to Dr. John Clephane in 1753, Hume wrote, "What would you have more? A Wife? That is none of the indispensable requisites of life. Books? That *is* one of them; and I have more of them than I can use" (B1, 377). On the other hand, there may have been a love interest between Hume and the Frenchwoman Comtesse De Boufflers, for just days before his death he wrote her a letter in which he stated, "I see death approach gradually, without any anxiety or regret. I salute you, with great affection and regard, for the last time" (B2, 514). Indeed, Ayer states, "She appears for a time to have been in love with Hume, and there is stronger evidence from their correspondence that he was in love with her" ("Hume," 195). Mossner notes a possible love affair with the Frenchwoman Marquise du Deffand and the Scot Nancy Orde, as well as mutual affection for several other ladies. Mossner infers that Hume was, in fact, a ladies' man (*Life of David Hume*, 566–70).

39. "I resolved to make a very rigid frugality supply my deficiency of fortune, to maintain unimpaired my Independency, and to regard every object as contemptible, except the improvement of my talents in literature" ("My Own Life," E/LF, xxxiv).

40. See "Of Civil Liberty," E/LF, 91–92. In a letter to Dr. John Clephane (1756), Hume speaks of the French elegance and then the following, "Were I to change my habitation, I would retire to some provincial town in France, to rifle out my old age, near a warm sun in a good climate, a pleasant country, and amidst a sociable people" (B1, 437). In 1765, Hume wrote a letter to Rev. Hugh Blair praising France and condemning England: "There is a very remarkable difference between London and Paris; of which I gave warning to Helvetius, when he went over lately to England, and of which he told me, on his return, he was fully sensible. If a man has the misfortune, in the former place, to attach himself to letters, even if he succeeds, I know not with whom he is to live, nor how he is to pass his time in a suitable society. The little company there that is worth conversing with, are cold and unsociable; or are warmed only by faction and cabal; so that a man who plays no part in public affairs becomes altogether insignificant; and, if he is not rich, he becomes even contemptible. Hence that nation is relapsing fast into the deepest stupidity and ignorance. But, in Paris, a man that distinguishes himself in letters, meets immediately with regard and attention" (B2, 268). Mossner notes that Voltaire called Hume "St. David" (*Life of David Hume*, 566).

41. Hume made the ludicrous comment that a certain author "corrupted his taste by the imitation of Shakspere," whose stage plays Hume called "barbarism" (letter to Joseph Spence, 1774, B1, 392). In two letters to Sir Gilbert Elliot (1769, 1770), Hume commented on the English, "I am delighted to see the daily and hourly progress of madness, and folly, and wickedness in England. The consummation of these qualities are the true ingredients for making a fine narrative in history, especially if followed by some signal and ruinous convulsion-as I hope will soon be the case with that pernicious people"! And, "Our government has become a chimera, and is too perfect, in point of liberty, for so rude a beast as an Englishman; who is a man, a bad animal too, corrupted by above a century of licentiousness" (B2, 431, 434).

expressions, called the common man vulgar or illiterate in classical learning.⁴² Regrettably, Hume held that males were superior to females and whites to non-whites.⁴³ Experience would teach him otherwise.

He wrote fluidly on economics, politics, population, immigration, sociology, psychology, banking, money, trade, commerce, labor, work, the performing arts, the press, religion and metaphysics,⁴⁴ industry, manufacturing, and numerous other subjects. He was astonishingly well-read, his opinions were well formulated, and much of his writing is as fresh and lucid today as it was 250 years ago. John Frame, in his magisterial history of Western philosophy, concurred with this assessment when he wrote that despite major weaknesses of Hume's philosophy, Frame considered the Scotsman "to be the clearest and the most cogent" philosophy of the modern philosophers.⁴⁵

---

42. EU, 161; P, 145.

43. "Of National Characters," E/LF, 208. In a footnote, Hume writes, "I am apt to suspect the negroes to be naturally inferior to the whites. There scarcely ever was a civilized nation of that complexion, nor even any individual eminent either in action of speculation. No ingenious manufactures amongst them, no arts, no sciences. Such a uniform and constant difference (between 'Germany' and 'southern people') could not happen, in so many countries and ages, if nature had not made an original distinction between these breeds of men." Martin Bernal, in *Fabrication of Ancient Greece*, argues that "most eighteenth century English speaking thinkers like David Hume were racists: They openly expressed popular opinions that dark skin colour was linked to moral and mental inferiority." Bernal argues that the above Humean quote "pioneered the view that there had been not one creation of man but many different ones" (203). I suspect that Hume thought the disparity in the races was due to external factors such as climate, topography, and history. Francis Williams was the black Jamaican poet to whom Hume referred as being "admired for very slender accomplishments, like a parrot who speaks a few words plainly" (Carretta, "Who Was Francis Williams?," 213). I would add that the overwhelming mindset of Europeans in the eighteenth century would agree with Hume, which doesn't make him right, but it does make him conventional. In this context, it should not be forgotten that Hume was a mild-mannered apostle of reason and humane sentiments. His common-sense approach to life contrasted deeply with the French Enlightenment love of the guillotine. Sadly, the Scottish cancel culture descended on Hume in 2020, and David Hume Tower at the University of Edinburgh has been renamed "40 George Square" for this one short footnote in one of his essays. It didn't make any difference to the Edinburgh morons that Hume called slavery "barbarous." Francis Williams himself owned slaves and is not recorded as opposing the slave trade or advocating abolition of the odious trade.

44. Numerous essays, including "Of Superstition and Enthusiasm," "A Note on the Profession of Priest," "Of the Immortality of the Soul," "Of Miracles," "The Natural History of Religion," "Dialogue Concerning Natural Religion."

45. Frame, *History of Western Philosophy*, 204.

Hume maintained that the American colonies were unjustly enslaved to England and rooted for our independence.[46] American evangelical Christians should dust off old Davey, claim him as a proud American, and see if his philosophy can be of assistance to Christian evangelical political conservatives today.

In chapter one, I will state my basic assumptions in approaching David Hume's philosophy as it relates to an evangelical approach to a pluralistic and secular social and political environment in a post-Christian culture.[47] Charles Taylor, in his massive study of secularism, has posited that there are three conditions of intellectual belief in the history of the Western world:

1. Pre-enlightenment or the enchanted phase, where Christianity was the DNA of Western culture,

2. Post-enlightenment, where Christianity was an option of faith in our Western culture,

3. Modernity, where Christian faith was impossible to sustain in our Western culture.

---

46. Hume's view of colonial America can, perhaps, be best seen in a summer 1775 correspondence between himself and William Strahan. Hume wrote, "Arbitrary power can extend its oppressive arm to the antipodes, but a limited government can never be upheld at a distance even where no disgusts have intervened: much less where violent animosities have taken place. We must therefore annul all the charters; abolish every democratical power in every colony; repeal the Habeas Corpus Act with regard to these; invest every governor with full discretionary powers; confiscate the estates of the chief planters; and hang three fourths of the clergy. [We must] lay aside all anger, shake hands, and part friends. Or if we retain our anger let it be only against ourselves for our past folly; and against that wicked madman Pitt, who has reduced us to our present condition." Strahan responded, "I differ from you *toto coelo* with regard to America. I am entirely for coercive methods with those obstinate madmen. I see nothing so very formidable in this business, if we become a little more unanimous, and could stop the mouths of domestic traitors, from whence the evil originated. Not that I wish to enslave the colonists, or to make them one job less happy than ourselves; but I am for keeping them subordinate to the British legislature; and their trade, in a reasonable degree, subservient to the interest of the mother country; an advantage she well deserves; but which she must inevitable lose, if they are emancipated, as you propose. I am really surprised you are of a different opinion" (B2, 477–78).

47. Much has been written about the secular or post-Christian society. The one indispensable study is Charles Taylor's *A Secular Age* (2007), but before Taylor there was Philip Hughes's *Christian Ethics in Secular Society* (1983), Carl F. H. Henry's massive, six-volume *God, Revelation and Authority* (1976), Grenz and Olson's *Twentieth Century Theology* (1992), Herbert Schlossberg's *Idols for Destruction* (1983), and David Wells's *God in the Wasteland* (1994) and *No Place for Truth* (1993). The situation is no better in Christian colleges, as James Davison Hunter has pointed out in his *Evangelicalism* (1993) and Naomi Schaeffer Riley in *God on the Quad* (2005).

In chapter two, I will discuss Hume's goal of doing true philosophy rather than false.[48] That is to say, I will try to explain what Hume's intention was in engaging in the philosophic enterprise at all.

In chapter three, I will briefly discuss the major tenets of Hume's learned philosophy.

In chapter four, I will be looking at Hume's conversible[49] application of his philosophic system to the culture:

> The Operations of the Mind may be divided into the learned and the conversible. The Learned are such as have chosen for their Portion the higher and more difficult Operations of the Mind, which require Leisure and Solitude, and cannot be brought to perfection, without long Preparation and severe Labour. The conversible World [have] a Taste of Pleasure, an Inclination to the easier and more gentle Exercises of the Understanding, to obvious Reflection on human Affairs and the Duties of common Life, and to the Observation of the Blemishes or Perfections of the particular Objects, that surround them.[50]

In chapter five, I will offer some conclusions and describe some possible applications to our present-day culture. I will begin with Hume's purpose, follow with a brief look at his epistemology and his moral theory (which leads to his theory of justice), and end with his political and social theory, focused on aspects of our current scene.

My emphasis is not on epistemology, moral theory, economics, or politics per se, but only as they apply to a general philosophy of culture. This is not to suggest that these were inconsequential subjects for Hume. On the contrary, he developed a well-thought-out system of economics and politics. My decision not to consider these topics in detail is a function of personal interest. Consequently, there is much about Hume's conversible philosophy that I will not be analyzing.

---

48. From time to time, Hume used the term vulgar to describe false philosophy, which was thinking generated by the common people or the general public.
49. That is, being able to be converted or applied or transposed.
50. "Of Essay Writing." E/LF, 533–34.

1

Preliminary Considerations about David Hume

In the age of Obama/Trump/Biden, political conservatism is in disarray. Conservative ideas are not being discussed at the highest level. When they are being discussed at any level, there is little seriousness about the discussion. Thus, a refresher course on the contribution of David Hume to American political thought is necessary.

It may be instructive to note how the term conservatism relates to the political order. The term is introduced into the English lexicon in 1830 by the Irish politician John Wilson Crocker (1780-1857) in an article entitled "International Policy" in the prestigious journal, *Quarterly Review*. He applied the term to the Tories, labeling them the Conservative Party. In France, the term was introduced into the political discourse by the theocrats Louis de Bonald (1754-1840) and François-René de Chateaubriand (1768-1848) in 1818 with their weekly journal *Le Conservateur*, which argued for "religion, the king, liberty, and Charter and respectable people." Bonald would emphasize obligations to God and to one's fathers. Both Bonald and Chateaubriand were serious Roman Catholics who followed Thomas Aquinas[1] in basing their theocratic political thought on the teachings of the church.

---

1. Aquinas based his political thought on the proposition that "since the beatitude of heaven is the end of that virtuous life which we live at present, it pertains to the king's office to promote the good life of the multitude in such a way as to make it suitable for the attainment of heavenly happiness, that is to say, the king should command those things which lead to the happiness of heaven and, as far as possible, forbid the contrary" (*On Kingship*, 4, 1, 15). Twentieth-century Thomist political conservatives include Jacques Maritain (1882-1973), Christopher Dawson (1889-1970), and Hilaire Belloc

For David Hume, social arrangements (i.e., institutions) become customary or habitual through usage. The conservative, on one hand, wants the government to strengthen and preserve these voluntary social institutions, since, by virtue of their custom and historicity, they are better adapted than anything else to provide satisfaction for the individual member of society. These voluntary associations (e.g., Rotary, church, social clubs, Chamber of Commerce, United Way, political parties, etc.) are natural, reasonable, and good.

The modern state, on the other hand, wants to annul the rights of every institution and association, except individual rights, because it cannot abide divided loyalties of the citizenry. As George Will has written,

> The Founders aimed to limit government by means of an institutional architecture of separated and rival powers in order to keep government on a short constitutional leash. The modern problem, Woodrow Wilson thought, was to unleash government so that it could be a properly efficient servant of the will of a harmonious people. It is telling that what Wilson hoped for in a government was "wieldiness." Who is to wield it? Experts.[2]

The danger of this massive attack on social conventions and institutions by the modern state is that it leaves the individual socially and politically naked in the face of an all-powerful, coercive, and jealous state apparatus. A coercive and jealous state is not a modern concept, since Samuel warned the Israelites against having a king a thousand years before Christ.[3]

Humean conservatism implies that freedom and equality are incompatible. The chief purpose of liberty is the protection of individual and family property, both material and immaterial, whereas the chief purpose of equality is that of redistribution of unequally gathered property and the juridical leveling of diverse contributions, which cripples the liberties of society's most productive and brightest members.[4]

Any society that fosters Humean customs and conventions also fosters traditions of artistic creativity, intellectual genius, and religious worship. Hume's society can be one that celebrates life that arises out of the age-old traditions or even the murky depths of religious faith—in other words, a society that celebrates idiosyncrasy, eccentricity, and non-conformity.

(1870–1953). Protestant ecclesiastical conservatives include Hugh Cecil (1869–1956), T. S. Eliot (1889–1965), and, interestingly for evangelicals, the Swiss neo-orthodox theologian Emil Brunner (1889–1966).

2. Will, *Conservative Sensibility*, 74.
3. Cf. 1 Sam. 8:10–18.
4. Cf. Matt 25, parable of the talents.

Social conventions and institutions provide the best counterforce to the hyper-individualism of the rights talk emphasis fostered by the liberal rationalistic state. Relying on the past for social inspiration and models readily brings the liberal reproach of reactionary, and fittingly and wonderfully so. For it is out of the rich history of human associations that Hume points us to the social institutions that resist the tide of naked individualism or overweening government. Indeed, we evangelical conservatives should embrace the term reactionary as an approbation, for we do react to untested rationalism in public policy. But we revel in our historical stream of human experience and relations, all under the developing guidance of our sovereign God. Christians believe in the biblical concept of the progressive movement of God's providence in history. We hold to the providential development of human civilization over time. Calvinism is a reforming theology within biblical revelation, conducive for understanding and appreciating Hume's ideas.

It is not politically profitable for the evangelical conservatives in the United States to neglect David Hume's contribution to an articulated philosophic and political conservatism that opposes the rationalized state or a theological political science.

Hume's emphasis on the value of convention and custom, expressed in voluntary social institutions that convey the social arrangement that arises from human nature or natural dispositions of mankind or natural principles,[5] is important. It is only through felicitous social arrangements that the individual's rights can be preserved. When conservatives stress Lockean individual and autonomous rights, we play into the statists' hand by eviscerating the protection which these agreeable social arrangements provide for the individual in the face of an all-powerful, aggrandizing modern rational Leviathan—the ultra-Hobbesian-Obama state, the armed, locked, and loaded crown (national government).

For Christian political conservatives, the need for strong intermediate social institutions (e.g., families, churches, schools, unions, trade associations, and clubs) is great, because they are the only things that can stand with cultural authority and autonomy against the presence of a strong, centralized, rationalized, and jealous government. Hume gives us the philosophic and prudential structure for such social protection for the individual and is perhaps part of the solution to Robert Putnam's warning that we are a nation that now likes to "bowl alone" in the loss of American community.[6]

---

5. Hutcheson, *Essay on the Nature*, 72, 75.
6. Putnam, *Bowling Alone*.

David Hume's insistence that personal identity is formed in the crucible of personal history, and that we know ourselves as we experience the world around us and our reaction to that world, can be a basis for the conservative view that we are what history makes us.

Conservatives must criticize abstract rationalists and their public policy formulations for subverting social habits, traditions, and institutions. In order to sustain civilization, we must be able not only to distinguish between good and bad, but also to cultivate a disposition to do good rather than bad. While many social conservatives properly look to Judeo-Christian teaching for that guidance, we ought, in an increasingly post-Christian age, leave open the option of looking to human experience as well. I have used this term post-Christian several times, and I need to defend my use of it.

There is a movement called theology of secularization which, in the words of John Frame, argues that we should "accept the development towards secularization" because it "affirms creation as something distinct from God, and man as its lord. The church should be understood in terms of the world, religion in terms of the profane, rather than vice versa."[7]

Note some representative observations and cultural expressions that that tend to confirm this interpretation of American contemporary life as post-Christian. I suspect Wells would have understood the attraction of the supernaturally themed Harry Potter books to today's millennials.

Theologian and activist Francis Schaeffer, whose influence with evangelical Protestant thinkers in the last third of the twentieth century is second only to that of C. S. Lewis,[8] writes, "Ours is a post-Christian world in which

---

7. Frame, *History of Western Philosophy*, 426. Note also Gutiérrez, *A Theology of Liberation*, and Cox, *Religion in the Secular City*. David Wells also applies the secular mindset to the church, but in his case, from a Reformed evangelical perspective: "What is external and sociological I have called *secularization*; what is internal and ideological I have called *secularism*. From the one perspective, what I am describing is the outlook and the values that arise in a society that is no longer taking its bearings from a transcendent order; from the other perspective, what I am describing is the track that modernization has taken within the human spirit in producing and authenticating contemporary values . . . among evangelicals, secularization has taken its toll on the their world, as well. Religious though they may be, evangelicals have found it difficult to think that God is working out his sovereign purposes in modern society. Secularism has flattened what is spiritual in society and, often, what is spiritual in the church. It has drained the human spirit, Christian and otherwise, of its capacity, as well as its need, to understand itself against the backdrop of what is eternal. Even among Christians, these secular habits of thought have become so ingrained as categories for evaluating the meaning of modern life, and distinctions between Good and Evil have become so remote" that supernatural themed novels "constitute an attempt to retrieve the lost understanding of God's providential presence in our world" (*God in the Wasteland*, 156, 180).

8. See Neuhaus's evaluation of Schaeffer in "Word on 'The Competition.'"

Christianity, not only in the number of Christians but in cultural emphasis and cultural results, is no longer the consensus or ethos of our society." He gives the major theological tenets of a post-Christian consensus as:

> the denial of the supernatural; belief in the all-sufficiency of human reason; the rejection of the fall; denial of the deity of Christ and his resurrection; belief in the perfectibility of Man; and the destruction of the Bible.

Schaeffer then remarks that "with this has come a nearly total moral breakdown.[9]

> Secularists' ruling assumption is man's independence—his capacity to understand and transform institutions as if human being were free of inherent evil and could build a just society without divine assistance. Ethicists consider human beings to be morally autonomous.[10]

David Hume did not believe in the fall of Adam and therefore the basic sinfulness of the individual. Rather, he argued that we do not inherently seek power and self-interest like Thomas Hobbes (1588–1679) maintained. Bluntly put, we Humean humans are born good and strive to be good throughout our lives.[11] This was not a very popular opinion in the Church of Scotland.[12]

James Hitchcock, professor of history at St. Louis University and a Roman Catholic, has written astutely of the secularism of contemporary America:

> The final stage of the [post-Christian society] is the media's exploitation of traditional American sympathy for the underdog. Judeo-Christian morality, although eroding for a long time and on the defensive almost everywhere in the Western world, is presented as a powerful, dominant, and even tyrannical system against which only a few brave souls make a heroic stand on behalf of freedom. Thus, secularists of all kinds and those who

---

9. Schaeffer, *Great Evangelical Disaster*, 29, 35–36.
10. Hoffecker, *Universe, Society, and Ethics*, xvii.
11. Hume, *Treatise on Human Nature*, book 3, part 2.
12. However, Hume was no atheist, maybe an agnostic, probably a deist. As Himmelfarb points out, "It was for good reason that the philosophes found Hume insufficiently atheistic" (Himmelfarb, *Roads to Modernity*, 39). Hume believed in the established church, particularly the Church of Scotland. He argued that Christianity had a salutary effect on people's lives and that "there must be an ecclesiastical order and a public establishment of religion in every civilized community" (H, 3:134–35).

deny traditional morality in words and behaviour are treated as heroes by the media.[13]

Mark Noll, in his seminal study, *A History of Christianity in the United States and Canada,* has concluded:

> Since World War II, the changes that have most significantly shaped North American culture have stressed technology instead of morality, personal enrichment instead of altruistic service, and the potential for individual development instead of the force of historical traditions. These secularizing forces have had a variety of effects.[14]

Peter Berger, Boston University sociologist, has written that the secularism of the post-Christian age is thoroughly evident in all aspects of our society:

> It affects the totality of cultural life and of ideation and may be observed in the decline of religious content in the arts, in philosophy, in literature and, most important of all, in the rise of science as an autonomous, thoroughly secular perspective on the world. Moreover, it is implied here that the process of secularization has a subjective side as well. As there is a secularization of society and culture, so is there a secularization of consciousness. Put simply, this means that the modern West has produced an increasing number of individuals who look upon the world and their own lives without the benefit of religious interpretation.[15]

There will be no peace between the ideas of biblical Christianity and the ideas of post-Christianity. Instead, there will be perpetual war and ideological conflict:

> Post-Christian paganism will always burn with a deadly hostility to the Galilean, because it was from him that it received its stigma, and never again can it face him with disinterested tolerance.[16]

Carl F. H. Henry, the dean of American evangelical theologians for the last half of the twentieth century, has enunciated certain social and philosophic features of America's post-Christian civilization:

---

13. Hitchcock, *What Is Secular Humanism?,* 84.
14. Noll, *History of Christianity,* 548.
15. Berger, *Sacred Canopy,* 107–8.
16. Thielicke, *Nihilism,* 94.

These factors—the extensive loss of God through a commanding spread of atheism, the collapse of modern philosophical supports for human rights, the brutish dehumanization of life which beyond abortion and terrorism could encourage also a future acceptance even of nuclear war, and a striking shift of sexual behavior that welcomes not only divorce and infidelity but devious alternatives to monogamous marriage as well—attest that radical secularism grips the life of Western man more firmly than at any time since the pre-Christian pagan era.[17]

Further evidence of our current post-Christian tendencies is given by William Johnson of Austin Presbyterian Theological Seminary, who reports that even some theologians are advocating a post-Christian concept of God:

Whereas earlier theologies, especially in the nineteenth century, virtually equated the reign of God with Western "progress," today our Western way of life seems to many to be an impediment to true progress as industrialization, consumerism, and technology pose a threat to Earth itself. This post-modern view of history has, in turn, led some theologians to an increasingly "post-Christian" view of God. These theologians see it as necessary to eliminate the worn-out belief in a sovereign but disaffected deity at work in human affairs. Such a portrait of God, they charge, has been used to rationalize the rankest sort of subjugation (Johnson's emphasis), with the reign of God being invoked to justify the ethnocentric proclivities of a privileged "us" against a reprobate "them" rather than the theocentric concern of Jesus Christ for the world-encompassing agenda of God.[18]

This post-Christian interpretation of subjugation finds expression in the writings of the influential liberal legal theorist Professor Laurence Tribe of Harvard. In 1988, Tribe, in his *American Constitutional Law*, interpreted the U. S. Constitution as containing what he called an "anti-subjugation principle," which Tribe maintains can be used to "break down legally created or legally reenforced systems of subordination that treat some people as second-class citizens."[19]

---

17. Henry, *Twilight of a Great Civilization*, 27. Among the many evangelical thinkers writing on this subject, the following have been found to be particularly noteworthy: Charles Colson, *Against the Night*; Os Guinness, *Gravedigger File*; Os Guinness, *Dust of Death*; Os Guinness, *American Hour*; Richard John Neuhaus, *Naked Public Square*; and Peter Jones, *Gnostic Empire Strikes Back*.

18. Johnson, "Reign of God," 128. Also writing from this perspective is David Ray Griffin, *God and Religion*.

19. Robert Bork sees this legal discovery as "unduly sweeping" since it makes the

Consider also the U. S. Supreme Court decision of June 1, 1993, upholding a lower court's ruling on the validity of reciting the Pledge of Allegiance in public schools.[20] An Illinois family challenged this civic ritual on the grounds that the phrase "one nation under God" was a violation of the First Amendment clause prohibiting the establishment of a religion. The Court stated that the contested phrase is "now understood as a form of ceremonial deism that has lost, through rote repetition, any significant content."[21] In other words, because the name God is culturally irrelevant, religiously impotent, and essentially meaningless, it is now permitted in cultural institutional discourse. The Court's reasoning, welcomed by many conservatives, impressively affirms the secular faith that presently predominates in our culture.[22]

David Ray Griffin, Claremont University professor of religion and a defender of the progress of post-Christian thinking, has noted that the revealed Christian worldview has fallen on hard times in academic circles:

> Having been the "queen of the sciences" in the Middle Ages, theology is now not generally counted among the intellectually respectable disciplines. A leading biologist [Stephen Jay Gould] jokes that only theology may exceed exobiology (the study of extraterrestrial life) in being a "great subject without a subject matter." The reference on an editorial page to an argument as "theological" usually means that the proponent defends a faith-commitment in the face of overwhelming disconfirming evidence, employs meaningless distinctions, or both.[23]

Constitution "apply to much private action, although it explicitly applies only to action by government" (*Tempting of America*, 202). The Tribe material comes from Bork, 199–206.

20. Robert Sherman vs. Community Consolidated School District 21 of Wheeling Township, IL. From US Court of Appeals, District 7, Docket No. 91–1684.

21. There is the argument made by such scholars as the late Harold O. J. Brown that since America was founded by deists, it could therefore be described as post-Christian from its inception. See Brown's *Reconstruction of the Republic*. Brown is more comfortable with biblical foundations than with Christian foundations for America's fundamental heritage.

22. See commentary in McAuliffe, "Secular Pluralism," 5–6.

23. Griffin, *God and Religion*, 1. Griffin writes, "[Theology] is now not generally counted among the intellectually respectable disciplines." He notes also that Richard Rorty once wrote that fortunately there was a period in our intellectual history "when religious intuitions were weeded out from among the intellectually respectable candidates for Philosophical articulation" and that, as a result, we are now freed from religious intuitionism (147n1). Griffin is citing Rorty's *Consequences of Pragmatism* (Minneapolis: University of Minnesota Press, 1982), xxxviii.

From a dispassionate observer of modern, secularized culture we have the views of Stanford sociologist Anthony Giddens. He notes that modernity makes both religion and tradition somewhat outdated:

> Most of the situations of modern social life are manifestly incompatible with religion as a pervasive influence upon day-to-day life. Religious cosmology is supplanted by reflexively organized knowledge, governed by empirical observation and logical thought, and focused upon material technology and socially applied codes. Religion and tradition were always closely linked, and the latter is even more thoroughly undermined than the former by the reflexivity of modern social life, which stands in direct opposition to it.[24]

Gidden's view would strike at Hume as well as the Scottish Presbyterian church, since Hume was an upholder of tradition. However, it is part of my thinking, contrary to Gidden's position, that Hume's philosophy can enable us to retain tradition, even if Christianity truly is waning. Interestingly, the term empiricist to describe Hume was not commonplace until long after Hume's death.[25]

All the foregoing manifestations of post-Christianity and reports of its influence have direct relevance to David Hume, since a major area that is immediately impacted by this secular sea change in ideology is that of social and cultural institutions and conventions. Harvey Cox, of Harvard Divinity School, wrote in 1964 that social institutions (e.g., churches, politics, universities, workplaces, etc.) have been gradually freeing themselves from religious control and influence for decades and have come into their own autonomy and inherent *raison d'être*. Cox argues that, as a result of widespread acceptance of the Enlightenment concept of a secular realm alongside the sacred realm, social institutions and ordinary life (Hume's common life) have been desacralized by a secular mode of existence. Cox claims this liberation is a desirable thing, since all the religious encumbrances of the past have been stripped away by our "secular mood" and we are now free to choose for ourselves.[26] This theme of the secularization of American life has more recently been picked up by Canadian philosopher Charles Taylor.[27]

---

24. Giddens, *Consequences of Modernity*, 109.

25. Brown, *From the Ancient World*, 215.

26. Cox, *Secular City*, 18–21. Cox writes, "Secularization implies a historical process, almost certainly irreversible, in which society and culture are delivered from tutelage to religious control and closed metaphysical world views. We are arguing that it is basically a liberating development" (20).

27. Taylor, *A Secular Age*.

I believe the verdict is in, and Cox and Taylor are correct: ordinary life in America can be characterized as post-Christian.

As for Hume's philosophical development, as a young man he discovered the works of Cicero, Seneca, and Plutarch. The latter posited that morality is based on our feelings or sentiments of approval or disapproval, not on religion or reason. Hume's intellectual journey through these thinkers was a personal philosophic awakening. He reported enthusiastically to Francis Hutcheson that the journey "opened up to me a new Scene of Thought."[28]

Hume based his entire body of work on the premise that the only true philosophic life was one in which the philosopher "lived," "talked," and "act[ed] like other people in the common affairs of life."[29] As he eloquently urged in the second *Enquiry*, "philosophical decisions are nothing but the reflections of common life, methodized and corrected."[30] From this premise is derived what Norman Kemp Smith has called the central theme of Hume's teaching: "the doctrine that the determining influence in human . . . life is feeling, not reason or understanding."[31]

Hume wrote that his common-life philosophy is true philosophy, since it conforms to what is. Any philosophy worthy of the name true philosophy must be based in ordinary, common experiences and impressions, i.e., the individual men and women engaged in "this commerce [true philosophy] must chiefly be furnished by conversation and common life."[32] True philosophy is genuine and authentic, since it matches what really goes on in the world of social involvements. False philosophy is alienated from common life, because it is based on abstract, autonomous rational principles: "speculations without the sphere of common life."[33] Unhinged from common life, false philosophy, flying under the color of rationalism, pretentiously judges, examines, and attempts to validate all thought. Hume called this the "fallaciousness and imbecility of reason."[34]

Emil Brunner, in Humean conservative fashion, writes,

---

28. Ironically, Hutcheson opposed Hume's appointment to the chair of Ethics and Pneumatic Philosophy in the University of Edinburgh as being "a very unfit person for such an office" (Hume's 1742 letter to William Mure [1718–1776], B2, 167). Mossner, *Life of David Hume*, 65.

29. T, 269; TM, 316.

30. EU, 162; P, 146.

31. Smith, *Philosophy of David Hume*, 11.

32. E/LF, 535, 570.

33. T, 271; TM, 318.

34. T, 186; TM, 237.

Tradition is not merely keeping alive the spiritual heritage of the past. Even more important, because more closely connected with the personal and social character of man, is the continuity of social values, such as custom, law, civil institutions, family tradition, public spirit and virtue. . . . Tradition is social rootedness, living togetherness, on the basis of common history, of family acquaintance through many generations. Tradition is for men in general what the house of the parents is for the child.[35]

Hume wrote in an essay: "But however intricate they may seem, it is certain, that general principles, if just and sound, must always prevail in the general course of things, though they may fail in particular cases; and it is the chief business of philosophers to regard the general course of things."[36] The devil is in the details, because that is where the application must be made.

In another essay, Hume tied the structure and functioning of society directly to principles enunciated in speculative philosophic, reasoning: "No party, in the present age, can well support itself without a philosophical or speculative system of principles annexed to its political or practical one."[37] It was in this "regarding the general course of things" that Hume fancied himself as a philosophic ambassador. He was to be the ambassador of true philosophy, having one foot in the philosopher's (the learned person's) court, and the other foot in the common person's (the conversible world's) court.[38] Mossner held that Hume's later essays are to be "regarded as a literary experiment towards the possible recasting of the philosophy of the ill-fated *Treatise*. Having failed to reach the public in a more learned form, perhaps he could do better in a more popular form."[39] And boy, did he become popular!

My conclusion is that Hume deserves recognition in today's marketplace of ideas as a premier philosopher whose ideas should be considered deferentially by evangelicals in a secular and hostile society. Hume offers a cogent system of thought that can be employed to maintain a national set of values and social culture that has enjoyed the affirmation of time. We are in

---

35. Brunner, *Christianity and Civilization*, 32–33.
36. "Of Commerce," E/LF, 254, 260.
37. "Of the Original Contract," E/LF 452, 465.
38. "I cannot but consider myself as a kind of resident or ambassador from the dominions of learning to those of conversation, and shall think it my constant duty to promote a good correspondence betwixt these two states, which have so great a dependence on each other" ("Of Essay Writing," E/LF, 533–35).
39. Mossner, *Life of David Hume*, 139.

a post-Christian[40] or secular culture[41] or culture of disbelief[42] in America, and Hume offers compelling philosophic argumentation that can be used in defense of a conservative cultural agenda that will sustain our unique and salutary American way of life.[43]

Before I get too far along with Hume, it needs to be said that when Hume speaks of Protestant Christianity, he uses the then common term enthusiasm to differentiate Scottish Presbyterianism from Roman Catholicism. So enthusiasm is the dog whistle for me as an evangelical Presbyterian to pay attention. The critique of religious enthusiasm was central to Hume's conservatism, far more central than a critique of Thomistic theory of the Catholic conservatives. Indeed, nineteenth-century French Catholic conservative political theorists like Louis de Bonald (1754–1840) and Joseph de Maistre (1753–1821),[44] who came after Hume, agreed in many respects with the Scotsman. For Hume, the danger of enthusiastic thinking was that enthusiasts take their bearings from divine revelation rather than experience and look to the God of the Bible for social ethics and norms. The anti-French revolutionist Maistre, agreeing with Hume, had it in for the Reformers, calling Luther and Calvin "arch innovators" and declaring that

---

40. The term post-Christian may have its contemporary genesis with historian Sydney Ahlstrom's description of the United States in the 1960s as being "post-Puritan, post-Protestant and post-Christian" ("Radical Turn").

41. The sociologist Peter Berger has led the scholarship in positing the notion that ours is a thoroughly secularized culture. Christian books denoting the secular age abound, but Catholic theologian Bernard Haring's *Faith and Morality in the Secular Age* is a fine example of the genre.

42. See the book by Yale legal scholar Stephen L. Carter, *Culture of Disbelief*, in which Carter notes that contemporary liberalism now views with suspicion people who talk about God in public: "More and more, our culture seems to take the position that believing deeply in the tenets of one's faith, represents a kind of mystical irrationality, something that thoughtful, public-spirited American citizens would do better to avoid. If you must worship your God, the lesson runs, at least have the courtesy to disbelieve in the power of prayer; if you must observe your sabbath, have the good sense to understand that it is just like any other day off from work" (6–7).

43. Sociologist James Q. Wilson argues in *Moral Sense* that "people necessarily make moral judgments, that many of those judgments are not arbitrary or unique to some time, place, or culture, and that we will get a lot further in understanding how we live as a species if we recognize that we are bound together both by mutual interdependence and a common moral sense" (xii). By moral sense, Wilson means an intuitive belief about how one ought to act when one is free to act voluntarily. He cites as his moral sense examples like sympathy, fairness, self-control, and duty. Furthermore, he claims his work is a continuation of Francis Hutcheson, David Hume, and Adam Smith. Thus, Wilson is a contemporary Humean and political conservative.

44. "There is no good that evil does not contaminate and corrupt; there is no evil that good does not curb and attack, in the ceaseless movement of all things toward a more perfect state" (Maistre, *On God and Society*, xl).

anyone who believed the *Confession of Augsburg* or the *Thirty-Nine Articles* believed in a "false religion written in a fit of delirium" that would soon pass away because these codes have no durability.[45] Interestingly, Anglican conservative theorists such as the theologian Richard Hooker (1554–1600) also suspected enthusiastic ideas.[46]

With the coming of the Enlightenment and the rejection of supernatural Christianity having much to say about how society is to be organized, Christian conservatives (meaning French Roman Catholic writers) began to nuance their arguments away from Christian doctrine and toward prudential utilitarian grounds. Even the darling of evangelical political theorists, Edmund Burke, realized that his audience wasn't interested in prooftexting their way to peace, prosperity, and social stability, so he began to de-emphasize enthusiasm.[47] Muller points out:

> While some conservative theorists have been religious believers, and most affirm the social function of religious belief in maintaining individual morality and social cohesion, none base their social and political argument primarily on conformity with ultimate religious truth.[48]

In fact, there is no necessary link between conservatism and religious belief, and most distinguished conservative theorists have been agnostic or atheist. Matthew Arnold (1822–1888), the son of the Anglican intellectual and educator Thomas Arnold, followed both Burke[49] and headmaster Arnold in his conservative commitment to the church, but he secularized it and thus gained popularity with the general public. Arnold jettisoned supernatural Christianity for a watered-down moralistic and aesthetic faith which, like his father, emphasized developing Christian gentlemen, i.e., practical goodness in one's personal life.[50] In a certain sense, America in the twenty-first century is ripe for the Arnold approach since we are in this

---

45. Maistre, *On God and Society*, 22–23.

46. Hooker, *Of the Laws of Ecclesiastical Polity*.

47. Burke wrote in *Tracts Relating to the Popery Laws* (1765), "In reality there are two, and only two, foundations of Law; and they are both of them conditions without which nothing can give it any force; I mean equity and utility. . . . Utility must be understood not of partial or limited, but of general and public utility, connected in the same manner with, and derived directly from, our rational nature" (as cited in Muller, *Conservatism*, 6).

48. Muller, *Conservatism*, 6.

49. Among many Burkean ideas which Arnold embraced would be the notion that individual liberty among the moral elite would not entail "doing as one pleases." The well-disciplined person does what is beneficial to others.

50. Arnold, *Culture and Anarchy*.

post-Christian secular age; and while we evangelicals might wish for a "thus saith the Lord" approach to public affairs, that is not what the Lord has given us. The public religion of the prayer breakfast movement may be more our cup of tea. It may cause us consternation, but a half loaf of Madison is better than no loaf. No more evangelical triumphalism, as journalist/academic Jon Meacham counsels:

> A true Christian ought to be more interested in making the life of the world gentle for others than he should be in asserting the dominance of his own faith.[51]

Interestingly, the Jewish Will Herberg argued, in tandem with John Davidson Hunter and Naomi Schaeffer Riley, that the church may be her own worst enemy in combating secularism. Granted, he was writing in 1960, and things have gotten more post-Christian since those halcyon days of Eisenhower:

> In the United States explicit secularism—hostility or demonstrative indifference to religion—is a minor and diminishing force; the secularism that permeates the American consciousness is to be found within the churches themselves and is expressed through men and women who are sincerely devoted to religion.[52]

However, theorists of all stripes have tended to agree[53] on the basic assumptions and tenants of classic conservatism:

- Human imperfection:[54] As Bonald has argued, we humans are created to be dependent on each other for guidance, direction, and affirmation.[55]

---

51. Cf. Meacham, *American Gospel*, and Lindsay, *Faith in the Halls of Power*.

52. Herberg, *Protestant, Catholic, Jew*, 271.

53. Kirk offers "six canons of conservative thought": 1. A belief that divine intent rules society as well as conscience, 2. Affection for the proliferating variety and mystery of traditional life, 3. Conviction that civilized society requires orders and classes, 4. Persuasion that property and freedom are inseparably connected, 5. Faith in prescription and distrust of 'sophisters and calculators,' 6. Recognition that change and reform are not identical, and that innovation is a devouring conflagration more often than it is a troch of progress *(Conservative Mind*, 7–8).

54. "Now we see but a poor reflection; then we shall see face to face. Now I know in part; then I shall know fully, even as I am fully known" (1 Cor 13:12). Cf. Job 37:16; Ps 147:5; Rom 3:10–11.

55. Bonald, *On Divorce*.

- Epistemological modesty: Because we are imperfect, Maistre points out the extent of our knowledge concerning the social and political world is limited and flawed.[56]
- Institutions: Because of our imperfections, we need human institutions, voluntary and involuntary, to provide "rules, norms, rewards and sanctions" for our flourishing.[57]
- Custom, habits, and prejudices: Hume and Burke argued that we imperfect humans relay on established moral rules, since we don't have time, energy, and intelligence to constantly create our own social rules.[58]
- Historicism and particularism:[59] We imperfect humans respect and participate in valuable institutions, which have been created, developed, and improved over time.
- Anti-contrarianism: Hume and Burke argued that we imperfect humans do not have the right to opt out of social and political obligations simply because we didn't voluntarily agree to certain relationships. We have been born into a "social contract not only between those who are living but between those who are living, those who are dead, and those who are to be born."[60]
- The utility of religion: There is a vital link between Christianity and conservatism (contra George Will). Christianity legitimizes the political state; provides comfort for imperfect humans while on earth, thus softening their anger and discontent; and acts as a prod to act morally with the incentive of eternal rewards in heaven.[61]
- The critique of abstractions: Conservatives are not opposed to scientific knowledge and analysis, but they oppose abstract theorizing divorced from experience and verifiability. That is one of the basics for Hume's skeptical view of religious enthusiasm.[62]

---

56. Cf. Isa 55:8.
57. Muller, *Conservatism*, 11; cf. Heb 10:25.
58. Cf. 2 Thess 2:15.
59. Cf. Heb 6:1; Gal 4:4.
60. Burke, *Reflections on the Revolution*, 101; cf. Heb 13:7–8.
61. Cf. Phil 3:14.
62. Cf. Col 2:8.

- The negative consequences of reformist action: Actions to serve humanity regardless of rational experience and history serve only to harm individual humans.[63]

It is not my purpose to explicate a Christian view of society and culture, nor to argue that American society is no longer in any way a Christian society. That task is quite beyond my focus. If America truly is in a post-Christian era, David Hume may very well offer conservative thinkers, both secular and religious, the rationale for a workable conservative view of culture, which, if they knew more about him, they would find congenial. Hence, he deserves greater attention and study by evangelical conservatives than he has heretofore been accorded.

David Hume wrote brilliantly on the need for cultural and social stability and security. His philosophy may be able to sustain the received benefits of the church's influence on the American way of life, despite our post-Christian condition.

Ironically, it is because we are in a post-Christian culture that Hume becomes even more important to Christian thinkers than he otherwise would be. If Hume is correct in stressing the stabilizing force of conventions, customs, and habits, a deliberate attempt to re-introduce Christianity into America's social institutions might be socially disruptive and dangerous. Hume wrote before the American republic was formed, and he did not foresee the great Christian influence in our early civil and social activities. But over the last 200 years these social institutions, such as churches, colleges, media, and charities, have been slowly desacralized, to the point where the forceful infusion of Christian principles into these now secular institutions would not be conducive to social stability and cohesion.

And here is an irony, for both the Humean and the Christian thinker: for many Christians, the Bible clearly teaches that a tranquil and stable (albeit free) society is one that they are to work to establish and maintain:

> Submit yourselves for the Lord's sake to every human institution, whether to a king as the one in authority or to governors as sent by him for the punishment of evildoers and the praise of those who do right. (1 Pet 2:13)[64]

In the Old Testament, Jeremiah conveys the word of Yahweh to His people dispersed in the pagan country of Babylon, "Also, seek the peace and prosperity of the city to which I have carried you into exile. Pray to the Lord for it, because if it prospers, you too will prosper" (Jer 29:7).

63. Cf. 1 Sam 13:11–14.
64. Cf. Rom 13:1–7; Titus 3:1.

In the gospel of Matthew, we see Jesus telling of Moses's having given permission for the previously forbidden practice of divorce in order to maintain social stability and justice. With the obstinacy of the people in mind, and in order that society would not be decimated by wholesale hypocrisy, lawlessness, and interpersonal devastation, Moses allowed divorce under certain prescribed circumstances.[65]

In a third biblical example, the apostle Paul exhorts all Christians that

> requests, prayers, intercession and thanksgiving be made for everyone-for kings and all those in authority, that we may live peaceful and quiet lives in all godliness and holiness. This is good, and pleases God our Savior, who wants all men to be saved and to come to a knowledge of the truth. (1 Tim 2:1–3)

These passages emphasize the ironic point that Hume provides philosophic defenses for a significant Christian ideal—a stable society—despite his religious skepticism.

It is Hume's skeptical writings on organized religion, of all his works, that have caused him the most trouble in conservative Christian circles. Orestes Brownson (1803–1876), considered by some conservatives to be one of the finest American Roman Catholic thinkers in the nineteenth century, called Hume a "chief of the modern infidel school."[66] From Burke onward, religious conservatives have defended religion as an integral part of their ideology. Hume's religious skepticism was so apparent that it has been difficult to include him in the pantheon of conservative gods.[67] He wrote such things as: "No character in human history is more dangerous than that of the [religious] fanatic; because he is entirely governed by his own illusions, which sanctify his most selfish views and passions."[68] And this from his essay "Of the Coalition of Parties":

> These consequences are the more to be dreaded, as the present fury of the people, though glossed over by pretensions to civil liberty, is in reality incited by the fanaticism of religion; a principle the most blind, headstrong and ungovernable, by which human nature can possibly be actuated.[69]

---

65. Cf. Matt 19:1–11.

66. Brownson, "Democracy and Liberty," 2:705.

67. The four-volume work entitled *The Wisdom of Conservatism*, edited by Peter Witonski of Washington University, includes selections of ninety-six thinkers from Thucydides to William F. Buckley, but Hume is only mentioned, not featured.

68. H, 5:492.

69. E/LF, 484–85, 500.

With such statements to his credit, it is no wonder that Hume is seen as "the best example we have of a secular and skeptical conservative."[70] It has been Hume's secularism that has separated him from Edmund Burke, Adam Smith, and their followers in the conservative movement. Hume refused to look upon religion as a force contributing to social stability, and orthodox religious assumptions played no part in his philosophy. However, it is this secular cast to Hume's philosophy that may offer the conservative the best defense for preserving the best of American culture in the face of the destructive liberal secular frontal assault on the traditions and customs of our post-Christian nation. Emil Brunner writes,

> The principle of tradition is deeply rooted in the Christian conception of life . . . all mankind is bound together with solidarity in creation and in sin. . . . In the Christian message, history is of capital importance. It is not surprising then, that tradition is the very essence of the Christian Church.[71]

For Brunner, the loss of a Christian social consensus means the loss of human tradition, which spells social disaster. Still, the New Testament scholar should have mentioned that our Lord warned against deifying tradition over against his word.[72] We must not use human traditions to cancel or nullify God's word.

The very essence of David Hume's thought is dependent on historical perspective because it is sequential. Hume sees common life as supplying us with the building blocks upon which to construct his philosophy. The notion that experiential impressions must precede ideas is distinctly historical and conservative, since it limits the freedom of the mental faculties to what can be evidenced in the experienced world. Nothing should be posited unless it can be tied to an impression; all abstract speculation and ideology is literally non-sense. Therefore, what goes before us, what has transpired in the past, creates the framework for our very understanding of ourselves, each other, and the world.

Hume's theory of causation is likewise dependent on historical succession. Certain events occur, and we come to expect certain others to follow. Since we are historical beings, we have a natural propensity[73] to look to the

---

70. Miller, *Philosophy*, 187.
71. Brunner, *Christianity and Civilization*, 30–31.
72. John 15:1–9.
73. Hume's propensities undergird his thought in his *Treatise On Human Nature*. Cf. "The Natural History of Religion," WOR, 117.

past for examples/types[74] and traditions.[75] We instinctively believe that what we call effects will follow what we call causes. Hume argued that we want (need!) to forge a connection between past and present.

Hume applied these epistemological concepts to common-life problems in his writings. His impressionistic epistemology builds naturally to a conservative view of society. That is, Hume believed that we must alter social relationships only in light of experience. What went on before has a presumption of utility and beneficence (as in *stare decisis*—"let the decision stand").

We can know nothing about present society (nor have a well-founded view of future society) that has not been impressed upon us by our past social arrangements. As humans we must revere the past, learning from it and emulating it, in order to act wisely in the present and future.

Human nature for Hume was a series of unexplained propensities in the individual. Throughout his writings, he referred to multiple propensities but never indicated from where these propensities come. They were just natural, innate feelings or sentiments that all of us have.[76] Of course, Christians believe in human propensities, but we have a source for them: the Creator. God has created us in his image with various propensities.[77] We humans were given God's propensities at creation, and while Adam's fall corrupted our propensities, they still reside in each individual. It is like Hume reverted to his childhood reading of *The Whole Duty of Man* with its checklists of moral virtues but never looked behind the checklist to see from where they come. So it was with his propensities.

With the mention of natural propensity, Hume introduced his notion that the individual has a multitude of born dispositions, proclivities, and propensities to naturally do or to think something. By way of summary:

- The propensity to believe that effects follow causes.[78] We habitually look to history, to the past for current guidance and truth. We

---

74. Cf. 1 Cor 10:6; 1 Tim 4:12, *typos*.

75. Cf. 2 Thess 2:15; 3:6, *paradosis*.

76. Gertrude Himmelfarb called this propensity a tendency and argued, "It was not, to be sure, an innate quality of human beings" (*Road to Modernity*, 35). I prefer to refer to propensities or innate qualities.

77. In Gen 1:27, "So God created man in his own image, in the image of God he created him; male and female he created them." The Hebrew preposition *be* (in) in the phrases *betsalmenu* (in our image) and *betsalmo* (in his image) should be taken as an instance of "*beth* essentiae" or "*beth* of the essence." In other words, essence could be substituted for image. Descartes said, "I am somehow made in his image and likeness."

78. "The Natural History of Religion," WOR, 117.

believe that what we call effects will follow what we call causes.[79] This is the a priori habit to think the same, customary way; I call it the habit of paradigm thinking.[80] Since impressions must precede ideas, we appropriate the sensible impressions through our memory and our imagination.[81] Our mind innately connects, separates, and even recombines ideas. This is the propensity to believe in the continuity of connecting (associating) the same ideas from the same impressions. Our mind innately connects, separates, and even recombines ideas:[82] "This supposition, or idea of continu'd existence, acquires a force and vivacity from the memory of these broken impressions, and from that propensity, which they give us, to suppose them the same; ... the very essence of belief consists in the force and vivacity of the conception."[83]

- The propensity to deify social arrangements, since these voluntary arrangements are the only pathway to self-identity. This is the innate desire to join in social arrangements. This is the natural urge to join others for common interest, since "men always seek society."[84] This spontaneous union of humanity is not only distinct from any political arrangement, but it may be, and often is, distinct from any clear consciousness of union at all. It is the sense of an objective common interest and purpose, to be served by common action.[85] This is the creation of a convention at work. Hume's doctrine of impressions, ideas, and associations through memory and imagination are key building blocks of his social theory, because he posited the notion that we can only legitimately form ideas about that which we perceive. Therefore, reliable and useful social arrangements are formed only in the slow flow of human conventions, habits, and associations. Furthermore, because we can have no certainty about causality, the notion of structuring society or manipulating social institutions through ideology to accomplish certain desired ends is a tenuous and humble undertaking. There is great social risk in rational social engineering, since we have no certainty in outcome. We can anticipate but not know the future.[86]

---

79. T, 187; TM, 238
80. EU, 43; P, 43
81. T, 8–9; TM, 56
82. T, 8–9; TM, 56.
83. T, 199; TM, 250. Cf. 1 Cor 10:6; 1 Tim 4:12, *typos* and traditions (cf. 2 Thess 2:15; 3:6, *paradosis*). Luke 8:15; 1 Cor 11:2; 15:2, *katecho* (hold firmly, keep).
84. T, 401–2; TM, 449.
85. T, 546; TM, 596.
86. Cf. Gen 1:26f; Eccl 3:11; Rom 1:18–19; 1 Cor 11:7; Jas 3:9.

- The propensity to see history as the key element in understanding the individual. This is the innate bent to imbue history with infallibility. We a priori give history greatness and normativeness.[87] This is the disposition to get our personal identity from our social habits, customs, conventions, and associations. Our own sense of identity is rooted in similar historical series of impressions. We come to know who we are only after we have experienced several separate yet connected impressions that form corresponding ideas in our mind. We are dependent on our past for our present interpretation of who we are and of what the future might be. The individual not only has a propensity to want to see a rational or even a divine plan at work in an orderly society, but he or she acquires identity in the very social habits, customs, and conventions of which he or she is a part.[88]

- The propensity to believe in an intelligent Author or Designer in the world, even if we can't prove it. This is the universal propensity to believe in invisible, intelligent power (i.e., causal principle originating from an unknown intelligent Designer) who/which has set a kind of mark or stamp on each individual.[89]

- The propensity to believe in an orderly world which is not chaotic or random, even if we can't explain why. Belief in this system of order is due to "a propensity in human nature, which leads into a system that gives [humans] some satisfaction."[90] But when no satisfactory explanation occurs, and it often did not for Hume, in order to "obliterate all these chimeras, I dine, I play a game of backgammon, I converse, and am merry with my friends . . . for three or four hours of amusement."[91]

- The propensity to that which is in one's self-interest. For Hume, the pursuit of personal interest for ourselves and our friends is basic to human nature.[92]

- The propensity to view public opinion (general opinion) as infallible and thus the authoritative guide to individual action.[93] Hume's moral theory was consensus-based, that is, based on public opinion: "The

---

87. T, 566; TM, 617.
88. Cf. Gen 1.
89. "The Natural History of Religion," WOR, 181.
90. "The Natural History of Religion," WOR, 117.
91. T, 1, 4, 7.
92. T, 491–92; TM, 543.
93. "Who do people say that I am?" (Matt 16:13); "He must have a good reputation with outsiders" (1 Tim 3:7).

general opinion of mankind has some authority in all cases."[94] Moreover, in order to be efficacious and supported by the public, "laws have, or ought to have, a constant reference to the constitution of government, the manners, the climate, the religion, the commerce, the situation of each society."[95] As Hume perspicuously observed in his essay "Of the First Principles of Government," government is supported only by the opinion of the governed.[96] First culture, then government.[97] Public opinion thus has the status, the authority of genuine and infallible knowledge!

- The propensity to be acquisitive. Hume believed that corruption, or "avidity of acquiring goods and possessions," is ineradicable in the human soul (a heritage of Scottish Calvinism?) and that no political convention such as a constitution is going to remove this greedy tendency. Consequently, it is the politicians' responsibility to constantly be vigilant over the public affairs of a nation and to make changes and alterations in the conventions of social life, in order to keep our avaricious tendency in check.[98]

- The propensity to impute good intentions in others, that is, to deny the fall of Adam. Insofar as people are human, their nature remains constant through the ages, as empirical observation confirms natural law. But at the same time, we are susceptible to changes through reflection (or education), custom and prejudice. So, while individuals stay the same, we are constantly changing: "We know, in general, that the characters of men are, to a certain degree, inconstant and irregular. This is, in a manner, the constant character of human nature."[99] The abstract changelessness of human nature is to be contrasted to its concrete, changing narrative. The central unifying principle of the constant Heraclitan (535–475 BC) social change is what Hume called

---

94. T, 552; TM, 603.

95. EM, 196; OC, 30

96. E, 29; LF, 32.

97. "I shou'd now appeal to popular authority and oppose the sentiments of the rabble to any philosophical reasoning. For it must be observ'd that the opinions of men, in this case, carry with them a peculiar authority and are, in a great measure, infallible. ... The general opinion of mankind has some authority in all cases; but in this of morals 'tis perfectly infallible. Nor is it less infallible, because [most] men cannot distinctly explain the principles, on which it is founded. Few persons can carry on this train of reasoning" (T, 552; TM, 603).

98. EU, 90; P, 83.

99. EU, 88; P, 82.

sympathy, including the innate propensity to recognize good intentions in other individuals.

- The propensity to observe moral rules out of a feeling of affinity (sympathy) for others. Artificial virtues are to morals what social rules are to politics—rules provide stability, uniformity, and probability. Human nature tells us that past observations are fundamental in predicting the future. We have a basic affinity for custom and order; therefore, any effective authority must rely on this natural affinity. Virtue is practiced because we naturally accept the discipline of such rules. In sum, authority is embodied in rules rather than in rule, in institutions and common practices rather than in persons.

- A propensity to seek freedom, security, and happiness. Government is to act as a facilitator, to use a present-day term, in order to coordinate, assist, and protect the independent center of power, loyalty, and authority resident in voluntary social institutions, which are the only valid expression of this natural human desire for freedom. Usually people will create a more satisfactory society, if left to themselves, than one that the government would impose on them. This propensity compels us to want to fend for ourselves without government interference.[100] Social peace and order preceded any written document because we can trace the propensity for civil agreement to the "innate nature of man."[101]

- A propensity to sympathize with others and therefore exhibit a benevolent attitude towards society. Voluntary institutions were seen by Hume to be a largely unreflective response to human experience, and thus were thought to be a natural guide to human corporate behavior. We humans just naturally like to socialize. Government is an important social institution because it helps to enforce observance of moral rules, and without such beneficial rules of conduct there would be no social stability. Observance of social rules of conduct is good for everybody. Well, almost everybody—except rule breakers. Government provides law and order, which have in the past proved useful in living our lives.

- The propensity to divide ourselves into social, racial, economic, religious, political factions. Hume divided social factions into personal

---

100. E, 457; LF, 471.

101. "Obedience or subjection [to government] becomes so familiar, that most men never make any enquiry about its origin or cause, more than about the principle of gravity, resistance, or the most universal laws of nature" (E, 454–56; LF, 468–70).

and real. A personal faction was "founded on personal friendship or animosity among such as compose the contending parties."[102] A real faction was founded on some real difference of interest (sentiment). Real factions were divided into three classifications: 1) Factions of interest. Factions which arise from "common interest are the most reasonable and the most excusable."[103] 2) Factions of principle.[104] Hume held that such parties "produce the greatest misery and devastation."[105] It is in this faction that Hume unflatteringly put Christianity.[106] Evangelical Christianity fits nicely into this category, as the biblically oriented sheep (enthusiasts) are led by the self-interested (superstitious) clergy. Haakonssen explains Hume's solution to this social problem: "The only way to deal with such factionalism was to enlighten the potential leaders of the factions. To this purpose Hume supported every move that could secure the inclusion of the clergy in the world of letters. Clergymen of taste and learning would tend to see issues of doctrinal theology as matters for discussion among the educated rather that reasons for social division."[107] 3) Factions of affection.[108] This real faction was "founded on the different attachments of men towards particular families and persons, whom they desire to rule over them. These factions are often very violent."[109] Violence comes with such personal and emotional commitments. Such governmental political parties are formed by the conflicting desires of different groups to have their country ruled by different parties (dynasties).[110]

* The propensity to reciprocity in social interaction, that is, to ignore the stranger and deal with friends.[111] Whether the strangers are foreign

102. "Of Parties in General," E, 55–56; LF, 56.

103. LF, 59.

104. E, 58; LF, 60.

105. J. Stewart, *Moral and Political Philosophy*, 203–4.

106. "The same principles of priestly government continuing, after Christianity became the established religion, they have engendered a spirit of persecution, which has ever since been the poison of human society, and the source of the most inveterate factions in every government . . . in modern times, parties of religion are more furious and enraged than the most cruel factions that ever arose from interest and ambition" (E, 60–61; LF, 62–63).

107. Haakonssen, "Structure of Hume's Political Theory," 70.

108. E, 58; LF, 59.

109. E, 61; LF, 63.

110. "Of the Rise and Progress of the Arts and Sciences," E, 116–18, 125; LF, 116–18, 124.

111. "Men being naturally selfish, or endow'd only with a confin'd generosity, they

or domestic, the economic message to big government is clear: No "injudicious tampering": Politicians and bureaucrats, mind your own business and let us mutually deal with each other.

- The propensity to be a moral agent. We are naturally moral beings who make moral judgments all the time, in all circumstances, and about all people.[112] Because basic human nature is universal, we can draw general moral conclusions from all societies and use all past ages to furnish, nourish, and embellish our own moral thinking. We can do nothing else but see how human nature has played itself out in recorded history, if we are to acquire a beneficial present moral society, as was set forth in Gen 9 as God's plan for a post-flood world.

∼

For Hume, what happened in the past is critical to our understanding of all aspects of the present, whether it be impressions leading to ideas, causal events leading to expected effects, personal separate impressions leading to self-identity, deity generating the natural universe, or past social arrangements leading to present social structures. For Hume, his philosophy was a great literary play: we are the subjects, history is the court, and custom is the king. Habit and tradition are the knights errant, and abstract ideology is the court jester, fit only for the dunce cap.

---

are not easily induc'd to perform any action for the interest of strangers, except with a view to some reciprocal advantage, which they had no hope of obtaining but by such a performance" (T, 519; TM, 571).

112. "Those who have denied the reality of moral distinctions, may be ranked among the disingenuous disputants; nor is it conceivable, that any human creature could ever seriously believe, that all characters and actions were alike entitled to the affection and regard of everyone.... There is no scepticism so scrupulous, and scarce any assurance so determined, as absolutely to deny all distinction between them [one man and another]" (EM, 170; OC, 1–2.) Hume's imputation of importance to the concept of general benevolence is seen in his concept of sympathy, which will be discussed later. Perhaps Hume picked up his notion of man's natural benevolent propensity from his reading of the early Greeks, such as Seneca, who wrote, "Nature bids me to be of use to men whether they are slave or free, freedmen or free born. Wherever there is a human being there is room for benevolence" (cited in Copleston, *History of Philosophy*, 1:431). In appendix 2 of the second *Enquiry,* Hume noted, "There is a principle, supposed to prevail among many, which is utterly incompatible with all virtue or moral sentiment .... This principle is, that all *benevolence* is mere hypocrisy, friendship a cheat, public spirit a farce, fidelity a snare to procure trust and confidence; and that while all of us, at bottom, pursue only our private interest, we wear these fair disguises, in order to put others off their guard, and expose them the more to our wiles and machinations" (EM, 295; OC, 137).

While many evangelical conservatives may wish "thus saith the Lord"[113] is enough ground for ordering a generally accepted epistemology, morality, and society, that is highly problematic in our present post-Christian secular age. David Hume's having grounded these things in historic experience and custom provides an intellectual framework to sustain a civil, tranquil, and quiet society in which to live a common life. While this is not a treatment on American political conservatism, it must be noted that in the mid-1970s, the conservative movement began to rapidly change from the so-called Old Right, focusing on anti-communism, limited government, and free enterprise to the so-called New Right, focusing on populism, family and conventional values, distrust of government, active evangelical involvement in politics, and single-issue campaigns.[114] Paul Gottfried opines that "perhaps the single most important element in the success of the New Right coalition was the involvement of evangelical Christians" led by Jerry Falwell and Pat Robertson in the 1970s.[115]

That is the state of the American conservative movement at the present time.

---

113. Cf. Isa 45:1; etc.
114. Viguerie, *New Right,* and Crawford, *Thunder on the Right.*
115. Gottfried, *Conservative Movement,* 98.

2

David Hume's True Philosophy

We may observe a gradation of three opinions, that rise above each other, according to the persons, who form them, acquire new degrees of reason and knowledge. These opinions are that of the vulgar, that of a false philosophy, and that of the true, where we shall find upon inquiry, that the true philosophy approaches nearer to the sentiments of the vulgar, than to those of a mistaken knowledge.[1]

We must cultivate true metaphysics with some care, in order to destroy the false and adulterate . . . to safeguard against deceitful and abstruse philosophy and metaphysical jargon.[2]

DAVID HUME WANTED TO offer the world a new perspective on philosophic theory. He attempted the discovery of the ultimate principle of intelligence or "mental powers and economy." He wanted to ascertain the "one operation and principle of the mind" which would be "general and universal."[3] He called his new philosophic perspective by various names: true philosophy,[4] true metaphysics,[5] moderate skepticism,[6] or, more descriptively, mitigated

---

1. T, 222; TM, 272.
2. EU, 12; P, 15.
3. EU, 14–15; P, 17.
4. T, 222; TM, 272.
5. EU, 12; P, 15.
6. T, 224; TM, 273.

skepticism or academical philosophy.[7] He spoke of his system as true because, as he traversed the "geography of the mind,"[8] he judged that his epistemology conformed to reality as it is experienced in the everyday world.[9]

Hume's quest for true philosophy was thus grounded in the authority and verifiable ability of common life, common practices, common recreations, or common experience.[10] The common man[11] lived in an experiential environment out of which human habits,[12] customs,[13] prejudices,[14] and associations[15] evolve. Common-life philosophy, therefore, is based on common-life experience. No ultimate principles can correctly be based on anything other than such experiences, "as they appear in the common course of the world, by men's behavior in company, in affairs, and in their pleasures."[16] "None of them [i.e., philosophers or artisans] can go beyond experiences, or establish any principles that are not founded on that authority" of experience.[17] Furthermore, Hume mocked philosophers "who never consulted

---

7. EU, 161–62; P, 145.

8. EU, 13; P, 16.

9. Cf. 2 Pet 1:3.

10. "All the philosophy, therefore, in the world, and all the religion, which is nothing but a species of philosophy will never be able to carry us beyond the usual course of experience, or give us measures of conduct and behavior different from those which are furnished by reflections on common life" (EU, 146; P, 132; see also T, 379; TM, 427).

11. T, 202; TM, 252: "what any common man means" (cf. T, 272; TM, 319; EM, 203; OC, 37). However, the fact that common life was the basis for philosophic thinking did not mean that any common person could do true philosophy. Hume was clear that the unreflective, "illiterate" person did not understand the authority and coherency of the idea of common life (EU, 161; P, 145). This idea is only understood by the self-conscious, reflective and skeptical thinker, that is, "all reasonable people" (EU, 125; P, 114), or those who were "wise and learned" (EU, 110; P, 100). Hume was no Philistine! Indeed, there seem to be three stages or gradations of philosophic understanding: the vulgar, the false philosopher, the true philosopher (T, 222; TM, 272).

12. "Reason is nothing but a wonderful and unintelligible instinct in our souls, which carries us along a certain train of ideas, and endows them with particular qualities, according to their particular situations and relations . . . habit is nothing but one of the principles of nature, and derives all its force from that origin" (T, 179; TM, 229).

13. "Custom, then, is the great guide of human life" (EU, 44; P, 45). Custom and habit are basically the same in the first *Enquiry*: "This principle is Custom or Habit" (EU, 43; P, 43).

14. "A fourth unphilosophical species of probability is that deriv'd from *general rules*, which we rashly form; to ourselves, and which are the source of what we properly call PREJUDICE" (T, 146; TM, 197).

15. T, 541; TM, 592–93; E, 54–74; LF, 54–72.

16. T, xxiii; TM, 46.

17. T, xxii; TM, 45.

experience in any of their reasonings, or who never searched for that experience, where alone it is to be found, in common life and conversation."[18]

All this common human activity creates an order of stability for the functioning of society. Hume energetically rejected rationalism and any other transcendent metaphysical system of thought, because they were not grounded in the common, customary experiences of humanity. Our knowledge and understanding reach no further than our experience.

Reason must operate completely within the world of common life, since the philosopher lives within the constraints of that world. While the philosopher might not like the limits of life as it is ordinarily experienced, that is all he genuinely has.[19] Thus, the philosopher is forced, if he is realistic, to face up to these limitations of knowledge. In his conclusion to book 1 of the *Treatise*, Hume acknowledges but laments this limitation of common-life philosophy.[20]

In short, Hume might have preferred some other philosophic vessel (perhaps rationalism, Pyrrhonic skepticism, or theology) to carry his ideas, and he acknowledges his unique system as being far from perfect. Yet he sallies forth with his true philosophy, for it is the best transport available for the onerous task of sailing the seas of human understanding.

While common life is to be the setting for a true philosophy, human nature, as it is played out in common life, is the script. Hume argued that human nature, despite all its weaknesses and limitations, will provide the only sure guide to a true philosophy. "Human nature is the only science of man."[21] His philosophy was an attempt to apply to the mind the experimental principles that Isaac Newton applied to the physical world.[22] The Christian Newton was one of Hume's principal heroes: "Newton; who trod

18. "Of Essay Writing," E, 569; LF, 535.

19. Cf. John 20:24–25.

20. "Methinks I am like a man, who having struck on many shoals, and having narrowly escaped ship-wreck in passing a small frith, has yet the temerity to put out to sea in the same leaky weather-beaten vessel, and even carries his ambition so far as to think of compassing the globe under these disadvantageous circumstances. The wretched condition, weaknesses, and disorder of the faculties, I must employ in my enquires, increase my apprehension" (T, 263–64; TM, 311).

21. Cf. Rom 2:14–16; Matt 15:19. T, 273; TM, 320.

22. "And as the science of man is the only solid foundation for the other sciences, so the only solid foundation we can give to this science itself must be laid on experience and observation" (T, xx; TM, 43). "So great is the force of laws, and of particular forms of government, and so little dependence have they on the humours and tempers of men, that consequences almost as general and certain may sometimes be deduced from them, as any which the mathematical sciences afford us" (E, 14; LF, 16; cf. EU, 83; P, 77–78). Hume eulogized Newton thusly: He was "the greatest and rarest genius that ever rose for the ornament and instruction of the species" (H, 4:434).

with cautious, and therefore the more secure steps, the only road which leads to true philosophy."[23] Hume wanted to be the Newton of the mind despite Newton's Christian mindset.

If examining human nature experimentally is the only correct way of studying humankind, then the history of how people have expressed their nature through history is critical to this study. As we look at human history, we see various customs[24] and conventions[25] that gradually develop, mostly unintended, over time. Customs determine conventions, traditions, and prejudices of the human moral world. Customs are not only epistemologically significant; they are also ontologically significant. Customs are, after all, the things philosophy will methodize and correct in order to gain an understanding of the world. Of course, Hume was writing in a Christian culture where there was general agreement on proper customs. His logic falls apart outside the Christian West where, for instance, honor killing is a custom in the Muslim world. All true philosophers are moderately skeptical, for they realize that they know only through the customary and imaginary process of association of ideas. Note that the Humean caution regarding cognitive certainty[26] reflects various biblical admonitions to be careful in pronouncements.

* 1 Cor 8:2: "The man who thinks he knows something does not know as he ought to know."
* 1 Cor 13:12: "Now we see but a poor reflection; then we shall see face to face. Now I know in part; then I shall know fully, even as I am fully known."
* Phil 3:12: "Not than I have already obtained all this, or have already been made perfect, but I press on to take hold of that which Christ Jesus took hold of me."

Thus, we see Humean mankind developing its own truths in the crucible of day-to-day associations, relationships, and involvements. There is, for Hume, a vast historical narrative of mankind as it has moved through

---

23. H, 2:373.

24. "Now as we call everything CUSTOM, which proceeds from a past repetition, without any new reasoning or conclusion, we may establish it as a certain truth, that all the belief, which follows upon any present impression, is deriv'd solely from that origin. . . . This custom operates before we have time for reflexion" (T, 102, 104; TM, 152–53).

25. "This convention . . . is only a general sense of common interest; which sense all the members of the society express to one another, and which induces them to regulate their conduct by certain rules" (T, 490; TM, 541).

26. T, 224; TM, 273.

the past and into the present. The future is yet unknown and unknowable, and therefore of relatively less importance. This notion about the future is crucial for understanding Hume's rejection of rationalism: since there is no sure way of knowing what effects present events will cause, we can profitably analyze only the past and usefully describe only the present. It is, of course, certainty about the future and not probability about it that Hume means to discount.[27]

A critical social concept in this common-life basis of philosophic musing was convention, which Hume understood to be a slowly evolving, virtually unconscious, non-promissory, natural agreement among individuals as to how they should be involved in and with the world around them and how they should structure their relationships.[28]

The gradual evolution of society creates conventional rules that are advantageous to people. Hume identified three such rules or "fundamental laws of nature": 1) stability of possession,[29] 2) transference by consent,[30] 3) performance of promises.[31] These are rules of social justice that would appear in some guise in any social contract, purposeful or not. Personal interest always would call for agreements. However, it must be stressed, even at the risk of repetition, that these social rules or conventions are not always conscious, deliberate agreements, but usually unconscious, casual utilitarian agreements of "common interest."[32]

Adherence to the rules is seen or somehow understood to be beneficial to society, while deviation from them is seen to be detrimental. Adherence is virtuous; deviation is vicious. The value of all such conventions is social utility, satisfaction, and blessing. Thus, history is a record of human conventions, most often unconsciously contrived to satisfy human needs and interests over a period.[33]

Conventions arise only when there is what Hume called a "common point of view," a matter of crucial significance in the development of morality.[34] These conventions are argued over and debated as time passes, and yet they are, on the whole, unreflective responses to the human condition. Thus, "the intercourse of sentiments, therefore, in society and conversation,

---

27. Cf. 2 Pet 1:20–21.
28. T, 490; TM, 541–42; cf. 2 Thess 2:15.
29. Cf. Matt 25:14–30.
30. Cf. 1 Tim 5:18.
31. Cf. Eccl 5:5; T, 501–26; TM, 553–75.
32. EM, 306; OC, 149.
33. Cf. 1 Cor 11:1–2.
34. T, 591; TM, 641.

makes us form some general unalterable standard, by which we may approve or disapprove of characters and manners."[35] Accordingly, moral conduct and its criteria are defined by human conventions, which have arisen by these unconscious processes.[36]

True philosophy is compared to a fox hunt in which not only is the fox (or conclusion) the goal of the hunt, but the very chase (the inquiry) itself is of value.[37]

The goal for Hume was to establish a system of thought that conformed to what was, that was satisfactory to the human intellect, and that was able to stand close examination by other philosophers.[38] Scottish realism at play!

True philosophy has the task of bringing out the principles and beliefs of the common life in a systematic, coherent, and understandable arrangement. False philosophy or modern philosophy,[39] grounded in rationalism, skepticism, vanity, or metaphysics, "arises either from the fruitless efforts of human vanity, which would penetrate into subjects utterly inaccessible to the understanding, or from the craft of popular superstition."[40] If false philosophy is so fruitless and incomprehensible then there is no reason to perpetuate it, for it is worthless.

Donald Livingston summarizes these points:

> True philosophy then, is distinguished from false in that it [acknowledges] the a *priori* structure of common life as a structure internal to its own activity. The true philosophy methodizes and corrects judgments made within the order of common life.[41]

DAVID HUME AND RATIONALISM

Warring against this common-life basis of philosophy is rationalism or the "autonomy principle," which holds that philosophy has the authority and ability to judge and prescribe, independently of the common life: "Reason first appears in possession of the throne, prescribing laws, and imposing maxims, with an absolute sway and authority."[42] Rationalism fancies itself to

35. T, 603; TM, 653.
36. Cf. 2 Thess 3:6.
37. T, 451; TM, 498.
38. T, 272; TM, 319–20.
39. T, 225–31; TM, 274–80.
40. EU, 11; P, 14; cf. EU, 165; P, 149.
41. Livingston, *Hume's Philosophy*, 25.
42. T, 186; TM, 237.

be freed from the vulgar, unreflective common life, which it characterizes as prejudiced, tradition-bound, and confused. In contradistinction, true philosophy presupposes the normative authority of the common life. True philosophy is at war against rationalism, because rationalism stands apart from the lessons of common life and arrogates to itself the authority to judge any part or all common life without regard for true human nature.[43] To the rationalist, reality is what pure reason holds it to be. However, this assumption generates serious difficulties.[44]

Hume's criticism of the theory of double existence also focused on its doublethink,[45] its twisting the meaning of words to mean the opposite of common usage: "Everyone [the modern philosopher] may employ *terms* in what sense he pleases."[46]

Hume thought that false philosophy was socially destructive. In the Introduction to the *Treatise,* he wrote that "we can give no reason for our most general and most refined principles, besides our experience of their

---

43. Cf. Titus 3:9–10.

44. A major flaw of modern, rationalistic philosophy is its espousal of a concept that Hume calls "double existence," which he considers to be monstrous and troublesome."(T, 215–16; TM, 265–66).

This is the "hypothesis of the double existence of perceptions and objects" (T, 215; TM, 264).

He characterizes this theory as due to the need to describe anything in two different ways in order to gain an understanding of it. First, rationalists must describe a thing in theoretical, abstract language pertaining to a "world of its own" (T, 271; TM, 318). Second, the thing must be described in the ordinary, concrete language of the common life, or as "things appear in the visible world"(T, 271; TM, 318). The rationalist's theory of double existence is meant to solve the problem of the relation between external objects and our perception of those external objects. The rationalists' chief question is: Do external objects have continued existence regardless of our perceptions? In other words, do trees in a forest exist if no one is there to look at them or hear them fall? Hume held that the rationalist vacillates between saying on the one hand, that our perceptions are interruptible and perishable, but, on the other hand, that they must have a continued existence and identity. To Hume, the rationalist invents the "double existence" of objects—as perceptions and as real external things. But to mention just one difficulty that rationalism generates: What rational grounds do we have for proposing a correlation of our perceptions with external objects which have never been experienced prior to the perceiving? Hume thinks it is all absurd (T, 211–18; TM, 261–68).

45. George Orwell, in his novel *Nineteen Eighty-Four,* refers to "Newspeak, doublethink, the mutability of the past" and has a Ministry of Truth with three slogans: "War is Peace, Freedom is Slavery, Ignorance is Strength" (25).

46. EM, 322; OC, 166. But the underlying motivation for such verbal manipulation may be that "whatever has the air of a paradox, and is contrary to the first and most unprejudiced notions of mankind is often greedily embraced by philosophers, as shewing the superiority of their science, which cou'd discover opinions so remote from vulgar conception" (T, 26; TM, 75; cf. T, 215; TM, 264–65).

reality."⁴⁷ The point is that common life alone provides us with internal principles for our thinking, which cannot be abandoned or even minimized without the abandonment or degradation of thought and communication itself. What we must do, to avoid such a social disaster, is to analyze common life in order to ascertain what is true thinking, i.e., true philosophy.

What is the cost, then, in terms of human suffering, of rationalism? Hume answered: misery, terror, absurdity, contradiction, and incomprehensibility.⁴⁸

True philosophy is the only thing that supplies a resolution to the quandaries engendered by abstract rationalistic investigations.⁴⁹

DAVID HUME AND EVANGELICAL (SUPERNATURAL) CHRISTIANITY

But rationalism is not the only enemy of true philosophy. Modern or popular religion,⁵⁰ i.e., supernatural Christianity, is also an enemy, for it too is grounded in something other than the common life. Biblical Christianity seeks its authority from metaphysical principles and therefore stands apart from ordinary experience. So, it is part of the false philosophy against which Hume argued.⁵¹ There is no social utility animating either rationalism or Christianity, only a commitment to metaphysical principles and dreams.

Hume tangentially referred to revealed Christianity as "sick men's dreams" and the "playsome whimsies of monkeys in human shape."⁵² For him, Christianity holds that history is under God's personal guidance and is

---

47. T, xxii; TM, 45.

48. T, 265–69; TM, 312–17; EU, 156–58; P, 141–42.

49. T, 269; TM, 317.

50. Popular religion is a term Hume used throughout his religious writings. For instance, "Thus it may safely be affirmed, that popular religions are really, in the conception of their more vulgar votaries, a species of daemonism; and the higher the deity is exalted in power and knowledge, the lower of course is he depressed in goodness and benevolence; whatever epithets of praise may be bestowed on him by his amazed adorers" ("The Natural History of Religion," WOR, 170). Popular religion is used in Hume's lexicon for revealed, orthodox, supernatural religion, as expressed in the Scottish Presbyterian Church. He also uses enthusiasm to express the same sentiment; note his essay "Of Superstition and Enthusiasm." It bears noting that the term enthusiasm was widely used in the seventeenth and eighteenth centuries to denote special inspiration or extravagant religious devotion. John Locke, in his "Essay Concerning Human Understanding," book 4, devotes a chapter to enthusiasm. So, Hume was in good and familiar taxonomical territory.

51. EU, 146; P, 132.

52. "The Natural History of Religion," WOR, 181.

moving towards a day of perfection. The grounding of this divine historical thesis is in a metaphysically received Scripture that is held to be beyond human judgment and criticism. Therefore, Christianity dogmatically teaches that political and social arrangements have an all-important future significance, but an unimportant past one. That is, Christian philosophers judge the present by the future completion of the ages, not by the past custom, tradition, and sentiment of the common life. Hume missed the biblical teaching about the authority and approval of certain traditions.[53]

Hume held that this future orientation of sacred history was impossible to accept rationally: "No new fact can ever be inferred from the religious hypothesis; no event foreseen or foretold; no reward or punishment expected or dreaded, beyond what is already known by practice and observation."[54] History is set in concrete. "In general, it may, I think, be established as a maxim, that where any cause is known only by its particular effects, it must be impossible to infer any new effects from that cause."[55] The point is that we can observe and testify to past divine working in history but have no warrant to assume that the future is going to be altered or guided by the providential hand in the same fashion.[56]

This exclusively future orientation of some Christian thinking correctly bothered Hume because it seemed to loosen the commitment of orthodox Christians, "these vain reasoners," to the present moral order.[57] Hume cited the example of the great Frenchman Blaise Pascal (1623–1662) to illustrate his point: "The most ridiculous superstitions directed Pascal's faith and practice; and an extreme contempt of this life, in comparison of the future, was the chief foundation of his conduct."[58]

53. Cf. Acts 28:17; 1 Cor 11:2, 23; 15:1–11; 2 Thess 2:5; 3:6.
54. EU, 146; P, 132.
55. EU, 145n; P, 131n.
56. In Job-like terms Hume queried: "I ask; who carried them [Christian philosophers] into the celestial regions, who admitted them into the councils of the gods, who opened to them the book of fate, that they thus rashly affirm, that their deities have executed or will execute, any purpose beyond what has actually appeared? (EU, 138; P, 125; Job 38; cf. Isa 40:12–31). "I answer that you have no reason to give it [i.e., justice of the gods] any particular extent, but only so far as you see it, at present, exert itself" (EU, 142; P, 128).
57. EU, 141; P, 127–28. This is a partial caricature of revealed Christianity, for the Reformed Scottish church preached of Christian involvement in society. Samuel Rutherford, professor of Latin and literature at Edinburgh in the seventeenth century, wrote *Lex, Rex, or the Law and the Prince, a Dispute for the Just Prerogative of King and People*, dealing more with political science than theology. For biblical texts disconfirming this Humean allegation, see Jer 29:4–9; Gen 18:16–33; Ezek 22:30; 1 Tim 2:1–4; etc.
58. EM, 343.

Livingston correctly notes a similarity between the rationalist and the Christian in that both are detached from the common life. The rationalist has his "timeless order of nature," and the Christian has his "future, perfect society as the standard of legitimacy."[59] Hume's Irish contemporary, Edmund Burke, writing with an appreciation for Christian metaphysics, saw the French Revolution as a rationalist-inspired struggle for absolute power over the institution of government, as opposed to a struggle for individual freedom. He argued that the French Revolution was the work primarily of French political intellectuals such as Jean-Jacques Rousseau (1712–1778), who did not have a stake in society and were even society's enemies.[60] Hume believed, contrary to Burke's Christianity, that it would be socially destructive for us to hold a fated view of the present that was dependent on metaphysical forces guiding and pre-ordaining the future. Such a view "reverses the whole course of nature," since, for Hume, the past was paramount and the future was problematic. As for Rousseau, who had insisted on the iniquity of all historically formed institutions and the absolute necessity for a present-day legislator to free the people from their institutional chains,[61] Hume would reply that it is from the past that we receive our normative narrative of the common life with its customs and standards. Like Tevye in *Fiddler on the Roof*, tradition is everything. Without the past, nothing of importance can be said about the present. The rationalist is conceited and the Christian imagines things[62] when they presume to judge the present from the viewpoint of their abstract systems.

Because Hume believed religion was a danger to the peace and harmony of society, he thought that religion and politics did not mix: "Nor have the political interests of society any connexion with the philosophical disputes concerning metaphysics and religion."[63] In his essay "Whether the British Government Inclines More to Absolute Monarchy or to a Republic," Hume referred to the sects of philosophy and religion that "excite such a ferment, and [are] both opposed and defended with such vehemence, that [they] always spread faster, and multiply [their] partizans with greater rapidity, than any old established opinion, recommended by the sanction of the laws and of antiquity."[64] In the second *Enquiry*, he wrote that modern

---

59. Livingston, *Hume's Philosophy*, 297.

60. Edmund Burke, *Reflections on the Revolution*.

61. Rousseau, "Of the Civil State," in *Of the Social Contract*, 18–19; "Of the Legislator," in *Of the Social Contract*, 36–40.

62. EU, 141; P, 128

63. EU, 147; P, 132

64. E, 51; LF, 50.

religion (e.g., Christianity) sought to control our whole conduct through an austere system of teaching of metaphysical rewards and punishments.[65]

Burkean scholar Francis Canavan points out other fundamental differences between Hume and Burke. Burke held that religion informed human nature about morals and that there existed an understandable and ordered universe that was discoverable through "our reason, our relations, and our necessities." In short, Burke accepted a doctrine of rational causality and the intelligibility of being.[66] Hume, on the other hand, did not accept a religious conception of morality, and he denied the possibility of a rational metaphysic, since he supposed that no real connection of objects with one another is discoverable by reason.

Hume believed that the metaphysical approach to politics or morals was inappropriate, because metaphysics tells us nothing about human experience and because metaphysical principles have no proven applicability to the common life.

In short, Christianity, for Hume, was a divisive and destructive system.[67] It created in its adherents a blind zealousness and ambition that was present in no other form of thought. A century later, during the Crimean War, Alfred, Lord Tennyson (1809–1892), would capture such religious fervency when he wrote of British cavalry: "Theirs not to make reply, / Theirs not to reason why, / Theirs but to do and die. / Into the valley of Death / Rode the six hundred."[68] The late great twentieth-century British conservative and follower of Hume Michael Oakeshott called revealed Christianity, "highfalutin metaphysical beliefs." He argued that those who use Christianity to legitimize a certain social order are potentially dangerous because they press government to do more than it should do. They "turn a private dream into a public and compulsory manner of living." Indeed, "the conjunction of dreaming and ruling generates tyranny," not unlike the rationalist ideal.[69] Hume's antagonism towards Christianity was also evidenced in sentiments such as the following: "He is a very honest man, said the prince of *Sallee*,

---

65. EM 341–42.
66. Canavan, *Political Reason of Edmund Burke*, 42–45.
67. T, 272; TM, 319; cf. E, 58–59; LF, 60.
68. Alfred, Lord Tennyson (1809–1892), "The Charge of the Light Brigade." In 1854, during the Crimean War, an English light-cavalry brigade of over six hundred men was led into a hopeless charge against well-protected batteries of Russian artillery at Balaklava. The blunder resulted in the deaths of well over two-thirds of the British soldiers. See Farwell, *Queen Victoria's Little Wars*, 68–84.
69. Oakeshott, "On Being Conservative," essay in *Rationalism in Politics and Other Essays*, 186, 194.

speaking of *De Ruyter*.⁷⁰ It is a pity he were a Christian."⁷¹ Ayer has written, "Hume is consistently hostile to Christianity, both on intellectual and on moral grounds."⁷²

Fittingly, some of Hume's antagonism towards orthodox Christianity may have come from his family custom and tradition. Mossner notes the extensive family connections that opposed the evangelical and Covenanter wing of the Protestant Scottish church.⁷³ The Calvinistic Covenanters received particularly harsh comments when Hume approvingly embraced the antisemitism of the Scottish Roman Catholic writer Andrew Michael Ramsey (1686–1743).⁷⁴

70. De Ruyter or De Ruiter was a seventeenth-century Dutch admiral who successfully engaged the British and French fleets. He was killed in a sea battle in 1676. A. T. Mahan calls De Ruyter "a great seaman" *(Influence of Seapower)*, 126–53.

71. The Natural History of Religion," WOR, 156

72. Ayer, "Hume," 204. Although Hume does not often refer to Montaigne, Montaigne's pyrrhonism had an influence on Hume, as did his religious skepticism. Hume urged in his essay "The Sceptic": "Assist yourself by a frequent perusal of the entertaining moralists: Have recourse to the . . . gaiety of MONTAIGNE" (LF, 179n). For his part, Montaigne wrote, "There is no hostility that excels Christian hostility" ("Apology for Raymond Sebond," in Frame, *Selections from the Essays*, 57n280).

73. Mossner, *Life of David Hume*, 12–13, 22.

74. "The God of the Jews is a most cruel, unjust, partial, and fantastical being. To accomplish the barbarous, partial degree of predestination and reprobation, God abandoned all nations to darkness, idolatry, and superstition, without any saving knowledge or salutary graces; unless it was one particular nation, whom he chose as his peculiar people. This chosen nation was, however, the most stupid, ungrateful, rebellious and perfidious of all nations. . . . For, in other respects, the bulk of Christians have continued as corrupt as the rest of mankind in their morals; yea, so much the more perverse and criminal, that their lights were greater. . . . It is true that all this makes God odious, a hater of souls, rather than a lover of them; a cruel, vindictive tyrant, an impotent or a wrathful daemon, rather than an all-powerful, beneficent father of spirits. . . . The grosser pagans contented themselves with divinizing lust, incest, and adultery; but the predestinarian doctors have divinized cruelty, wrath, fury, vengeance and all the blackest vices" ("The Natural History of Religion," WOR, 171–73). Is there not a sense of Feuerbach's anthropological God in the last part of this Humean approved statement? I believe so. See Feuerbach, *Essence of Christianity*, 228. Interestingly, Francis Fukuyama comments that the rationalistic French Revolution institutionalized a Christianized state in Ramseyian anthropomorphic terms: "The modern liberal democratic state that came into being in the aftermath of the French Revolution was, simply, the realization of the Christian ideal of freedom and universal human equality in the here-and-now. It constituted a recognition that it was man who had created the Christian God in the first place, and therefore man who could make God come down to earth and live in the parliament buildings, presidential palaces, and bureaucracies or the modern state" (Fukuyama, *End of History*, 199). Hume believed that polytheism was more consistent with the origin and growth of religion, more tolerant, and therefore more useful to a secure and peaceful society, than monotheism (e. g., Christianity). He held that monotheism has a god who is more intolerant, jealous, judgmental, revengeful, and demanding than

Still, Hume did have a family tradition of sympathy with the Scottish Presbyterians. He had an uncle whose father was hanged as a Covenanter by the Scottish crown.[75] And Mossner does relate a tale of apparent false accusation in a paternity suit against Hume by one Agnes Galbraith, which the leadership (session) of his parish church, the Kirk of Chirnside, dismissed, with a rebuke for Miss Galbraith. So, the evangelical Presbyterians was prepared to be somewhat scrupulous with Hume despite its theological differences.[76]

It seems that Hume made a decision early in his life to pursue fame and ideological autonomy from the Scottish Presbyterian church at the expense of other personal goals or accomplishments. He speaks of "my love of literary fame, my ruling passion,"[77] a "certain Boldness of Temper" to resist "any Authority,"[78] and that it is only through philosophic musings that the "greatness and elevation of [the] soul is to be found."[79]

With these fundamental moral choices made early on, Hume could brush off his strong dislike of revealed Presbyterian Christianity as an unimportant personal character flaw, for he states that his passionate love of fame "never soured my temper (humour)," nor did it cause him to be "susceptible of enmity."[80] I suspect, however, that he would have received an argument as to the latter claims from many Presbyterians in Scotland and England during his day. Hume somewhat disingenuously stated that he "wantonly exposed" himself to religious factions,[81] yet he postponed publishing his essay "On Miracles" in the *Treatise* for years,[82] and his essays "On Suicide" and

---

the gods of polytheism ("The Natural History of Religion," WOR, 145–46).

75. Mossner, *Life of David Hume*, 33.

76. Mossner, *Life of David Hume*, 81–83.

77. E, 615; LF, xl. In his second *Enquiry*, Hume wrote approvingly of the love of fame, "A desire of fame, reputation, or a character with others, is so far from being blamable, that it seems inseparable from virtue, genius, capacity, and a generous or noble disposition" (265).

78. Letter to Dr. George Cheyne, cited in Smith, *Philosophy of David Hume*, 14. This sentiment is, of course, a common one, found in many of the revolutionary philosophers such as Descartes, Rousseau, and James.

79. Letter to Michael Ramsay, 1727 (B1, 15).

80. E, 615; LF, xl.

81. E, 615; LF, p. xl.

82. Hume's essay on miracles caused considerable consternation from the theological quarters and pastoral theologians such as Thomas Rutherford, William Adams, George Ridpath, Philip Skelton, John Douglas, Richard Price, John Leland, and especially the Calvinist George Campbell, son of Colin Campbell. William Warburton inveighed against dear "Davie" in print. Warburton wrote to Rev. Richard Hurd, "I will trim the rogue's [Hume's] jacket, at least sit upon his skirts." He called Hume "a puny

"Of the Immortality of the Soul" were not published until after his death, for fear of further offense to the church. In any case, with his dismissal of evangelical Christianity as, at the very least, nonsense, and more probably evil, Hume misinterpreted Christianity,[83] and had the practice of cherry-picking disagreeable factions of the church that displeased him in order to characterize the whole. This should not be surprising, since eighteenth-century Scotland bore the influence of the great Scottish Calvinist preachers and theologians from two previous centuries.[84] Hume simply could not escape their influence over Scottish thought, so he ran from it.

Hume's biographer, Mossner, reinforced Hume's faction-characterization of Christianity. Mossner, no friend of eighteenth-century Presbyterians, cites Hume's notation of James Beattie of Marischal College; John Brown of Haddington; William Warburton, bishop of Gloucester; and John Witherspoon of Paisley (and later Princeton) for particular reproach.[85] To refute the Hume/Mossner caricature, it should be noted that James Beattie

---

Dialectician from the North who came to the attack with a beggarly troop of routed sophisms" (Mossner, *Life of David Hume*, 326).

83. I have noted from time to time some specific areas where Hume's criticism of orthodox Christianity is misdirected, since some of his own ideas are prefigured in biblical texts, including some of his criticisms.

84. For instance, George Wishart (1513–1546), John Knox (1514–1572), Andrew Melville (1545–1622), Robert Bruce (1554–1631), Alexander Henderson (1583–1646), Robert Baillie (1599–1662), Samuel Rutherford (1600–1661), John Brown of Wamphray (1610–1679), George Gillespie (1613–1648), and Ebenezer Erskine (1680–1754).

85. For Mossner's comments on Beattie, see *Life of David Hume*, 577–82; for his comments on Brown, see 308–9; for his comments on Warburton, see 123, 289–90, 323–26; and for his comments on Witherspoon, see 336–37, 356, 368. The Scottish Presbyterians during the eighteenth century split into two groups: the Moderates and the Popular Part or Highflyers. The Moderate Presbyterian Party found poetry, drama, literature, and philosophy engaging vehicles of religious expression almost as the same authority as the Bible. These liberals believed that every person had the right, even obligation, to interpret the Bible and cared more about the graceful delivery and expression of sermons, speeches, and writings than content. The Popular Party were Westminster confessing Calvinists. Witherspoon was a leader in the Popular Party and took the opportunity to mock and criticize the Moderate Party, led sometimes by Witherspoon's friend Alexander Carlyle. While we have no positive evidence that he ever met Hume, Witherspoon read and commented on Hume's writings. In 1756, Witherspoon wrote an essay entitled "Essay on Justification," in which he calls Hume's enumeration of virtues "an insult upon reason itself" because Hume included such "virtues" as "wit, genius, health, taper legs, and broad shoulders." (T, 3–4). In 1766, Witherspoon moved from Scotland to America to become the president of a new college, College of New Jersey (Princeton). Garry Wills argues that "Witherspoon was probably the most influential teacher in the entire history of American education. His pupils included a president of the United States, a vice-president, 21 United States senators, 29 members of the House, 12 state governors, 56 state legislators and 33 judges, 3 on the Supreme Court" (Wills, *Explaining America*, 18).

(1735–1803), professor of moral philosophy at Marischal College in Aberdeen, was a romantic, orthodox Christian poet and philosopher who challenged Hume at several points.[86] Perhaps Beattie's most telling criticism was against Hume's evident racism, as contained in Hume's essay "Of National Character." Beattie brought orthodox Christianity to bear on this unfortunate area of Hume's philosophy.[87]

As for John Brown (1722–1787) and William Warburton (1698–1779), while it is agreed that both of them had contentious spirits, Brown left a legacy of a learned Scottish clergy and professional class for generations of service to the English-speaking world; and Warburton was a Shakespearean and Lockean scholar, an Anglican bishop, a friend and champion of the English poet Alexander Pope, and an early and outspoken opponent of the British slave trade.[88] John Witherspoon (1723–1794) became the first president of Princeton University in the American colonies, a New Jersey member of both Continental Congresses, and the only clergyman and academic to sign the Declaration of Independence. In short, some of the key men who opposed Hume's view of Christianity were not uneducated, fringe rustics, but persons of deep learning, piety, and social involvements, the very characteristics Hume most admired and praised.

In his essay "Of Parties in General," Hume wrote, "Sects of philosophy, in the ancient world, were more zealous than parties of religion; but, in modern times, parties of religion are more furious and enraged than the most cruel factions that ever arose from interest and ambition," and

---

86. Beattie himself was challenged in his criticism of Hume by no less than Immanuel Kant: "It is positively painful to see how utterly [Hume's] opponents, Reid, Oswald, Beattie, and lastly Priestley, missed the point of the problem; for while they were ever taking for granted that which he doubted, and demonstrating with zeal and often with impudence that which he never thought of doubting, they so misconstrued his valuable suggestion that everything remained in its old condition, as if nothing had happened. . . . I should think that Hume might fairly have laid as much claim to common sense as Beattie and, in addition, to a critical reason (such as the latter did not possess)" (Kant, *Prolegomena*, 6–7). Hume, not surprisingly, called Beattie a "bigotted silly Fellow" in a letter to John Strahan in 1775. Alvin Plantinga and Nicholas Wolterstorff may have the final word for evangelicals on Thomas Reid and Hume in their book *Faith and Rationality*: "The ghost of David Hume seemed safely enough laid to rest by the likes of Reid and [William] Paley, so that the key question for the apologist was not natural religion, but revealed religion, that is, the Bible" (229).

87. Beattie, *An Essay*, 479ff. See John Immerwahr's "Hume's Revised Racism" for this feature of Beattie's contribution.

88. In a long essay entitled "Of the Populousness of Ancient Nations," Hume argued that "domestic slavery is more cruel and oppressive than any civil subjection whatsoever" and "slavery is in general disadvantageous both to the happiness and populousness of mankind" (*Essays* [Miller], 383, 396).

Christianity "engendered a spirit of persecution" that was poisonous and fractious to society.[89]

Sabine opines that "the influence of Hume has been the most potent solvent of religious dogmatism that modern philosophy has produced."[90] Hume believed that metaphysical reasoning in political affairs leads to intractably opposed viewpoints where there is no common ground between the groups. For metaphysicians, seeking compromise and conciliation is to be a traitor and heretic. For religious metaphysicians, to press their own cause is to press God's cause, and no wavering is to be tolerated. All enemies are to be extirpated, perhaps with fanfare.[91] Prescient observations applicable to the twenty-first century, as radical Muslims allow no deviation from strict conformity to their twisted doctrines and dogmas.

Hume argued that Christianity created social factions and sects by its very nature of being metaphysical.[92] He wrote in "Of Parties in General": "As much as legislators and founders of states ought to be honored and respected among men, as much ought the founders of sects and factions to be detested and hated; because the influence of faction is directly contrary to that of laws."[93] In a wonderfully insightful passage in his *History*, Hume wrote that Charles I (1600–1649, King of England and Scotland and enemy of Reformed clerics) correctly saw the association between religion and politics, in that he understood "that when he was contending for the

89. E, 60–61; LF, 62–63

90. Sabine, 721.

91. "Of Parties in General": "After Christianity became the established religion, they have engendered a spirit of persecution," "Christendom the scene of religious wars and divisions," "but in modern times, parties of religion are more furious and enraged than the most cruel factions that ever arose from interest and ambition" (E, 59–61; LF, 62–63). "Of Superstition and Enthusiasm": "My *second* reflection with regard to these species of false religion [e.g., Quakers, independents, Presbyterians] is, *that religions, which partake of enthusiasm are, on their first rise, more furious and violent than those which partake of superstition [e.g., Roman Catholic], but in a little time become more gentle and moderate.* The violence of this species of religion, when excited by novelty, and animated by opposition, appears from numberless instances; of the *anabaptist* in GERMANY, the *camisars* in FRANCE, the *levellers* and other fanatics in ENGLAND, and the *covenanters* in SCOTLAND" (E, 78; LF, 76–77).

92. Hume apparently missed the biblical injunction for believers to reason with their neighbors. See Isaiah 1:18 (*yakach*, reason), and Job 13:6 (*tokachath*, reason), and Acts 17:2; 18:4, 19, where reason is the translation for *dialegomai*. There are many other biblical references exhorting Christians to be reasonable and rational in their thinking and public discourse.

93. E, 55; LF, 55. Cf. H, 4:91–92: "In all former ages, not wholly excepting even those of Greece and Rome, religious sects and heresies and schisms had been esteemed dangerous, if not pernicious, to civil government, and were regarded as the source of faction and private combination and opposition to the laws."

surplice, he was in effect, fighting for his crown and even his head." He was particularly agitated against Presbyterian clergymen who opposed him from the pulpit.[94]

What are the costs to human common life of metaphysical or supernatural religious thinking? Hume listed intolerance, vengefulness, unruly social factions and divisions, and absolutized governmental policies.

DAVID HUME AND SKEPTICISM

There was yet a third enemy of common-life philosophy, and that was skepticism. Much of the antagonism against Hume has come as a result of what seems to his opponents to be a pronounced skepticism. Even before Hume died, James Beattie's attempted refutation of Hume's skepticism, *The Nature and Immutability of Truth in Opposition to Sophistry and Scepticism* (1770), went through eleven editions in just ten years! Most Humean scholars credit Norman Kemp Smith's work in 1941 with a counter interpretation which holds that Hume was not such a rank and excessive skeptic after all. Smith argues against Hume's being a philosophical "subversive skeptic"[95] or a malicious skeptical thinker.[96] For Smith, Hume was not primarily a skeptic, but rather a philosophical naturalist, in that he offered, in place of rationalism, Cartesian doubt, and metaphysical certitude, a causal theory of how instinct, habit, and feeling determine belief. Smith argues that while Hume was positing his true philosophy, he had to destroy excessive Pyrrhonian skepticism in the process.[97]

---

94. H, 5:546. "[The king wrote] that unless religion was preserved, the militia would be of little use to the crown; and that if the pulpits had not obedience which would never be it Presbyterian government was absolutely established, the king would have but small comfort of the militia. This reasoning shows the king's good sense, and proves his attachment to Episcopacy, though partly founded on religious principles, was also, in his situation, derived from the soundest views of civil policy. In reality, it was easy for the king to perceive, by the necessary connection maintained at trifles and important matters, and by the connections maintained at that time between religion and politics, that when he was contending for the surplice, he was in effect fighting for his crown, and even, for his head. Few of the popular party could perceive this connection. Most of them were carried headlong by fanaticism; as might be expected in the ignorant multitude."

95. As D. C. Stove wrote in "Hume, the Causal Principle, and Kemp Smith," as cited in Livingston, *Hume's Philosophy*, 26.

96. As John Randall Jr. argued in "David Hume: Radical Empiricist and Pragmatist," as cited in Livingston, *Hume's Philosophy*, 26.

97. Whelan also argues that Hume is not primarily a skeptic but is instead a positivist, in that Hume advances "doctrines that I believe may best be grasped under the general headings of *order* and *artifice:* the order that we create or impose on our cognitive

David Norton notes that Hume treated five kinds of skepticism: ethical or moral, religious, Cartesian, Pyrrhonian, and academic.[98]

Hume's opposition to moral and ethical skepticism was clearly enunciated. Concerning religious skepticism, Hume did not devote a great deal of specific intellectual weaponry. That he was a skeptic regarding organized religion has been shown clearly and unequivocally from his writings;[99] but his system did not stress religious skepticism, although he applied it that way to some extent in his essays and his *History*. He did state in his first *Enquiry* that "the *Skeptic* is another enemy of religion."[100] And the term skeptic does appear frequently in his *Dialogues*. One reference from his *History* will illustrate his religious skepticism—or, at any rate, the extreme care which he recommended when one is examining extraordinary claims:

> It is the business of history to distinguish between the miraculous and the marvellous; to reject the first in all narrations merely profane and human; to doubt the second; and when obliged by unquestionable testimony, as in the present case [i.e., Joan of Arc] to admit of something extraordinary, to receive as little of it as is consistent with the known facts and circumstances.[101]

On Cartesian skepticism, we find Hume criticizing Descartes and his antecedent skepticism, which stresses universal doubt, as being impossible to attain and sustain.[102] Still, Hume did not completely dismiss Cartesian skepticism, for it can provide "a necessary preparative to the study of philosophy, by preserving a proper impartiality in our judgements, and a weaning our mind from all those prejudices, which we may have imbibed from education or rash opinion."[103] Moderate skepticism is good. Indeed, we will see that moderation in all things, including skepticism, is a Humean watchword.

---

and moral worlds through habitual adherence to the rules that are constitutive of mental and social artifices" (*Order and Artifice*, 4).

98. Norton, *David Hume*, 244.

99. Hume clearly is a skeptic about religious systems, such as organized Calvinism. But he was not skeptical about natural religion, which is based on a natural belief in some sort of first cause. This view is suggested in the *Dialogues*. It conforms to the Smith interpretation of Hume as a naturalist, rather than a radical skeptic.

100. EU, 149; P, 135.

101. H, 2:389

102. EU, 149–50; P, 135–36.

103. EU, 150; P, 136.

On to Pyrrhonian skepticism. What we know of it comes from the writings of Sextus Empiricus, a third-century philosopher.[104] Hume described Pyrrhonian skepticism in his first *Enquiry* as a fallacious system of thought, which holds the unfitness of the individual's mental faculty to reach any fixed determination about anything.[105] In short, one can't know anything about anything for certain. In his *Treatise*, Hume argued against such skepticism by calling it "total skepticism" and a "fantastic sect."[106]

The threat to civil life from Pyrrhonian skepticism was the debunking of common-life morality. In Hume's *Dialogues*, Cleanthes criticizes Philo's (more like Hume's) excessive skepticism as a potential justification for the state to unduly intrude into the affairs of society.[107] If Pyrrhonianism attacked only revealed religion, it would not have caused Hume much concern. But Pyrrhonianism attacked much more; it attacked the very idea of a moral, religious view of life. With this religion of skepticism, the Pyrrhonian could wreak havoc on the very humanness of humanity, and this Hume could not passively permit. Indeed, skepticism would leave the individual with nothing to believe, nothing to hold on to, no compass for making life's decisions. Hume had Philo state in the *Dialogues* that he is a person "who has himself no fixed station or abiding city, which he is ever, on any occasion, obliged to defend."[108] If one doesn't stand for something, one will fall for anything.

What is the cost to human common life of extreme or excessive Pyrrhonic skepticism? Hume replied that it was anxiety, lethargy, and even the end of human life itself.[109]

---

104. Sextus also called Pyrrhonism the Sceptic discipline, the zetetic discipline for searching, the ephectic discipline for suspending, or the aporetic discipline for doubting. Sextus included five basic points in an outline of Pyrrhonism. First, Pyrrhonists "do not make any positive assertion that anything we shall say is wholly as we affirm it to be." Second, they "merely report accurately on each thing as our impressions of it are at the moment." Third, Sextus divides philosophers into three camps: a) those who "claim to have discovered the truth" (the Dogmatists); b) those who say, "finding the truth is an impossibility" (the Academics); and c) those who are still searching for the truth (the Sceptics). Fourth, Pyrrhonism "is an ability to place in antithesis, in any manner whatever, appearances and judgements, and thus—because of the equality of force in the objects and arguments opposed—to come first of all to a suspension of judgment." Fifth, after a "suspension of judgment" on matters of opinion has been achieved, then one can move on to the attainment of "mental tranquility" ("an undisturbed and calm state of soul") because of being able to be intellectually disengaged. See Hallie, *Scepticism*, 31–34. I am indebted to Norton's *David Hume* for helping here.

105. EU, 150; P, 136.

106. T, 183; TM, 234.

107. D, 190–191.

108. D, 249.

109. EU, 160; P, 144.

Hume, however, believed that Pyrrhonism does not stand much of a chance to take a permanent hold of the individual, because it goes against the grain of human nature.[110]

Finally, if Hume's skepticism was not moral or Cartesian or Pyrrhonistic, and only secondarily religious, what kind of skepticism was it? Hume described it as mitigated, academic, or moderate.[111] Hume's academic skepticism recognized that human nature is not easily quantifiable or understandable, so a degree of philosophic humility is warranted. Hume, whose common-life philosophy was based on "the nature of human life," was keenly aware of the "universal perplexity and confusion which is inherent in human nature."[112] Philosophic ambivalence is the Humean order of the day.[113]

Hume's celebrated, much criticized, and perhaps misunderstood skepticism was based on his conviction that all our distinct perceptions are of distinct existences, and that the connection between these perceptions is not known to be real but only imagined, that is, facilitated through our imagination. For Hume, this lack of knowable connection was serious enough, but it seemed to threaten our perception of individual identity and our knowledge of the existence of the external world. Does philosophy provide a connection to these individual distinct perceptions?[114]

---

110. EU, 160; P, 144. Living on Main Street will make a person wiser than living in the sheltered groves of academe. Hume gave his final answer to Pyrrhonism in the "action, and employment and occupations of common-life philosophy" (EU, 158–59; P, 143; cf. D, 191). "Pyrrhonism['s] . . . undistinguished doubts are, in some measure, corrected by common sense and reflections" (EU, 161; P, 145). And "nothing can be more serviceable" in "freeing us from the impossibility" of the "Pyrrhonian doubt" than "the strong power of natural instinct" (EU, 162; P, 146).

111. EU, 40–41; P, 41.

112. EU, 161; P, 145–46.

113. In the same section of the first *Enquiry*, Hume wrote of this academical skepticism: "There is, indeed, a more mitigated scepticism or academical philosophy, which may be both durable and useful, and which may, in part, be the result of this pyrrhonism or *excessive* scepticism, when its undistinguished doubts are, in some measure, corrected by common sense and reflection . . . which is best adapted to the narrow capacity of human understanding. . . . This means these philosophers set themselves at ease and arrive at last . . . at the same indifference . . . which true philosophers by their moderate scepticism [attain]" (T, 224; TM, 273). "In general, there is a degree of doubt, and caution, and modesty, which, in all kinds of scrutiny and decision, ought for ever to accompany a just reasoner" (EU, 162; P, 146). Indeed, Hume hopes that his brand of skepticism will "inspire [dogmatic reasoners] with more modesty and reserve, and diminish their fond opinion of themselves, and their prejudices against antagonist" SEU, 161–62; P, 145–46).

114. EM, 223; OC, 58.

Hume asked on what ground, if any, can we justify our belief in the existence of ourselves and of externalities? Are we forever confined to an understanding of causality by subjectivity, personal propensity,[115] and private beliefs? Hume's answer was, basically, that the problem of justification does not really arise, for, "We may well ask, What causes induce us to believe in the existence of body? but 'tis vain to ask, Whether there be body or not? That is a point, which we must take for granted in all our reasonings."[116]

We may not have cognitive certainty, but that is not critical for living our lives in or understanding our world. We simply do the best we can with what we have: "'Tis impossible upon any system to define either our understanding or sense; and we must but expose them farther when we endeavor to justify them in that manner. . . . Carelessness and inattention alone can afford us any remedy."[117]

Hume continued with this key statement about his skepticism:

> Another species of mitigated skepticism which may be of advantage to mankind, and which may be the natural result of the Pyrrhonian doubts and scruples, is the limitation of our enquires to such subjects as are best adapted to the narrow capacity of human understanding.[118]

What he was saying is that we should limit our inquiries to those things within the scope of our faculties and experience, and that even though we should suspend dogmatic assertions, we should not and cannot suspend belief: "While we cannot give a satisfactory reason, why we believe, after a thousand experiments, that a stone will fall, or a fire burn; can we ever satisfy ourselves concerning a determination, which we form. . . ?"[119]

This philosophic disengagement[120] stemming from Hume's mitigated skepticism was given further expression in his anti-supernatural religious writings.[121]

---

115. Hume's notion of various human propensities is kin to Konrad Lorenz's "The Great Parliament of Instincts," elucidated in his book *On Aggression*. Note especially chs. 6 and 13. However, instinct for Lorenz is a neurophysiological function of the human developed through evolution, and not habituation developed through social interaction like it is for Hume.

116. T, 187; TM, 238.

117. T, 218; TM, 268. Cf. John 20:29; 1 Cor 13:12; 2 Cor 4:18; 5:7; 1 John 3:2.

118. EU, 162; P, 146.

119. EU, 162; P, 146. Cf. 1 Tim 1:4; 4:7; 2 Tim 2:23; Titus 3:9.

120. This concept of Hume's system being one of disengagement is ably argued by Siebert, *Moral Animus*, 170–96.

121. "The whole is a riddle, an enigma, an inexplicable mystery. Doubt, uncertainty, suspence of judgment appear the only result of our most accurate scrutiny, concerning

Early in *The Natural History*, Hume commended "a manly, steady virtue, which either preserves us from disastrous melancholy accidents, or teaches us to bear them"[122] as an alternative to the superstitions of revealed religion. His natural-religion concept of a first cause gets us started, but the rest is up to us as a human community.

So Hume, to prepare the way for setting forth his true philosophy, needed to dispatch with vigor the contending philosophies that failed to satisfy the reality of the common life of human understanding. He proposed in their place his mitigated skepticism, academical skepticism, common life philosophy, or true philosophy. Part of this was what he called his learned system of thought, formulated by "the higher and more difficult operations of the mind that require leisure and solitude, and [that] cannot be brought to perfection, without long preparation and severe labour."[123] It is to a summary of the main features of that system that I now turn.

---

this subject. But such is the reality of human reason, and such the irresistible contagion of opinion, that even this deliberate doubt could scarcely be upheld; did we not enlarge our view, and opposing one species of superstition to another, set them a quarrelling; while we ourselves, during their fury and contention, happily make our escape into the calm, though obscure, regions of philosophy" ("The Natural History of Religion," WOR, 182).

122. "The Natural History of Religion," WOR, 178.

123. E, 568; LF, 533.

3

David Hume's Learned Philosophy

The Operations of the Mind may be divided into the learned and the conversible. The Learned are such as have chosen for their Portion the higher and more difficult Operations of the Mind, which require Leisure and Solitude, and cannot be brought to perfection, without long Preparation and severe Labour. The conversible World [have] a Taste of Pleasure, an Inclination to the easier and more gentle Exercises of the Understanding, to obvious Reflection on human Affairs and the Duties of common Life, and to the Observation of the Blemishes or Perfections of the particular Objects, that surround them.[1]

DAVID HUME TOOK GREAT pains in breaking down just how humans think and put together ideas. For him, the past was crucial in understanding knowledge, language, ethics, and politics.[2] He was a philosopher guided by history because, for his moral world, common-life philosophy has a reference to the past deeply imbedded in it. That is, it feeds off the past for nourishment and growth. Since the past was so important to Hume, historical narrative also was important, for it is only through narratives that social impressions can be turned into enduring ideas. Early events, based on impressions and recounted through stories, create ideas. These, in turn, produce other ideas, which give us meaning and significance about the human condition as it has been lived out in common life.[3] We can understand

1. E/LF, "Of Essay Writing," 533–34.
2. Cf. Job 8:8–10; Ps 18:3–4; Eccl 1:9; Rom 15:4; etc.
3. T, 146; TM, 196.

things only after they have occurred, and we can understand the present only considering later occurrences, when what had been the present has become past. These future impressions are important for a correct comprehension of the present.[4] This theme of the importance of history is woven throughout Hume's learned philosophy.

Several of Hume's key epistemological foci are fundamental in understanding his social theory:

* Hume's notions of impressions, ideas, and associations created the grounding for his doctrine of social convention and habits.
* His view of causality led him to postulate a common-life approach to social arrangements, and his view of the religious propensity[5] in individuals served him as he argued for a type of deified cultural structure which has no room for a revealed deity.
* Hume's notion of the self portrayed individual identity as integrally connected to the past and present society, and so history is a key element in understanding the individual's importance in social functioning.

DAVID HUME AND IMPRESSIONS, IDEAS, AND ASSOCIATIONS

Fundamental to Hume's philosophy is the notion that the content of the mind arises from experience. His generic name of this content is perceptions, which are divided into impressions and ideas. Impressions come, in various ways, from objects, while ideas come from impressions. We see this expressed in what Hume called the first principle of his "science of human nature":[6]

> We shall here content ourselves with establishing one general proposition, That all our simple ideas in their first appearance are derived from simple impressions, which are correspondent to them, and which they exactly represent.[7]

---

4. Carl L. Becker, in his book *The Heavenly City of the Eighteenth-Century Philosophers*, demonstrates the use of posterity in the thinking of the philosophers of the eighteenth century. He specifically mentions the contribution of Hume.

5. Cf. Gen 1:26f; Eccl 3:11; Rom 1:18–19; 1 Cor 11:7; Jas 3:9

6. T, 7; TM, 54.

7. T, 4; TM, 52.

Without impressions, there can be no ideas. Furthermore, simple ideas, to which this first principle refers, can be combined into complex ideas, which therefore need no separate, additional impression in order to exist.[8] For Hume, there was no such thing as an innate idea in the Cartesian sense, that is, an idea before an impression.[9]

Hume held that these impressions, which precede ideas, are more lively, vivacious, and forceful than the faint, pale, and weak corresponding ideas.[10] Simple ideas are only copies of previous impressions.[11] This means that impressions differ intrinsically from ideas by the internal characteristics of their strength or liveliness, as well as externally in terms of their origin.

Hume appealed to shared values, judgments, descriptions, and meanings to frame his philosophy. He maintained that the language of common, ordinary, everyday life was clear, concise, and authentic in describing the empirical world. He contrasted that clear, common-life language with the language of philosophy, which he said was controversial, confused, and obtuse.[12]

Since, in Hume's opinion, there were no genuinely abstract ideas, all ideas must be concrete and derived from concrete things. Without this concretizing of all ideas in experience we are left with spurious concepts and notions which have no necessary connection to reality. Anyone can posit anything, however foolish, and claim to be wise.[13]

For Hume, there were two types of impressions as well as two corresponding types of ideas: those of sensation and those of reflexion. Impressions from sensation, which pertain to the outer world, arise "in the soul originally, from unknown causes." Impressions from reflexion (reflection), pertaining to the inner world, arise "in great measure from our ideas," which have arisen, in turn, from impressions of sensation. He wrote that "the impressions of reflexion, *viz* passions, desires, and emotions, which

---

8. T, 3; TM, 51.

9. EU, 22; P, 24. Hume does note "one contradictory phaenomenon" which may disprove his thesis—that of the idea of the missing shade of blue in a "continual gradation of shades." Having generously supplied a contradiction, he nevertheless concludes: "this may serve as a proof, that the simple ideas are not always derived from the correspondent impressions; tho' the instance is so particular and singular, that 'tis scarce worth our observing, and does not merit that for it alone we should alter our general maxim" (T, 6; TM, 53).

10. T, 1–2; TM, 49.

11. EU, 19; P, 22.

12. EU, 21; P, 24.

13. T, 72; TM, 120; cf. 1 Cor 2; Col 2:8; 1 Tim 6:20.

principally deserve our attention, arise mostly from ideas."[14] So, we have a circular or spiral theory of understanding that goes something like this: impressions from external things lead to corresponding ideas, which in turn lead to corollary impressions of reflection, which lead to other ideas, and so on and so on. Furthermore, the engine of a thought is fueled by our imagination and memory.

Hume maintained that human passions, which are a type of impression or reflexion, are the initial stimuli of human actions: passion is to action somewhat as simple impression is to ideation. Human passions arise as a direct response to other features of human experience (hunger, fear, etc.), yet they are themselves the true active, generating factors in human behavior. Hume wrote, "Reason is, and ought only to be the slave of the passions and can never pretend to any other office than to serve and obey the [passions]."[15] What he ironically meant by this is that an active, generating principle (passions) cannot be controlled by a passive, inert principle (reason).[16] Perhaps Shakespeare said it best, "The brain may devise laws for the blood, but a hot temper leaps o'er a cold decree."[17]

If we know primarily by impressions, and impressions are perceptions, can we know anything besides our immediate experience? Hume answered, yes, we can know by association of simple ideas. He explained this process by stating that as impressions occur, they prompt memories of 1) similar impressions (resemblance), 2) contiguous impressions that happened nearby or at the same time, and 3) cause and effect. This happens because of a mental associating quality he described as a "gentle force";[18] it pushes the mind to pass from one idea to another idea based on these three relational qualities.[19]

In Hume's discussion of how the human mind unites the "continual succession of objects," and of the human "propensity to renew the same act or operation" in associating ideas, he focused on custom or habit as the critical faculty of human nature.[20] Hume's theory of association of ideas is one of the connecting chains of historical narrative which creates social and cultural continuity and, therefore, stability.

---

14. T, 8; TM, 55.
15. T, 415; TM, 462.
16. T, 457; TM, 509; cf. T, 413, 415; TM, 460–62.
17. Portia in Shakespeare, *Merchant of Venice*, 1.2.
18. T, 11; TM, 58.
19. T, 12–13; TM, 60.
20. EU, 43; P, 43.

Now if an impression continues to recur, must it be from the same object? Hume answered: no, it can be from similar objects. It is a matter of constancy of impressions over time. If these impressions occur frequently and regularly, the imagination will believe the object continues to exist even when it does not.

Memory alone acquaints us with the verifiable continuity and extent of this succession of perceptions: "This supposition, or idea of continu'd existence, acquires a force and vivacity from the memory of these broken impressions, and from that propensity, which they give us, to suppose them the same; . . . the very essence of belief consists in the force and vivacity of the conception."[21] Since impressions must precede ideas, we appropriate the sensible impressions through our memory and our imagination.[22] Our imagination connects, separates, and even recombines ideas.[23]

Simple ideas, as we earlier noted, can be combined into complex ideas, which Hume, following Locke, classified into substances, modes, and relations.[24]

Relations are important. Hume divided them into seven major kinds: 1) resemblance, 2) identity, 3) relations of time and place, 4) proportion in quantity or number, 5) degrees in any quality, 6) contrariety, and 7) causation. He further divided these seven relations into two classes: relations which "depend entirely on ideas, which we compare together" (Kant later

21. T, 199; TM, 250; cf. Luke 8:15; 1 Cor 11:2; 15:2 (*katecho*, hold firmly, keep).

22. T, 8–9; TM, 56.

23. Hume maintained that the similarity of objects eventually is seen by the imagination as an identity. Because the imagination is lazy (T, 215; TM, 265), it seeks to do the easy thing, and the easy thing is simply to make believe or feign that the objects continue to exist, even when the impressions are interrupted or terminated (T, 208; TM, 258). It is more difficult for the imagination to distinguish between distinct impressions than to "mistake the one for the other" and allow the impressions to coalesce into a single idea. Likeness, therefore, becomes sameness. The lazy nature of human imagination coincides with Hume's understanding of humans as primarily conservative, stable beings in that we derive personal satisfaction in the routine, the habitual, the customary modes of thought and action (cf. John 18:39; 1 Cor 8:7; 11:16 [*sunetheia*, habit]). But we do not just playfully make believe the objects exist; we earnestly believe they do. Consequently, the imagination imparts all the vivacity of an impression of an object to the feigning of the existence of the object even when actual sense perception is absent. Therefore, reality is rendered to the unperceived! Fiction becomes supposed fact (cf. 2 Kgs 6:15–17; Acts 7:55–56; 10:9–16). The imagination is now able, by analogy, to transfer this supposed reality to those objects that have not had the constancy and coherence to develop a tested impression. In sum, the way the unreal perceptions present themselves to our senses resembles that of constant and coherent real objects (T, 216; TM, 265).

24. T, 13; TM, 60. Modes (T, 16–17; TM, 63–64) and substances (T, 16–17, 234; TM, 282) are relatively unimportant for our discussion.

termed these relations analytic) and relations that "may be changed without any change in the ideas"[25] (Kant termed these relations synthetic).[26] Hume placed four of the relations—resemblance, contrariety, degrees in any quality, and proportion in quantity or number—in the class of relations which "depend entirely on ideas which we compare together" because they are "discoverable at first sight" and fall more properly under the province of intuition than demonstration. These four relations are the foundation of science, since we can "pronounce them [certain] at first sight without enquiry or reasoning."[27]

Of the remaining three Humean relations—identity, relations in time and place, and causation—it is "only causation, which produces such a connexion, as to give us [probable] assurance from the existence or action of one object, that 'twas followed or preceded by any other existence or action."[28]

This relational scheme is the basis for the so-called Hume's Fork,[29] which was given expression at the end of his first *Enquiry*:

> If we take in our hand any volume; of divinity or school metaphysics, for instance; let us ask, Does it contain any abstract reasoning concerning quantity or number? No. Does it contain any experimental reasoning concerning matter of fact and existence? No. Commit it to the flames: for it can contain nothing but sophistry and illusion.[30]

This is an exclusive either/or proposition. Hume's philosophical relations are pitched on a fork: propositions are either logically verifiable ("abstract reasoning") or else they are empirically verifiable ("experimental reasoning"). If not either, they are nonsense. It is with his fork that Hume skewers both the rationalist and the evangelical (supernaturalistic) Christian.

Hume held that we can have awareness of a relationship either between ideas or between matters of fact. Relationship between ideas involves the domain of certainty, including mathematics and logic. This is genuine knowledge: self-evident, intuitive, or deductive. A problem for Hume, however, is that such knowledge (mathematics, for instance) is only empty, abstract, formal truth that tells us nothing about reality, about existence,

---

25. T, 69; TM,117; EU, 28–29.

26. For Kant's discussion of analytical and synthetical judgments see *Critique of Pure Reason*, Introduction, ch. 4.

27. T, 70; TM, 118.

28. T, 73; TM, 121.

29. Cf. Antony Flew, *David Hume,* esp. ch. 3.

30. EU, 165; P, 149.

about factuality. It may give us certainty, it may give us "truth,"[31] but it does not give us morality or beauty or virtue for the common life. However, we do have the faculty to compute for commerce, which was critical for Hume's social theory. It is important to the common life of the merchant who must keep track of expenses and income and billing procedures.[32]

Awareness of a relationship between matters of fact provides no genuine knowledge, but it does give us non-trivial information about existence and reality, which is properly called belief. While belief provides no certainty, it does provide guidance. It gives us usable insights for our lives. Scottish philosopher and Kantian scholar Norman Kemp Smith remarks that Hume made a clear distinction between knowledge (which is of ideas) and belief (which pertains to facts). Each goes its own way and concerns its own world: knowledge "yields the higher type of assurance; but belief more deeply concerns man as an active, and therefore moral, being."[33]

The relationship between matters of fact is crucial for an understanding of Hume's notion of convention. It is always possible to conceive of the contrary of a matter of fact (i.e., statistics are what you make of them), whereas it is impossible to do so with a logical comparison of ideas (i.e., you cannot dispute an idea). In the comparison of ideas, no facts need to exist: facts do not matter; only formal logic counts. In the relationship between matters of fact, however, facts are supreme: they do matter. Cause and effect surely is important, but instances of it cannot be established without doubt. Hume called the cause and effect connection a human convention.[34] However, as we shall see later, it is not a purely arbitrary connection.

As I noted earlier, conventions, for Hume, were rough general rules that have proven themselves over the ages to be useful and beneficial to humans, although sometimes their usefulness is not readily apparent. Conventions, he maintained, are necessary for the smooth functioning of society. They are inescapable, because empirical factors and common sense require some such arrangements. Individuals habitually and unreflectively use them, abide by them and rely on them for social and personal stability. But—and this is important—because it is a "matter of fact," no convention can be proved to be essential or necessary. A contrary convention may turn out to be better suited for society. Only time can tell. This leaves open the door for gradual reform of social institutions, which are conventional in

---

31. T, 180; TM, 231.
32. T, 166; TM, 216; T, 71; TM, 119; T, 181; TM, 232.
33. Smith, *Philosophy of David Hume*, 68.
34. EM, 306; OC, 149.

Hume's sense.³⁵ This is the bedrock of a conservative vision of social modification and value systems. History is king.

DAVID HUME AND HISTORY

In an important portion of the *Treatise,* Hume discussed the different effects in comparing future and past events and near and far objects. He posited five rules of perception:

1) Our imagination would rather enjoy the present than the past or the future.

2) Our imagination moves in sequence from one object to another.

3) Our imagination likes the future more than the past, even though the past is the source of its content.

4) Our imagination is inspired and invigorated with tempered opposition.

5) Our imagination is enlarged and delighted with the contemplation of any great object.³⁶

The remote past has an aura of greatness, but this occurs only because the imagination has a propensity to imbue it with such. The greatness and the normativeness of the past are determined, a priori, by an original propensity of the mind to imbue greatness³⁷ and not by some contrived empirical standard of greatness. It is all in our head! While the past is normative and authoritative, one is nonetheless sometimes forced to re-evaluate it using present standards.³⁸

I have already shown the importance for Hume, in many contexts, of the historic ordering of events, and so we should not be surprised to see his association of ideas understood in terms of historic narrative. All ideas are narratively associated by succession.³⁹ Every object is conceived as being in time and related to us, whereupon this narrative propensity is triggered. Hume always stressed the narrative association of ideas.⁴⁰

---

35. Cf. Gen 41:46–49; Dan 6:3–4; Exod 18.
36. T, 427–38; TM, 474–84.
37. Cf. Gen 1.
38. T, 566; TM, 617.
39. This association is not random but rather seen from the self's view of the present, with both prior and posterior events encompassing the self and sometimes even comprising parts of it.
40. "In narrative compositions the events or actions which the writer relates, must be connected together, by some bond or tye; they must be related to each other in the

What Hume was saying here is that history is like a chain-link fence that cannot be broken without damage being done to the fence. Of course, history is also—to continue the analogy—somewhat like a web, with numerous strands crisscrossing each other in various patterns of interdependency in the flow from past to present and future.

Hume was a relativist in that he viewed history from the perspective of the present and therefore held that history changes as the present moves to the past. The historian's point of view is always advancing into the future, with new events and more narrative associations being created and more stories being told. In a sense, distant history is always being re-interpreted as these new, more recent ideological and institutional associations take place. Still, the changes are slow and methodical, the chain-link fence is never breached, and the web very gradually acquires new strands that blend in with the old.

Because experiential concepts are codified in the conventional language of common life, they are very stable. And stability is critically important for Hume. This is one advantage that common-life philosophy has over metaphysical philosophy (e.g., rationalism). Experiential concepts change slowly and there is time for broad social consensus in important areas of social arrangements and structures.[41] With the rapid changes brought on by modernity, however, one is tempted to wonder if we have consensus-building time. Still, with human nature being universal and uniform,[42] I believe Hume would give a resounding *Yes!* to the question.

Because experience is the key to human conceptual paradigms, Hume's empirical philosophy looks backwards for its meaning. That is, simple ideas are derived from simple past impressions, and complex ideas are derived either from complex past impressions or from various simple impressions that generate simple ideas that our imagination combines into complex

---

imagination, and form a kind of *Unity* . . . the historian traces the series of actions according to their natural order, remounts to their secret springs and principles, and delineates their most remote consequences. He chuses for his subject a certain portion of that great chain of events, which compose the history of mankind: Each link in this chain he endeavors to touch in his narration. . . . Not only in any limited portion of life, a man's actions have a dependence on each other, but also during the whole period of his duration from cradle to the grave; nor is it possible to break off one link, however minute, in this regular chain, without affecting the whole series of events which follow" (Hume, *Essays* [Green and Grose], 2:19–20).

41. This is somewhat similar to the old eighteenth-century Princetonian view for an incremental implementation of abolitionist policies, which is partly a child of the Scottish philosopher Thomas Reid's (1710–1796) common sense realism philosophy. Reid rejected the fundamental empirical premise of his contemporary Hume (cf. Frame).

42. Again, Gen 1.

ideas. Indeed, his theory of concept formation is called historical empiricism by one commentator.[43] This concept is critical for a stable, conservative view of culture.

I turn now to Hume's celebrated analysis of causality, which also is dependent on the past and the association of ideas.

DAVID HUME AND CAUSE AND EFFECT

Hume defined causation in this way:

> We may define a cause to be an object, followed by another, and where all the objects similar to the first are followed by objects similar to the second. Or in other words where, if the first object had not been, the second never had existed.... We may form another definition of cause, and call it, an object followed by another, and whose appearance always conveys the thought to that other.[44]

In looking for an underlying explanation of causal relationships, Hume came up empty-handed.[45] He asked: What produces this following of one object by another? He answered, "We have no idea;"[46] the underlying causes are "concealed from us,"[47] they are "secret powers."[48] If they exist at all, they are not comprehensible to us, though we witness and measure their presumed results.

Christians know where causality comes from because cause and effect is taught throughout the Scriptures as God's economic way of being sovereign over his creation and letting us know how to live prudent lives. Every time we find "therefore," we find cause and effect. Jesus taught causality.[49] In fact, there are many passages teaching causality.[50]

Hume gives two examples of such powers: inertia and gravity.[51]

43. Livingston, *Hume's Philosophy*, 94.
44. EU, 76–77; P, 72.
45. T, 157–59; TM, 207–9; EU, 76–78; P, 72–73.
46. EU, 74; P, 70.
47. EU, 32–33; P, 34.
48. EU, 33–34; P, 35.
49. Cf. Matt 7:24–27; John 6:44; etc.
50. Cf. Exod 20:5–6; Num 32:23; Deut 30:19; Prov 1, 2, 8, 29; Eccl 8:11–12; Amos 6:3–7; Rom 1, 2, 6, 8; Gal 6:7–8; Jas 4:7.
51. Inertia: EU, 73n; P, 69n. Gravity: Luke 5:37–39; 24:49; 1 Tim 5:11–13; 1 Sam 20:18ff.

What Hume was doing in his account of the causal relationship is consistent with his empirically based true philosophy. He was describing, not prescribing. He was extracting rules of thought from what he experienced. He was codifying common, ordinary life. As he wrote at one point, we pronounce objects to be connected, but we cannot explain how they come to be connected.[52] At best, we note that the connection does occur. We state what is and not what, for underlying metaphysical reasons, ought to be.

As mentioned earlier, matters of fact are controlled by the experiential law of cause and effect, which Hume said had four relational earmarks: contiguity, priority or succession, constant conjunction, and necessity.[53] The first three earmarks are easy to understand, i.e., there can be no spatial gaps between the cause and the effect, the cause must be part of the effect's past, and there must be a regular temporal association between them.

However, the fourth earmark, necessity, bears some explanation. "There is a NECESSARY CONNEXION to be taken into consideration; and that relation is of much greater importance than any of the other [three] above-mention'd."[54] This fourth earmark, necessity, posed a problem, since Hume did not believe we could know solely from experience that a certain cause must have a certain effect or that a certain effect must always be the result of a certain cause. Causal claims pertain to matters of fact, the denial of which is not self-contradictory. Only definitions and mathematical formulas have necessity. They give us "knowledge of relations of ideas." What he posited in place of knowing that a cause necessitated a certain effect was the "force and liveliness of the perception" or feeling that a cause necessitated a certain effect.[55] There is the custom[56] or the principle of association[57] in the sequence of events; but there is no knowable necessity, in the nature of things, that a certain effect must follow a certain cause. One expects the cause to be followed by the effect. But this is mere probability, not genuine natural necessity. We cannot know for certain that, in the past or in the

52. EU, 75; P, 71. Raeburne Heimbeck agrees with this interpretation in his *Theology and Meaning*: "Hume's analysis of causality is not what it attempts to be and not what it is advertised to be, namely a *conceptual* analysis. It is not in fact an analysis of the *meaning* of causal expressions but instead an analysis of the grounds for making causal statements or of the evidence required for proving causal statements. Hume is guilty of conflating statements which give the grounds for believing (evidence for asserting) causal statements with statements which give the meaning of causal statements" (155–156n).
53. T, 75–77; TM, 123–26.
54. T, 77; TM, 125.
55. T, 86; TM, 134.
56. T, 183; TM, 234.
57. T, 97, 183; TM, 145.

future, given antecedents have had or will have the consequences that they presently have.[58] We cannot know for sure that the sun will rise tomorrow, even if we strongly expect it to do so.[59] Nor can we know for sure that certain social actions will, of necessity, cause certain social results. Social ideology cannot be supported by Hume's causal necessary connexion.

The key for this feeling of expectation is again the association of ideas. Hume wrote that "necessity [as we comprehend it in experience] is nothing but that determination of the thought to pass from causes to effects and from effects to causes, according to their experienc'd union."[60] "Necessity is something, that exists in the mind, not [necessarily] in objects."[61] "The necessity or power, which unites causes and effects, lies in the determination of the mind to pass from the one to the other."[62]

We can never experience the actual process in which one event is produced from another, nor do we perceive in any one impression any power to bring another impression or idea into being. In fact, there is no difference between the concept of power and the concept of the exercising of power: "The distinction, which we often make betwixt *power* and the *exercise* of it, is equally without foundation."[63] The concepts of necessity, force, power, and efficacy result from an internal, personal need to suppose there are genuine links between matters of fact. Belief in objective necessity has no source in sense impressions[64] but only in the laws of our own psychology. We naturally believe it. However, we do have a genuine idea of necessary connection in causation. It is derived, not from an impression of sensation, but from an impression of reflection, viz. of an expectation, due to constant conjunction, that one event will follow another. Most people are not aware that the idea originates in this way, so they project it out onto the facts, misconstruing it as a real connection between the causal terms, when it is a feature of their own minds which arises as they interpret experience. In sum, so far as Hume could know, there is no real necessary connection between objects in cause and effect. But it is nevertheless meaningful to speak as if there were.

---

58. Contra Jer 33:17–21, which says that Yahweh's covenant with King David and the Levites is as reliable as his sovereign control over day and night.

59. EU, 26–27; P, 28. Contra the predictability of the created order in Gen 8:22; Job 24:19; Eccl 1:4–5; Jer 17:8; 33:25; John 16:2–3.

60. T, 166; TM, 216.

61. T, 165; TM, 216. Contra Heb 8:3 (*anankaios*, necessary).

62. T, 166; TM, 216.

63. T, 171; TM, 222.

64. Contra Luke 9;22–24.

This suggests George Berkeley's famous claim that we should "think with the learned but speak with the vulgar."[65]

Hume concluded his discourse on causality with a breathtakingly boldly nihilistic statement, which bears quoting in full:

> According to the precedent doctrine, there are no objects, which by the mere survey, without consulting experience, we can determine to be the causes of any other; and no objects, which we can certainly determine in the same manner not to be the causes. Anything may produce anything. Creation, annihilation, motion, reason, volition; all these may arise from one another, or from any other object we can imagine. Nor will this appear strange, if we compare two principles explain'd above, *that the constant conjunction of objects determines their causation, and that properly speaking, no objects are contrary to each other, but existence and nonexistence.* Where objects are not contrary, nothing hinders them from having that constant conjunction, on which the relation of cause and effect totally depends.[66]

If we cannot know or presume anything for certain in the future, how can we construct a social theory on anything but experience? Any proclaimed certain social ideology is, de facto, excluded for Hume.

Did Hume, by this, deny that there is an ultimate causal principle? By no means! What he held was that while we do not have knowledge or internal understanding of such a principle as it is, we do have an external understanding, i.e., we can observe the circumstances and the presumed effects of an ultimate principle. But the nature and the origin of such original causal powers is a secret, hidden from our view: "We are placed in this world, as in a great theatre, where the true springs and causes of every event are entirely concealed from us."[67]

---

65. "Treatise Concerning the Principles of Human Knowledge," in Berkeley, *Principles*, 45–46, para. 51. This reference, which is in quotes in Berkeley's text, probably comes from Francis Bacon's *On the Dignity and Advancement of Learning* (first published in 1605), book 5, ch. 4: "Men may imagine they have a command over words, and can easily say they will speak with the vulgar, and think with the wise" (158). In other editions, Bacon's quote appears in book 2, ch. 14, para. 11.

66. T, 173; TM, 223.

67. "The Natural History of Religion," WOR, 117. In this view, Hume was reflecting the limited understanding he attributed to his hero, Newton: "While Newton seemed to draw off the veil from some of the mysteries of nature, he showed at the same time the imperfections of the mechanical philosophy; and thereby restored her ultimate secrets to that obscurity, in which they ever did and ever will remain" (H, 4:374). Hume was indeed the Newton of the mind. (However, John Locke, also a follower of Newton, was Hume's predecessor in this respect.) Cf. Deut 29:29; Job 28:20–21; Isa 55:8–9.

DAVID HUME AND INTELLIGENT DESIGN

Hume was not content, however, to leave the original causal point in a nether world of cognitive nothingness. He inferred that the wider universe had an intelligent designer, an "invisible, intelligent power in nature," "the author of nature," "the sovereign mind," "intelligent cause or author."[68]

The order of the universe proves an omnipotent mind.[69] Moreover,

> The generality of mankind . . . acknowledge mind and intelligence to be, not only the ultimate and original cause of all things, but the immediate and sole cause of every event which appears in nature.[70]

In the "Letter from a Gentleman to His Friend in Edinburgh," written in 1745 by Hume, he declared,

> Wherever I see order, I infer from Experience that there hath been a designer and contrivance. And the same Principle which leads me into this inference, when I contemplate a Building, regular and beautiful in its whole Frame and Structure; the same Principle obliges me to infer an infinite perfect Architect from the infinite Art and Contrivance which is displayed in the whole Fabrick of the Universe.[71]

Hume was applying for a position at the University of Edinburgh in moral philosophy and was being opposed by the Scottish Presbyterian William Wishart (1691–1753).[72] Rev. Wishart wanted the same job and vigorously opposed Hume's religious skepticism, leading the charge against him by circulating a list of dangerous propositions contained in Hume's *Treatise*. Hume's responsive letter addressed to his friend in Edinburgh was a point-by-point defense of the propositions contained in his *Treatise*. He didn't get the Edinburgh job nor any job at a Scottish university.

Hume argued that belief in this system of order is due to "a propensity in human nature, which leads into a system that gives [humans] some satisfaction."[73]

68. All in WOR.
69. T, 633n; TM, 211n.
70. EU, 70; P, 66; cf. "The Natural History of Religion," WOR, 135, 180.
71. Para. 2 in Hume, "Letter from a Gentleman."
72. Wishart, a Presbyterian moderate, had a distinguished name but was not related to the Scottish reformer George Wishart (1513–1546). See Baird, *Thunder Over Scotland*.
73. "The Natural History of Religion," WOR, 117. "The universal propensity to believe in invisible, intelligent power [i.e., causal principle originating from an intelligent

We may therefore conclude that Hume believed in a being who authored and sustained an orderly system of nature and that humans have a propensity to find that orderly system in nature and to attribute it to an intelligent power.

> Were men let into the apprehension of invisible, intelligent power by a contemplation of the works of nature, they could never possibly entertain any conception but of one single being, who bestowed existence and order on this vast machine, and adjusted all its parts, according to one regular plan or connected system.[74]

Hume's belief, of course, was decidedly different from evangelical (revealed) Christianity. Institutional religious convictions spring, for Hume, from the common life of humanity. Humans want to believe in a transcendent being that orders society; therefore, they create religious conventions and rituals to embody this human predilection.[75] Nevertheless, those in the intelligent design movement have an advocate in secular philosophy with David Hume.

Hume stated the "contraries of nature become proofs of some consistent plan and establish one single purpose or intention, however inexplicable and incomprehensible."[76] However, the apostle Paul tells us the answer to nature is available for all to see and understand and it is not incomprehensible.[77]

---

designer] if not an original instinct, being at least a general attendant of human nature, may be considered as a kind of mark or stamp, which the divine workman has set upon his work" ("The Natural History of Religion," WOR, 181). There is more than an echo of Descartes here, for Descartes, in the third *Meditation,* wrote, "The only remaining alternative is that [the very clear proof that God indeed exists] is innate in me, just as the idea of myself is innate in me. And indeed, it is no surprise that God, in creating me, should have placed this idea in me to be, as it were, the mark of the craftsman stamped on his work. . . . I am somehow made in his image and likeness" (Descartes, *Philosophical Writings,* 2:35).

74. "Origin of Polytheism," WOR, 113. Hume, employing Occam's razor, continued, "All things in the universe are evidently of a piece. Every thing is adjusted to every thing. One design prevails throughout the whole. And this uniformity leads the mind to acknowledge one author, because the conception of different authors serves only to give perplexity to the imagination without bestowing any satisfaction on the understanding ("Origin of Polytheism," WOR, 113). "The whole frame of nature bespeaks an intelligent author; and no rational enquirer can, after serious reflection, suspend his belief a moment with regard to the primary principles of genuine Theism and Religion" ("The Natural History of Religion," WOR, 107).

75. "The Natural History of Religion," WOR, 130, 181.

76. "General Corollary," WOR.

77. Cf. Rom 1:20, Gen 1; Ps 19:1; Isa 48:13; John 1:3; etc.

Hume's epistemology of impressions and ideas was a deliberate assault on the concept of the mind or self as an entity separate from its perceptions.[78] That is, he argued that we do not ever perceive such an entity as self. We perceive only ideas and impressions; and mind, from a practical viewpoint, is merely a name for a series of such perceptions. In fact, the collected impressions and ideas are the only things that we can experience of the mind. We cannot know the mind as a single entity, we can know only its perceived constituent parts. We infer self through the faculty of our memory, which strings together past impressions, thereby giving us various ideas comprising our sense of personal identity: "The mind is a kind of theater where several perceptions successively make their appearance; pass, re-pass, glide away, and mingle in an infinite variety of postures and situations."[79]

Self or mind is more like a stream of consciousness than any stable set of impressions. Princeton University professor George Will describes Hume's concept of personal identity as "a constantly changing kaleidoscope of experiences and impressions."[80] We are constantly reinventing ourselves in a gradual and imperceptible process. Thus, the reality of self as we know it, like all history, is partially a result of our imagination, says Hume. Our understanding of our personal identity is like a chain-link fence: we cannot break off one link without affecting the whole web of personal impressions. Hume, of course, did not apply his streaming epistemology to sexual identity, but he anticipated that he would be employed in defending the freedom, indeed the requirement, that each individual determine his/her/their self. Still, Hume's notion of moral conventionality could keep him in the conservative camp during the current sexual war raging in Western societies.

DAVID HUME AND MORALITY

> The only object of [moral] reasoning is to discover the circumstances on both sides, which are common to [estimable or blamable] qualities; to observe that particular in which the estimable qualities agree on the one hand, and the blamable on the other; and thence to reach the foundation of ethics, and find those universal principles, from which all censure or approbation is ultimately derived. As this is a question of fact, not of abstract science, we can only expect success, by following the

---

78. T, 160; TM, 209–10.
79. T, 253; TM, 301.
80. Will, *Statecraft as Soulcraft*, 62.

experimental method, and deducing general maxims from a comparison of instances.[81]

With this eighteenth-century linguistic construction, Hume posited that morality is founded on what exists in society. What ought to be is based ultimately on what is.[82]

Hume believed that morality cannot be determined by a *priori* obligations,[83] by reason,[84] or by any religious higher power.[85] As I have previously noted, he believed morality was a matter of passion, of pleasure and pain. "An action or sentiment or character is virtuous or vicious; why? because [an action or sentiment or character] causes a pleasure or uneasiness of a particular kind."[86] In other words, to think of actions as right or wrong is simply to have passions or feelings of a certain sort of approval or disapproval towards them.[87] Morality is a matter of the heart: "The approbation or blame which then ensues, cannot be the work of the judgment, but of the heart; and is not a speculative proposition or affirmation, but an active feeling or sentiment."[88] Thus, morals become linked to passions or feelings and not to cognitions exclusively. There are no things good or evil in themselves, or actions right or wrong in themselves, whose moral quality are independent of our attitude to them. As the Oxford political philosopher John Plamenatz comments, "Things are good and bad . . . because the contemplation of them causes pleasure or displeasure to the persons who observe them or who think about them."[89]

Concerning the human desire for pleasure or happiness, James Bonar Scottish lawyer and scholar (1751–1821) noted, "The ordinary action of men in managing the affairs of life, and in pushing their way in the world, involves the holding up before the mind's eye of an idea of a pleasure; and

---

81. EM, 174; OC, 7.

82. This does not mean, however, that changes in the status quo are never desirable or justifiable.

83. T, 473; TM, 525.

84. T, 458; TM, 510.

85. D, 203.

86. T, 471; TM, 523.

87. T, 471; TM, 523.

88. EM, 290; OC, 131. Alexis de Tocqueville, in his *Democracy in America* (1835), referred to "habits of the heart" as they formed the character of a culture or national community. One hundred fifty years later, Robert Bellah picked up on this theme and published his best seller, *Habits of the Heart*, which explored the traditions, customs, etc., of individual Americans in shaping our national culture. Neither book references Hume, and I have found no reference to Hume's influence, if any, on Tocqueville.

89. Plamenatz, *English Utilitarians*, 25.

this idea of a pleasure constitutes a desire and excites an action."[90] Hume referred to this desire for pleasure or happiness in at least two different essays.[91]

Why do Hume's virtues generate approval? Because they are socially useful, beneficial, and acceptable. Hume advised us to "consult common experience."[92] That is, an action is virtuous because it has a "tendency to public interest," a "tendency to promote [a person's] interest and satisfaction," or a "tendency to the happiness of mankind and of particular persons."[93] Hume held that morality is artificial and conventional,[94] in that it follows an implicit agreement, between and among individuals, that each will promote the common or public interest.[95] Innate tendencies or propensities do, however, have a place in his moral theory, even if subsidiary.[96]

90. Bonar, *Philosophy and Political Economy*, 110–11. Bonar was the son of the prominent Free Church of Scotland minister Rev. Andrew Bonar and the nephew of the hymnist Horatius Bonar.

91. In his essay "Of Refinement in the Arts," he wrote: "Human happiness, according to the most received notions, seems to consist in three ingredients: action, pleasure, and indolence (or repose)" (E, 276; LF, 269). In his essay "Of Parties in General," Hume had this statement about happiness: "As to practical arts, which encrease the commodities and enjoyments of life, it is well known, that men's happiness consists not so much in an abundance of these, as in the peace and security with which they possess them; and those blessings can only be derived from good government" (E, 54; LF, 54–55). Note also, "Of the Rise and Progress of the Arts and Sciences" (E, 114; LF, 113). In the *Dialogues*, Hume had Pamphilus give another cause of human happiness: "the two greatest and purest pleasures of human life [are] study and society" (OC, 186). Finally, in the first *Enquiry*, Hume wrote of yet another cause of happiness: "I am sensible, that, according to the past experience of mankind, friendship is the chief joy of human life" (EU, 140; P, 127). So, Hume's list of pleasurable sentiments includes avarice, action, pleasure, repose, peace, and security—which are brought about by commerce and good government.

92. T, 487; TM, 538.

93. T, 589–90; TM, 639–40.

94. T, 496; TM, 548.

95. T, 497; TM, 548.

96. Like non-human animals, Humean individuals are creatures of instinct. We have animal-like faith in our senses and depend on them (as animals do) to function in our world. In his chapter on "The Origin of Ideas" in the first *Enquiry*, Hume defined innate as that which is "original or copied from no precedent perception" (EU, 22n; P, 24). With this definition in mind, Hume contended that "all our impressions are innate, and our ideas not innate." Furthermore, he stated that powerful sentiments such as "self-love, resentment of injuries, or the passion between the sexes" are innate, since they are inherent in human nature (EU, 22n; P, 24). So, animal instinct, and not reason or religion, governs our lives. Sympathy is one of these instincts—it is an indispensable tool in creating personal and social morality (T, 577; TM, 628). Cf. Rom 1. Hume argued that genuinely moral approbation comes from the disinterested (E, 269; LF, 263 or impartial (T, 583; TM, 634) observer in accordance with the universal sentiment

To Hume, true philosophy, history, and common life were all bound together in a whole cloth of experience: "The study of history confirms the reasoning of true philosophy; . . . shewing us the original qualities of human nature."[97] He believed that a correct observation of humanity, including such diverse groups as Chinese, Persians, and Italians,[98] would reveal certain common, innate human characteristics[99] leading to proper morality.[100]

Moreover, he wrote of the "constant and universal principles of human nature," alluding to the intimate connection between morals, politics, and history and suggesting a striking analogy between the moral philosopher and the natural scientist.[101]

In short, human nature remains the same in the abstract, in broad fundamental ways. The overwhelming number of ordinary actions by most men can be predicted based on one's observations of one's own common-life society. All humans, of all ages, are characterized in our human nature by the principles of association, sympathy, propensities, and passions, such as "ambition, avarice, self-love, vanity, friendship, generosity, public spirit." These are the "constant and universal principles of human nature," grounded for us

---

of sympathy: "We may presume, that [sympathy] also gives rise to many of the other virtues; and that qualities acquire our approbation, because of their tendency to the good of mankind" (T, 578; TM 628). In order that we prevent ourselves from being in a constant state of situational fluctuation in the "approbation of moral qualities," which would naturally lead to "continual [moral] contradictions," Hume posited that we need to "fix on some steady and general points of view," or "choose some common point of view" (T, 591; TM, 641). This fixation would provide us with a "more steady judgment of things" (T, 581; TM, 632; cf. EM, 229; OC, 64). We find this "distant view of reflection" in the natural, universal nature of humans (cf. Gen 9:5–6). Hume's quality of disinterest may be defined as the contemplation of an action unaffected by any hope of benefit or fear of injury likely to happen to the contemplator, or a person to whom the contemplator is not indifferent. Indeed, morality, for Hume, could even be defined crudely as a spectator sport ("The hypothesis which we embrace is plain. . . . It defines virtue to be whatever mental action or quality gives to a [disinterested or impartial] spectator the pleasing sentiment of approbation; and vice the contrary (TM, 289; OC, 129).

97. T, 562; TM, 613.
98. T, 379; TM, 427.
99. EU, 83; P, 77.
100. "[That subject] implies some sentiment common to all mankind, which recommends that same object to general approbation, and makes every man, or most men, agree in the same opinion or decision concerning it. It also implies some sentiment, so universal and comprehensive as to extend to all mankind, and render the actions and conduct, even of the person the most remote, an object of applause or censure, according as they agree or disagree with that rule of right which is established" (EM, 272; OC, 110; cf. E, 382; LF, 378).
101. EU, 83–84; P, 78.

in empirical historical testimony and emanating from the "regular springs of human actions and behavior."[102] It is in this same light that Hume spoke of natural virtues, such as sympathy, benevolence, generosity, etc., which are "entirely natural, and have no dependence on the artifice and contrivance of men."[103] These virtues are self-evident, and no one can doubt"that they are good for society.[104] This was Hume's version of natural law.[105]

Does this uniformity of human nature springing from historic patterns of behavior mean individuals and societies are nothing but automatons, mindlessly going through the steps of a pre-ordained and regimented common life, particularly from the designing Author of nature? Not at all! Social and historic circumstances significantly modify the public display of human nature. Hume referred to the "diversity of characters, prejudices, and opinions" among individuals, which results in a variety of conduct. In a wonderfully evocative illustration of this combination of unity and diversity, form and freedom, he compared human nature to the Rhine and Rhone Rivers:

> The Rhine flows north, the Rhone south; yet both spring from the *same* mountain, and are also actuated, in their opposite direction, by the *same* principle of gravity. The different inclinations of the ground, on which they run, cause all the difference of their courses.[106]

In a letter to Francis Hutcheson in 1739, Hume posited utility as the mark and test of virtuosity: "Now I desire you to consider if there be any quality that is virtuous, without having a tendency either to the public good or to the good of the person who possesses it. If there be none without these tendencies, we may conclude that their merit is derived from sympathy."[107] This quote leads us to another important consideration for Humean moral theory: morality is based, in part, on the natural selfish impulse of the individual. That is, our benevolent interest is causally grounded in self-centeredness. Since the virtue or rightness of an action comes from public utility and benefit, some sort of self-interest, which public utility and benefit serve, is the engine which drives Hume's moral theory. That is, I ought to do

---

102. EU, 83; P, 78; cf. T, 113; TM, 162; E, 560; LF, 565 ("Of the Study of History").
103. T, 574; TM, 625.
104. T, 578; TM, 629.
105. Cf. Ps 19; Jer 25:5–6; Rom 2:12–16.
106. EM, 333; OC, na.
107. B1, 115.

something because, at some level, it is in my own non-other-directed, that is selfish, interests to do so.[108]

However, an ought statement never follows directly from premises from which ought is absent. This contention is the so-called Hume's Moral Law.[109] What Hume was stating in his moral law, as some ethicist logicians such as R.M. Hare (1919-2002) would argue, is that there is a categorical difference between describing and prescribing, even though a prescription must have some descriptive content.[110] We cannot deduce a moral conclusion, which is prescriptive, from a mere description. An imperative conclusion can come only from an imperative premise. There is no other possibility. Hume was so confident in this logical formulation that he boldly stated, "I am persuaded that this small attention wou'd subvert all the vulgar systems of morality."[111]

108. EM, 278; OC, 118; EM, 280; OC, 119; T, 487-88; TM, 539-40.

109. "In every system of morality, which I have hitherto met with, I have always remark'd, that the author proceeds for some time in the ordinary way of reasoning, and establishes the being of a God, or makes observations concerning human affairs; when of a sudden I am surpriz'd to find, that instead of the usual copulations of propositions, *is*, and *is not*, I meet with no proposition that is not connected with an *ought*, or an *ought not*. This change is imperceptible; but is, however, of the last consequences. For as this *ought*, or *ought not*, expresses some new relation or affirmation, 'tis necessary that it shou'd be observ'd and explain'd; and at the same time that a reason should be given, for what seems altogether inconceivable, how this new relation can be a deduction from others, which are entirely different from it" (T, 469; TM, 521). R. M. Hare defines what he calls Hume's Law as follows: "In this logical rule [that the conclusion of an argument can be an imperative if and only if at least one premise is an imperative], again, is to be found the basis of Hume's celebrated observation on the impossibility of deducing an 'ought' proposition from a series of 'is' propositions—an observation which, as he rightly says, 'would subvert all the vulgar systems of morality,' and not only those which had already appeared in his day" (Hare, *Language of Morals*, 29). See also Flew, *David Hume*, 45, 144-49.

110. See R. M. Hare, *Language of Morals* and *Moral Thinking*. Could this reticence to declare himself more often in matters moral come from his early reading of Cicero, for the Roman lawyer wrote, "Those who ask for my own opinion on every question merely show excessive curiosity" (Cicero, *Nature of the Gods*, 73)?

111. T, 470; TM, 521. Hume himself, however, sometimes seems to have violated this principle, for he used historical custom and tradition (is) to generate conventions (ought). For instance, in transferring property through the principle of *accession*, Hume moved away from the descriptive statement "We acquire the property of objects of *accession*" (the common life rooting for this statement is given in a footnote: "We shall proceed to explain ... by examples from common life and experience" [T, 509n; TM, 561]) to the prescriptive statement or rule: "And this principle is of such force as to give rise to the right of accession" (T, 509n; TM, 561). Hume appears to have violated his own moral law again when he argued a form of government has moved from the descriptive (custom) to the prescriptive (obligatory) as noted above (cf. T, 566; TM, 617). Another example of violation is noted by James Q. Wilson: "[Hume] says that justice

is a convention invented by man to make him more secure in his possession of property. Without rules governing the ownership and transmission of property, social life would be impossible. But why do men form society? Because of their natural impulses, especially sexual attraction and the children that result from sexual union. Fine, this makes rules governing the *existing* distribution of property—the rules of justice, if you will—useful. But why should men care about the *future* transmission of their property? Because, Hume answers, of 'the natural affection, which they bear their children.' And what does that affection imply? A 'duty, the care of children.' Here Hume derives an 'ought' statement from an 'is' statement scarcely eight pages after asserting that this cannot be done" (Wilson, *Moral Sense*, 238). Still, one could argue that Hume was merely describing the causes which produced the ought, the right, the obligation, rather than a logical deduction from certain premises.

As I have noted, Hume argued—and this is a leading feature of his moral theory—that human morality implies "some sentiment common to all mankind" and a "common point of view" in language use (EM, 272; OC, 110–11). There must be agreement about general moral precepts. He held that the "very nature of language" implies approbation or disapprobation, regardless of which language is being spoken. That is, when one uses the word virtue, or its equivalent in any language, one is praising and implying that the praise would be universal. Thus, moral power is more evident in language than in rules (E, 234; LF, 229).

There may be a problem for Hume here: in deciding what words in other languages are equivalent to virtue, part of our criterion may be this praising function. If so, Hume's view here seems to beg the question. It appears to be circular. Moral language is fixed by convention (EM, 306; OC, 149). Language developed historically to facilitate the communication of social needs, goals, beliefs, and intentions. It therefore is not only a convention itself, but also makes possible all the other human conventions. In order to do that, language had to have a publicly agreed-upon set of understandings or, as Hume wrote, "some steady and general points of view" (T, 581; TM, 632). The meanings of words are given in their use in the stable conventions of language: "The very nature of language guides us almost infallibly in forming a judgment of this nature [framing a moral distinction]" (EM, 174; OC, 6). In a crucial paragraph, Hume used the example of the expression "I promise" to illustrate the so-called performative use of language, which is entirely conventional yet both "steady and general":

When a man says he promises anything, he in effect expresses a resolution of performing it; and along with that, by making use of this form of words, subjects himself to the penalty of never being trusted again in case of failure. A resolution is the natural act of the mind, which promises express (T, 522; TM, 74).

J. L. Austin, two hundred years later, developed his "theory of Illocutionary forces which makes use of performative utterances to indicate that the utterances are the performance of some act and not the report of its performance" (Urmson, "John Langshaw Austin").

In an insightful passage, Hume seems to have suggested that the verbalizing of moral instruction is the basis for moral action. He wrote in his second *Enquiry*, "The end of all moral speculations is to teach us our duty; and, by proper representations of the deformity of vice and the beauty of virtue, beget correspondent habits, and engage us to avoid the one, and embrace the other" (EM, 172; OC, 4). Loyola University scholar John Danford, in an article on Humean morality, states, "Hume seems to have concluded that the only satisfactory foundation for morality is neither science nor theology, but rhetoric" (Danford, "Surest Foundation of Morality," 148). (The University of Chicago conservative thinker Richard M. Weaver would have agreed, for he authored

Hume held that our moral beliefs are neither innate (unlike the universal principle of human nature) nor a product of reason ("reason is only the slave of passions") but rather of cultural evolution (i.e., they are an artifact). In this process of evolution, what proved to be conducive to more effective human effort survived, and the least effective was superseded. It was a survival of the fittest among human conventions; it was a sort of moral Darwinism in action, described by Hume a century before Charles Darwin (1809–1882) wrote.[112]

There are two types of moral conventions:

1. rules of justice (conventions that regulate property)[113]

2. rules that regulate politics (conventions dealing with political legitimacy;[114] political rules will be discussed later)

For now, a brief look at rules of justice. Of these artificial or conventional rules of morality or virtue, justice is the most important. Hume called justice an artificial virtue because it "produces pleasure and approbation by means of an artifice or contrivance, which arises from the circumstances and necessity of mankind. Of this kind I assert justice to be."[115] We approve of justice because conventions established by us further our common interests.[116]

This common interest or public good can never be achieved without an interest in others' well-being: "Thus self-interest is the original motive to the establishment of justice: but a sympathy with public interest is the source of the moral approbation, which attends that virtue."[117] Self-interest is the first and critical step in our moral ladder leading to public interest. First me, then you. I take the oxygen mask before I give it to you.

---

a very influential book, *The Ethics of Rhetoric,* in 1953. Interestingly, Weaver makes no mention of Hume's contribution to the connection between rhetoric and morals in his book.) If Danford is correct that rhetoric is the footing for human morality, and I believe there is merit to his contention, then past experience is the masonry for the rhetorical foundation, for Hume stated in his first *Enquiry*: "It is only experience, which teaches us the nature and bounds of cause and effect and enables us to infer the existence of one object from that of another. Such is the foundation of moral reasoning, which forms the greater part of human knowledge, and is the source of all human action and behavior" (EU, 164).

112. Cf. "The Legal and Political Philosophy of David Hume," by F. A. Hayek, in Chappell, *Hume.*

113. T, 502–34; TM, 553.

114. T, 534–69; TM, 585.

115. T, 477; TM, 529.

116. T, 490; TM, 541–42; cf. T, 500, 533; TM, 551, 585.

117. T, 499–500; TM, 551.

Self-interest is an instinctive guiding principle that causes us to eschew reason, trust the senses, and rely on the limited knowledge that sensible perceptions give us. The Humean concept of sympathy, however, is the tendency for a passion that exists in another person to generate a like passion in us. It is our innate, instinctive capacity to feel with another his or her well-being or distress without our having specific affection for him or her. It is through sympathy that we communicate our internal passionate selves to others.

However, self-interest will cause social problems of injustice and disturbance. How does a society guard against the socially destabilizing influence of self-interest and egoism? By social rules: "It is only a general sense of common interest; which sense all the members of the society express to one another, and which induces them to regulate their conduct by certain rules."[118] These rules are required because the spirit of benevolence or sympathy is not forceful enough, natural enough in the individual to "counterbalance the love of gain and render men fit members of society."[119] Therefore, legal restraint is required, enforced by government. Hume wrote that the "infirmity of human nature becomes a remedy to itself" by providing the provision for this negligence through a remote and powerful government. We cannot cure human nature, but we can change human society, and so social rules, enforced by government, become a necessity to ensure justice.[120] Government, however, need not have more power than this function requires.

These artificial rules of justice benefit all of society.[121] Hume implored us to "consult common experience" to see that this is true.[122]

HUME AND PRIVATE PROPERTY

For Hume, justice and property were conceptually interdependent.[123] He defined property as "such a relation betwixt a person and an object as permits him, but forbids any other, the free use and possession of it, without

118. T, 490; TM, 541
119. T, 492; TM, 543; cf. Gen 3; Rom 5.
120. Cf. Rom 13:1–7.
121. "By society all man's infirmities are compensated; and tho' in that situation his wants multiply every moment upon him, yet his abilities are still more augmented, and leave him in every respect more satisfied, and happy, than 'tis possible for him, in his savage and solitary condition, ever to become" (T, 485; TM, 537).
122. T, 487; TM, 538.
123. Harrison's *Hume's Theory of Justice* was valuable for me at this stage.

violating the laws of justice and moral equity."[124] Personal possessions need to have publicly agreed upon rules of preservation in order to stabilize ownership and civil harmony against natural inconveniences. These inconveniences are that:

1) An individual wants more goods than are easily available from the hand of nature.

2) An individual "never attains a perfection in any particular art."

3) An individual's "force and success are not at all times equal."

4) An individual is not entirely benevolent in his dispositions, and so we will not agree to let each person have such goods as will "satisfy every one's desires and necessities." An "opposition of passions, and a consequent opposition of actions is necessarily produced for scarce resources."

5) An individual can wrest property fairly easily from one set of hands to another.[125]

If property ownership is so tenuous, is there any real and rational way of preserving ownership in society? Hume identified for analysis three theoretically possible types of property distribution:[126]

1) Distribution according to the virtue of each recipient. The problem here, however, is two-fold: individual character constantly changes and is uncertain, and virtue is constantly being debated, since we have "no determinate rule of conduct."

2) Distribution according to how one used to distribute.[127] Hume maintained this idea has the same weakness as the first.

3) Distribution so that everybody gets an equal portion. This approach seems to commend itself because "wherever we depart from this equality, we rob the poor of more satisfaction than we add to the rich, and . . . the slight gratification of a frivolous vanity, in one individual, frequently costs more than bread to many families."[128]

However, Hume argued against equal distribution as being impractical and pernicious to human society for three reasons:

---

124. T, 310; TM, 360. David Miller's work was very helpful in this section.
125. T, 484–89; TM, 536–40.
126. EM, 192–94; OC, 25–27.
127. T, 514; TM, 566.
128. EM, 194; OC, 27; cf. Acts 2:44–45; 4:32–35.

First, the basic differences in the individuals' "art, care, and industry will immediately break that equality."

Second, "the most rigorous inquisition is requisite to watch every inequality on its first appearance"; i.e., the Hobbesian Leviathan state would be required to do this watching. Thomas Hobbes (1588–1679) argued (before Rousseau) in his masterpiece *Leviathan* (1651) that society's civil peace and social unity are best achieved by the establishment of a state apparatus through a social contract. Hobbes's ideal state was one ruled by an absolute power responsible for protecting the security of the commonwealth and granted sovereign authority to guarantee the common defense.

Third, equality destroys social hierarchy and authority and levels all power to an ineffectual state.[129] Hume here argues like a true pre-Burkean conservative. He argues even like a true Scottish Presbyterian: "The laborer's appetite works for him; his hunger drives him on."[130]

Instead of these three anti-social methods of property distribution and acquisition, Hume advocated five rules which determine property, conforming to his fundamental notion of habit, custom, and convention, expressed in his version of the origin of private property: property rights arose in a "savage and solitary condition" when individuals, seeing presumed advantage for joining together, "seek each other's company, and make an offer of mutual protection and assistance." In order to protect each individual from the "avidity and selfishness" of human nature, they agree to "mutual restraint and forbearance." The methods of protection to be employed are Hume's five rules:

1) Possession: "Everyone continue to enjoy what he is at present possess'd of."[131]

2) Occupation: "The first possession always engages the attention most."[132]

3) Prescription: "Possession during a long tract of time conveys a title to any object."[133]

4) Accession: "We acquire property of objects when they are connected in an intimate manner with objects that are already our property."[134]

---

129. EM, 194; cf. Exod 20:15, 17; Deut 19:14; etc.
130. Cf. Prov 16:26.
131. T, 503; TM, 555.
132. T, 505; TM, 557.
133. T, 508; TM, 56.
134. T, 509; TM, 560.

5) Succession: One's "possessions shou'd pass to those, who are dearest to them, in order to render them more industrious and frugal."[135]

What was Hume's justification for these five rules of property distribution? It arose from his concepts of association of ideas and of imagination.[136] And how does the imagination suggest these rules to us? By the operation of cause and effect.[137]

It is important to note that Hume's rules of property were like everything else he advanced—evolutionary, inasmuch as they are subject to the customs and habits of a society. Consequently, his having noted that these rules are frivolous and products of our imagination shows that Hume realized they needed to be adopted to various circumstances and social situations. Indeed, he made plain that property restitution be allowed and injustice be discouraged in property allocation.[138] Just how this is to be done Hume left unsaid and presumably up to each society.

One can imagine that through social groupings and cultural change, impressions are made and ideas form that cause property laws to be modified to fit the nature of current society. In his *Treatise*, Hume went so far as to say that only a stable society gives the freedom for property laws to change for the enjoyment of the once dispossessed.[139] Change will come but only in its time and only incrementally.

Hume understood human nature remarkably well, for he noted the natural weakness or the "narrowness of the soul" of the individual[140] which leads to avidity and selfishness, etc. Additionally, he clearly understood the natural greed in the human heart that helps to explain the power and success of modern-day advertising. That is, we don't want what we don't know we can have, but we do want what we do know we can have.[141] We prefer a bird in the hand to two birds in the bush. By creating false expectations of

---

135. T, 510-11; TM, 561. In a footnote in his second *Enquiry*, Hume calls these rules "very frivolous": "What possessions are assigned to particular persons; this is, generally speaking, pretty indifferent; and is often determined by very frivolous views and considerations" (EM, 309n; OC, 152n; cf. T, 501-13; TM, 553-64; EM, appendix 3, 309n; OC, 152).

136. T, 504-5n; TM, 556n.

137. T, 504n; TM, 555n. By the relations of resembling, contiguity, correspondence.

138. T, 505; TM, 556

139. "The same love of order and uniformity, which arranges the books in a library, and the chairs in a parlour, contributes to the formation of a society, and to the well-being of mankind by modifying the general rule concerning the stability of possession" (T, 504n; TM, 556).

140. T, 537; TM, 588.

141. Cf. Matt 12:34; 15:18; etc.

unmerited property transfers, society will be destabilized and all hope of property enjoyment destroyed.[142]

SUMMARIZING THOUGHT

Hume's doctrine of impressions, ideas, and associations through memory and imagination are key building blocks of his social theory, because he posited the notion that we can legitimately form ideas only about that which we perceive. Therefore, reliable and useful social arrangements are formed only in the slow flow of human conventions, habits, and associations. Furthermore, because we can have no certainty about causality, the notion of structuring society or manipulating social institutions through ideology to accomplish certain desired ends, is a tenuous and humble undertaking. There is great social risk in rational social engineering since we have no certainty in outcome; we can anticipate but not know the future. The individual not only has a propensity to want to see a rational or even a divine plan at work in an orderly society, but also acquires identity in the very social habits, customs, and conventions of which he or she is a part. So, any social theory which is truly humane must consider the impact on the individual of social change and the slowness with which such change will consequently take place.

I move now to consider selected aspects of Hume's true philosophy in popular form.

---

142. T, 503; TM, 554.

4

David Hume's Conversible Philosophy

The Operations of the Mind may be divided into the learned and the conversible. The Learned are such as have chosen for their Portion the higher and more difficult Operations of the Mind, which require Leisure and Solitude, and cannot be brought to perfection, without long Preparation and severe Labour. The conversible World [have] a Taste of Pleasure, an Inclination to the easier and more gentle Exercises of the Understanding, to obvious Reflection on human Affairs and the Duties of common Life, and to the Observation of the Blemishes or Perfections of the particular Objects, that surround them.[1]

THERE IS YET ANOTHER human propensity of which Hume spoke, and that is a propensity to join others for common interest, or as Hume wrote, "men always seek society."[2] While we may not know exactly how this social cohesion takes place, we do know that it functions "by a kind of *presensation;* which tells us what will operate on others, by what we feel immediately in ourselves."[3] Bonar has a word at this point: "There is no [social] contract or promise, but a 'common sense of interest.'"[4] This spontaneous union of humanity is not only distinct from any political arrangement, but it may be, and often is, distinct from any clear consciousness of union at all. It is the sense of an objective common interest and purpose, to be served by

1. "Of Essay Writing," E/LF, 533–34.
2. T, 401–2; TM, 449.
3. T, 332; TM, 382.
4. Bonar, 124; Humean quote is from T, 490; TM, 541.

common action; but the solidarity is not always clearly understood, still less does it always imply a bond of conscious sympathy.⁵ This is the creation of a convention at work.

How authoritative is this propensity to join? Hume claimed that the common person's public passion and sentiments are to be taken with the utmost seriousness: "I shou'd now appeal to popular authority and oppose the sentiments of the rabble to any philosophical reasoning. For it must be observ'd that the opinions of men, in this case, carry with them a peculiar authority and are, in a great measure, infallible."⁶ Public opinion thus has the status, the authority of genuine and even infallible knowledge. For Hume, the mob ruled. Hume's apotheosis of it had significant implications for his conception of civil arrangements, which I will discuss later.

Hume believed no one to be an island.⁷ We are social creatures. Indeed, in order to know ourselves, we must relate to external objects, including other humans: "Ourselves, independent of the perception of every other object, is in reality, nothing: For which reason we must turn our view to external objects."⁸ "Men always consider the sentiments of others in their judgments of themselves,"⁹ for "the minds of men are mirrors to one another, not only because they reflect each other's emotions, but also because those rays of passions, sentiments and opinions may be often reverberated."¹⁰ Moreover, "we can form no wish, which has not a reference to society."¹¹ In short, the individual and society are almost as one, and the individual has a clear existential dependence on society.¹² Once again Hume's thought is mirrored in biblical teaching. The individual believer receives much of his or her identity and role in life from his or her position in the body of Christ.

---

5. T, 546; TM, 596.

6. T, 546; TM, 598. "The general opinion of mankind has some authority in all cases; but in this of morals 'tis perfectly infallible. Nor is it less infallible, because [most] men cannot distinctly explain the principles, on which it is founded. Few persons can carry on this train of reasoning" (T, 552; TM, 603).

7. As did the seventeenth-century English poet John Donne: "No man is an Hand, intire of it selfe; every man is a peece of the Continent, a part of the maine; if a Clod bee washed away by the Sea, Europe is the lesse, as well as if a Promontorie were, as well as if a Mannor of thy friends or of thine owne were; any man's death diminishes me, because I am involved in Mankinde; And therefore never send to know for whom the bell tolls; It tolls for thee" (*Devotions upon Emergent Occasions*. XVII).

8. T, 340; TM, 390.

9. T, 303; TM, 354.

10. T, 365; TM, 414.

11. T, 363; TM, 412.

12. As well as an ontological rooting in society.

Each individual has a unique function and value.[13] We know ourselves only as others know us.[14]

Because of the social nature of humanity, personal relationships are crucial in governing. Consequently, Hume argued in his essay "Of the Independency of Parliament" for the efficacy of the "good old boy" system in politics.[15] This notion was expressed when Hume embraced the all-male European aristocracy. Given his ambiguous view of women,[16] Hume would have been an active Rotarian in the days before the U. S. Supreme Court in 1987 forced Rotary International to admit women into the all-male clubby sanctuary of its meetings. Furthermore, as Haakonssen notes,

> Hume believed that landed property was a stabilizing influence on government. Since real estate could not be removed from the country, the landed interest was the interest of the country.[17]

The power of the crown to appoint members of the House of Commons to positions in the military and civil service, to confer titles and honors, and in other ways to appeal to the interests and the pride of members of the parliament, is the best safeguard against the abuse of democratic power. After all, for Hume, our social dimension notwithstanding, the pursuit of personal interest for ourselves and our friends was basic to human nature.[18] This is another Hume propensity. He believed that corruption, or "avidity of acquiring goods and possessions," is ineradicable (a heritage of Scottish Calvinism?) and that no political convention such as a constitution is going to remove this tendency. Consequently, it is the politicians' responsibility to constantly be vigilant over the public affairs of a nation and to make changes and alterations in the conventions of social life, in order

---

13. See Rom 12:4–8 and 1 Cor 12:12–27 for major biblical passages.

14. Cf. Prov 26:12; 2 Cor 10:12; 1 John 4:19–22.

15. "The crown has so many offices at its disposal, that, when assisted by the honest and disinterested part of the House, it will always command the resolutions of the whole, so far, at least, as to preserve the ancient constitution from danger. We may, therefore, give to this influence what name we please; we may call it by the invidious appellations of corruption and dependence; but some degree and some kind of it are inseparable from the very nature of the constitution and necessary to the preservation of our mixed government" (E, 45; LF, 45).

16. Hume does not treat the subject of women separately from men except in a short section of *A Treatise of Human Nature* (book 3, part 2, section 12), "Of Chastity and Modesty," which could be called old-fashioned but not sexist. Indeed, Christians would find nothing amiss in Hume's comments. The ambiguity comes because Hume does not treat women in the same fulsome fashion as he does men.

17. Haakonssen, "Structure of Hume's Political Theory," 372ff.

18. T, 491–92; TM, 543.

to keep the tendency toward corruption in check. Hume believed that the aristocratic-led democracy was by natural propensity basically more intelligent and moral, due to breeding and education, than tribal or primitive political arrangements.

However, the only reliable guide to cultural changes in the political arena is through experience and experimental reasoning.[19]

In discussing a particular historical incident, Hume remarked, "The country party should have made some concessions to their adversaries, and have only examined what was the proper degree of this dependence, beyond which it became dangerous to liberty."[20] What he was advocating here was a political application of influence. With the peddling of influence through family, patronage, bribes, contracts, etc., the crown would be able to keep the British government functioning in a stable fashion. This constitutes a strong argument against the rationalist desire for reform-to-perfection, in favor of a customary "it's who you know, not what you know" kind of government functioning. Hume's influence could well be used to defend big-city political machines[21] and tightly controlled political parties as social vehicles to maintain his ultimate social goal: a stable urban society. He expressed his frustration over an absence of the "good old boy" network in a revealing letter to the French economist and politician Anne-Robert Jacques Turgot (1727–1781): "A minister here can amass no fortune, being checked in every little abuse; he can give little employment to his own friends, favourites and flatterers, but must bestow all offices on those who by their votes and credit may support government."[22] So much for civil service that is proving its inadequacy, since there is the opportunity of a change of government personnel after every election!

The political machine conception, resulting in a new mechanistic political language, "lies at the origins of modern constitutionalism." Under the influence of Hume's ideas "what matters most is not the moral quality of the rulers but the structure of the institutions within which the rulers operate."[23]

When individuals are fully integrated into society, society's activities are fully interdependent and integrated. One part of society cannot be healthy, vibrant, and productive while another part is sick, anemic, and unproductive. These points are implicit in Hume's essay "Of the Rise and

---

19. EU, 90; P, 83.
20. "Of the Independency of Parliament," E, 45; LF, 45.
21. Hume even uses the phrase "political machine" in two of his essays, "Of Some Remarkable Customs" and "Idea of a Perfect Commonwealth."
22. June 1768.
23. Wootton, "Liberty, Metaphor, and Mechanism," 210.

Progress of the Arts and Sciences," in which he wrote of the emergence of refined spirits, genius, and cultivated people through social intercourse.[24]

Constant Noble Stockton, professor of philosophy emeritus at the University of Wisconsin, notes that, for Hume, "changes in the social, cultural, and moral level of a community are in the cause, or at least the condition, of its political and constitutional development."[25] In the essay "Of the Rise and Progress of the Arts and Sciences," Hume confirmed this interpretation.[26]

Furthermore, Hume believed that public and private life were intertwined in social improvement. He wrote that "industry, knowledge, and humanity, are not advantageous in private life alone: They diffuse their beneficial influence on the *public,* and render the government as great and flourishing as they make individuals happy and prosperous."[27] Hume was speaking here not of the size of government but rather of its "degree of perfection" and its capability of supporting the "ornament[s] and pleasure[s] of life." As society is more refined through this process, Hume argued that

> knowledge in the arts of government naturally begets mildness and moderation, by instructing men in the advantages of humane maxims above rigor and severity which drive subjects into rebellion, and make the return to submission impracticable, by cutting off all hopes of pardon.

Thus, an increase in civilization will soften the tempers of men and sustain a civil environment where authority will be less severe. Finally, if all else fails, there will be independent and stubborn factions to resist an "ill modelled government."[28] Always incrementalism, gradualism, and social evolution!

Having argued for the importance of sociability, Hume nevertheless was insistent that you and I, through custom, prejudice, sentiment, passion, and emotion, can make a difference, even in a social sea. Hume cited the example of the rise of Homer, who made an impressive difference in ancient Greece.[29] In the essay "Of Parties in General," he cited legislators and founders of states as worthy of honor, since they "secured the peace, happiness and liberty of future generations."[30]

---

24. E, 114–15; LF, 114.
25. Stockton, "Economics," 314.
26. E, 116; LF, 115.
27. "Of Refinement in the Arts," E, 279; LF, 272.
28. E, 280–83; LF, 273–76.
29. "Of the Rise and Progress of the Arts and Sciences," E, 115; LF, 114.
30. E, 54; LF, 54.

How did Hume explain this individual influence against the mass influence in society? In his aforementioned essay "Of the Rise and Progress of the Arts and Sciences," he argued that it is only by chance that the great leader will arise, but the group contribution is predictable because of gradual and reasonable customs and habits.[31] Hume's point here was that knowable general principles usually can be applied to group behavior but often not to individual behavior. He illustrated this by contrasting the rise of the Commons in England with the reign of various French monarchs.[32] James Bonar comments:

> Taking men not as individuals but as communities, caprice may be disregarded, for it will not disturb general reasonings and prevent general conclusions. In other words, the actions of men in communities will have a uniformity on which investigation may count, and a logic in it which they may decipher.[33]

If the social world is one of passion, thought, opinions, sentiments, emotions, judgments, and desires, then historical narrative is critical in the weaving of the tale of humankind, and association of ideas is fundamental in creating and maintaining this story of human nature. Humankind's role is universalistic in that, insofar as people are human, their nature remains constant through the ages, as empirical observation confirms natural law. But at the same time, we are susceptible to changes through reflection (or education), custom, and prejudice. So, while individuals stay the same, we are constantly changing. "We know, in general, that the characters of men are, to a certain degree, inconstant and irregular. This is, in a manner, the constant character of human nature."[34] The abstract changelessness of human nature is always in conflict with life's concrete, changing narrative. The central unifying principle of the constant Heraclitan[35] changing is what Hume calls sympathy, including the innate propensity to recognize good intentions in other individuals.

We must attempt to distill the timeless rules and lessons from the past while discarding the temporal settings. This is a cautionary word to those of us in the twenty-first century who would disregard the maxims of the

---

31. E, 112–13; LF, 112.

32. E, 113–14; LF, 113.

33. Bonar, *Philosophy and Political Economy*, 121.

34. EU, 88; P, 82.

35. Heraclius, the Greek philosopher (535–475 BC), is best known for his doctrines that things are constantly changing (universal flux) and that opposites coincide (unity of opposites). "No man ever steps in the same river twice, for it's not the same river and he's not the same man."

ancients because they do not fit today's political sensitivities and pieties. Scripture is not silent about the wisdom of the ancients.[36] In his essay "Of the Standard of Taste," Hume asked, "Must we throw aside the pictures of our ancestors, because of their ruffs [sleeve frills for men] and farthingales [hooped petticoats for women]"? He answers no, because the thought or imagination of one generation is valuable for all future generations.[37] Didn't Isaac Newton (1643–1727) tell us that we all stand on the shoulders of past giants (our grandparents)? And Hume read Newton.[38]

Human individuals live in a narrative world that is filled with associations, and they can understand this narrative world only by thinking narratively. They must understand the association of ideas and abstract out of these associations some principles to judge narrative thinking, so that they can modify their thought intelligently. As noted earlier, "philosophic decisions are nothing but the reflections of common life, methodized and corrected"[39] into conventions. These conventions, which are developed over time, must be brought to light by judgment and analysis working through a grid of historical narrative. Numerous authors have agreed with Hume's conviction that all philosophers must, in effect, be historians.[40]

Arguing against the rationalistic Platonic theory of double existence to society, Hume drew the lesson that double existence creates the social concept of a duality: the imperfect, visible society vs. the perfect, invisible one. According to this rationalistic approach, the principal task of the political philosopher is to structure the visible, concrete, imperfect society to match the invisible, abstract, perfect one, as far as possible. The visible society is time-dependent, narrative-bound, and contingent on various other factors, whereas the invisible society is timeless, above history, and not contingent on anything. However, Hume's verdict was that the Greek-inspired invisible

---

36. Heb 11:2 says, "This is what the ancients were commended for," and Jer 18:15 states, "Yet my people have forgotten me; they burn incense to worthless idols, which made them stumble in their ways and in the ancient paths. They made them walk in bypaths and on roads not built up."

37. E, 252–53; LF, 246–47.

38. T, "Experimental Method of Reasoning"; 10–13; 13–17; "Introduction," 43; 173; EU, 5–16, esp. para. 9, p. 14; EM 174.

39. EU, 11; P, 146.

40. Livingston, *Hume's Philosophy of Common Life*, 248: "The philosopher, properly conceived, is himself a historian, firmly rooted in some narrative order and subject to its authority."

society is an illusion.⁴¹ This false philosophy of double existence encourages the enthusiast:⁴²

> [It leads him to] ridicule everything, that has hitherto appeared sacred and venerable in the eyes of mankind. Reason, sobriety, honour, friendship, marriage, are the perpetual subjects of their insipid raillery; and even public spirit, and a regard to our country, are treated as chimerical and romantic. Were the schemes of these anti-reformers to take place, all the bonds of society must be broken, to make way for the indulgences of a licentious mirth and gaiety.⁴³

To reiterate an earlier observation: what Hume chiefly opposed in rationalism is that it rejects a historic, narrative-based philosophy in favor of a metaphysical one that has no loyalty to, or grounding in, or even applicability to common life. This metaphysical philosophy bases its morality on reason or revelation and then tries to force that morality on humanity, regardless of the realities of human nature. To the rationalist, history, custom, tradition, and the common life have no value or authority in determining the moral order of human society. Hume deplored such dangerous arrogance. So, we should be neither rationalists nor metaphysicians, but empiricists.

Because social cohesion is so important, factions within society that divide and rend the social fabric are to be opposed. Consequently, Hume devoted some of his most original work to a study of social factions and their attendant dangers.

DAVID HUME'S CONCEPT OF FACTIONS

Hume divided social factions into personal and real.

A personal faction is "founded on personal friendship or animosity among such as compose the contending parties." Personal factions arise most easily in small states, where "every domestic quarrel . . . becomes an affair of state. Love, vanity, emulation, any passion, as well as ambition and resentment, begets public division." Furthermore, "men have such a propensity to divide into personal factions, that the smallest appearance of real difference will produce them." Factions (parties) begun with real differences

---

41. T, 224; TM, 273.
42. EM, 343.
43. "Of Moral Prejudice," E, 573; LF, 538.

on a personal basis often "continue even after that difference is lost," because the sentiment is personal.[44]

A real faction is founded on some real difference of sentiment or interest. Real factions are divided into three classifications:

1) Factions of interest. Factions that arise from common interest "are the most reasonable and the most excusable."

2) Factions of principle. Factions of principle, "especially abstract speculative principle, are known only to modern times, and are, perhaps, the most extraordinary and unaccountable *phenomenon*, that has yet appeared in human affairs."[45] Hume held that such parties "produce the greatest misery and devastation." It is in this faction that Hume put Christianity, and he was not very subtle as to his views on religious parties.[46] Hume declaimed that "in modern times, parties of religion are more furious and enraged than the most cruel factions that ever arose from interest and ambition."[47] Canadian political scholar and politician John Stewart notes that while people are comforted and pacified by similar opinions held by neighbors and friends, they are agitated and disturbed by commensurate doubt and criticism held by those around them. Thus, Humean society is vulnerable to factious fury from the pulpit or the parliament and thus destabilized society.[48]

3) Factions of affection.[49] The third type of real faction, that coming from affection, is "founded on the different attachments of men towards particular families and persons, whom they desire to rule over them. These factions are often very violent."[50] Such governmental parties are formed by the conflicting desires of different groups to have their country ruled by different dynasties. It was this type of factionalism that eventually evolved into the Hanover line versus the Stuart line of succession to the crown. Hume held that when one line had ruled for a sufficiently long period, then, in order to keep peace, custom would dictate presumption should go to that line.

44. "Of Parties in General," E, 55–56; LF, 56.

45. E, 58; LF, 60.

46. "The same principles of priestly government continuing, after Christianity became the established religion, they have engendered a spirit of persecution, which has ever since been the poison of human society, and the source of the most inveterate factions in every government" (LF, 62).

47. E, 60–61; LF, 62–63.

48. J. Stewart, *Moral and Political Philosophy*, 203–4.

49. E, 58; LF, 59.

50. E, 61; LF, 63.

The competing factional claims of specific versus general interest was of concern to Hume in government as well as morals. One of the ways this competition plays itself out is in the crafting of laws. Factions, special interests, private and public interests, partial and impartial interest, local and national interests—all compete for attention in the civic arena. Hume believed that general, impartial, national laws were the only remedy for an unstable government. There must be general laws and statutes in order to balance the particular cases and smooth out the inconveniences in a society in a stable manner.[51] It is the general laws that provide the "source of all security and happiness" and liberty for society.[52]

Furthermore, reason should play a part in crafting the nation's laws. Hume held that general laws were more rational than special ones because they were more normative, fitting the circumstances of the whole rather than a part. He wrote in his essay "Idea of a Perfect Commonwealth" that "reason can prevail over the whole. Influence and example being removed, good sense will always get the better of bad among a number of people."[53] Reason here evidently accords with the definition given in "A Dissertation on the Passions," where Hume analyzed reason as "nothing but a general and calm passion which takes a comprehensive and a distant view of its object and actuates the will, without exciting any sensible emotion."[54]

Hume's public factions and interests were to be used by the wise magistrate to balance competing claims and powers in government. He observed in his essay "Of the Independency of Parliament":

> Political writers have established it as a maxim, that, in contriving any system of government, and fixing the several checks and controls of the constitutions, every man ought to be supposed a knave, and to have no other end, in all his actions, than private interest. By this interest we must govern him, and, by means of it, make him, notwithstanding his insatiable avarice and ambition, cooperate to public good.[55]

However, Hume disagreed with the cynicism of these political writers and amended their maxims:

> It is, therefore, a just political maxim, that every man must be supposed a knave; though, at the same time, it appears somewhat

---

51. "Of the Rise and Progress of the Arts and Sciences," E, 116–117; LF, 116.
52. E, 118, 125; LF, 118, 124.
53. E, 509; LF, 523.
54. Hume, *Essays* (Green and Grose), 4:161.
55. E, 40–41; LF, 42.

strange, that a maxim should be true in politics which is false in fact. But to satisfy us on this head, we may consider, that men are generally more honest in their private than in their public capacity, and will go greater lengths to serve a party, than when their own private interest is alone concerned.[56]

University of Michigan Law School professor Don Herzog comments on this passage: "Taken as private individuals, men may be fairly honest; they may be driven by a concern for the regard of others. But politics is a distinct context, and the distinction makes a difference."[57] Hume would then argue that because politics is indeed a distinct context and a distant context, social institutions need to be nurtured to thwart the political ambitions of the legislators. In private life, human conduct is fenced by social approval or disapproval. In fact, personal identity is largely determined by the interaction and moral responses of those around one. However, politicians are bereft of this social control, for they interact only (or primarily) with other politicians, often of their own political persuasion, and so they lack the conventional checks and balances on their conduct. Consequently, a formal constitution is indispensable for the self-identity of the politician and the safety of the citizenry. That is why a good constitutional government can even make statesmen out of bad people.[58]

Finally, Hume drew a salutary conclusion in favor of a system of interest-bound checks and balances which distributes power among several courts and orders in order to produce a wise and happy government.[59]

DAVID HUME AND DEMOCRACY

Hume had a fear of unbridled democracy. Too much liberty was a bad thing, because it too often led to corruption, factions, and social self-destruction.[60]

---

56. E, 42–43; LF, 42–43.

57. Herzog, "David Hume: Crusading Empiricist, Skeptical Liberal," in Dascal and Gruengard, eds., *Knowledge and Politics*, 74.

58. "But a republic and free government would be an obvious absurdity, if the particular checks and controuls, provided by the constitution, has really no influence, and made it not the interest, even of bad men, to act for the public good. Such is the intention of these forms of government, and such is their real effect, where they are wisely constituted" ("That Politics May Be Reduced to a Science," E, 14; LF, 15–16).

59. E, 43; LF, 43.

60. "Idea of a Perfect Commonwealth," E, 508; LF, 522. Note also the following: "There is no quality in human nature, which causes more fatal errors in our conduct, than that which leads us to prefer whatever is present to the distant and remote, and makes us desire objects more according to their situation than their intrinsic value"

Madison shared Hume's suspicion of direct democracy. In the "Fifty-Fifth Federalist," Madison wrote, "Had every Athenian citizen been a Socrates, every Athenian assembly would still have been a mob." Hume wrote something similar: "Cardinal de Retz says that all numerous assemblies, however composed, are mere mob and swayed in their debates by the least motive."[61] Madison thought that it is the legislature that needs to be checked, not the executive.

Hume understood that monarchy, by its very nature, recognizes social bonds and constitutive groups in society, whereas democracy tends to supplant this social structure with individual freedom and the atomizing of the national population. Democracy leads to egalitarian society, which Hume believed to be destructive to order and stability. He believed that wide direct participation in public affairs is not conducive to self-restraint and emotional control. Furthermore, equality among citizens leaves no room for deference, civility, and respect in social intercourse. In his essay "Of the Rise of the Arts and Sciences," Hume spoke of "polite deference and respect, which civility obliges us either to express or counterfeit towards the person with whom we converse." By way of example, Hume approvingly wrote of Cicero and Atticus, "[The latter] is a humble admirer of [Cicero], pays him frequent compliments, and receives his instructions, with all the deference which a scholar owes to his master."[62]

Interestingly, Hume's theory of understanding (i.e., that impressions lead to ideas) did not allow him to invoke clear, simple ideas of society, since one can never have a clear impression of society as such. Individuals, however, do provide impressions to the mind, and therefore particular factions of individuals, i.e., voluntary institutions, can generate complex ideas of society. Individual humans can be studied, and from the observations a science of human nature (and, to a limited extent, a science of society, i.e., sociology) can be inferred. Hume was not content to let social applications of his philosophy always go unstated, so social institutions, composed of individuals, came to be the chief component in his sociology. However, even though individuals are the ultimate particulars on which social institutions

---

(T, 538; and the space and time section, T, 427–38); "That Politics May Be Reduced to a Science," E, 17; LF, 18; "Whether the British Government Inclines More to Absolute Monarchy, or to a Republic," E, 52, LF, 52. Hume did pen a couple of thoughts which seem to argue against a dogmatic assertion of an anti-democratic spirit. He wrote in his essay "Of Civil Liberty," "I am apt, however, to entertain a suspicion, that the world is still too young to fix many general truths in politics, which will remain true to the latest posterity" (E, 89; LF, 87).

61. "Idea of a Perfect Commonwealth," LF, 523.

62. E, 129–30; LF, 128–29.

are founded, democratic individualism nevertheless is not viable within Hume's vision.

DAVID HUME AND THE CHAMBER OF COMMERCE

While a little nervous about voting rights, Hume did not fear wealth. He believed that prosperity and civilization are intertwined. He wrote in "Of Refinement in the Arts" that "riches are valuable at all times"[63] and that "luxury is preferable to sloth and idleness."[64] Furthermore, the love of money abounds in ages of knowledge and refinement, and "industry, knowledge, and humanity are linked together, by an indissoluble chain."[65] In another essay, Hume tied the world of inventor/entrepreneur/merchant to the world of politics when he rhetorically asked, "Can we expect that a government will be well modelled by a people, who know not how to make a spinning wheel, or to employ a loom to advantage?"[66] Hume also wove the whole cloth of social arrangements in order to sew together commerce, politics, the arts, and general culture.[67]

Society is transformed, and social institutions are developed over time to accommodate the changes. These new institutions and conventions are, of course, a product of ordinary and evolutionary common life and custom. As society evolves, so do social manners. And as social manners change, the entire civil structure of the country changes correspondingly. "[This] change of manners," wrote Hume, "was the chief cause of the secret revolution of government and subverted the power of the barons."[68] In this way, a stable democracy was born, with the establishment of the House of Commons, through a quiet, secret change of public manners over time. Furthermore, Hume believed that commerce had a natural tendency to beget social order and civility. For him, commerce was the answer to the natural fractiousness of human society.[69]

63. E, 282–83; LF, 276.
64. E, 287–88; LF, 280.
65. E, 277–78; LF, 270–71.
66. E, 280; LF, 273.
67. H, 4:413–14; see also H, 3:71–72.
68. H, 4:375.
69. "Laws, order, police, discipline; these can never be carried to any degree of perfection, before human reason has refined itself by exercise, and by an application to the more vulgar arts, at least of commerce and manufacture" (E, 280; LF, 273). In an intriguing (and anti-clerical) passage, Hume refers to faithful Christians as customers: "No regard will be paid to truth, morals, or decency, in the doctrines inculcated. Every tenet will be adopted that best suits the disorderly affections of the human frame.

Hume stressed the increase in sociability which was stimulated by refinements in the mechanical and liberal arts, to which commerce had led. For Hume, commerce fosters not greed but industry, knowledge, sociability, and humanity in the individual human and in society in general. In short, he was a fan of the Edinburgh Chamber of Commerce.[70]

Regarding the social merits or benefits of international commerce and trade, Hume praised it in his essay "Of Commerce" as creating more industry and "delicacies and luxuries" for each trading nation, to say nothing of making each kingdom more powerful, richer, and happier.[71] Foreign trade stimulates employment, housing, a labor pool, and greater selection in personal possessions; it fosters human happiness in general. Its chief advantage, however, is that once under way, it carries us on to "farther improvements, in every branch of domestic trade as well as foreign trade" itself.[72] Perhaps Hume provided the first cogent defense of the benefit of the multi-national corporation.[73]

Adam Smith, Hume's Scottish friend and confidant,[74] agreed with Hume's ground-breaking thinking in tying the conventions of commerce and manufacturing to other social goods, such as liberty. Smith wrote that "commerce and manufacturing gradually introduced order and good government, and with them the liberty and security of individuals. Mr. Hume

---

Customers will be drawn to each conventicle by new industry and address, in practising on the passions and credulity of the populace" (H, 3:129).

70. "The more these refined arts advance, the more sociable men become nor is it possible, that, when enriched with science, and possessed of a fund of conversation, they should be contented to remain in solitude, or live with their fellow-citizens in that distant manner, which is peculiar to ignorant and barbarous nations. They flock into cities; love to receive and communicate knowledge; to show their wit or their breeding; their taste in conversation or living, in clothes or furniture. Curiosity allures the wise; vanity the foolish; and pleasure both. Particular clubs and societies are everywhere formed: both sexes meet in an easy and sociable manner; and the tempers of men, as well as their behavior, refine apace. So that, beside the improvements which they receive from knowledge and the liberal arts, it is impossible, but they must feel an increase of humanity, from the very habit of conversing together, and contribute to each other's pleasure and entertainment" (E, 277–78; LF, 270–271).

71. E, 269–70; LF, 263.

72. E, 270; LF, 264.

73. Nicholas Phillipson, whose book *Hume* first brought this Humean focus to my attention years ago. I believe it bears greater study as we continue in a global village economy.

74. Smith wrote to William Strahan in 1776 on the occasion of Hume's death, "Upon the whole, I have always considered him, both in his lifetime and since his death, as approaching as nearly to the idea of a perfectly wise and virtuous man, as perhaps the nature of human frailty will permit" (LF, xlix).

is the only writer who, so far as I know, has hitherto taken notice of it."[75] Dugald Stewart concluded that the "political discourses of Mr. Hume were evidently of greater use to Mr. Smith than any other book that had appeared prior to his lectures."[76]

American Founding Father John Adams famously wrote,

> I must study Politicks and War that my sons may have liberty to study Painting and Poetry Mathematicks and Philosophy. My sons ought to study Mathematicks and Philosophy, Geography, natural History, Naval Architecture, navigation, Commerce and Agriculture, in order to give their Children a right to study Painting, Poetry, Musick, Architecture, Statuary, Tapestry and Porcelaine.[77]

DAVID HUME AND BIG GOVERNMENT

Hume was wary of government taking too active a role, an "injudicious tampering" role, in both domestic and international commercial affairs. In his essays and his *History*, he argued against the dangers of big government upsetting the salutary cultural effects of free and unfettered trade. In his *History*, he made abundantly clear his view opposing governmental interference in the economic workings of society.[78]

We see an indication of humankind's natural propensity for reciprocity when Hume wrote: "Men being naturally selfish, or endow'd only with a confin'd generosity, they are not easily induc'd to perform any action for the interest of strangers, except with a view to some reciprocal advantage, which they had no hope of obtaining but by such a performance."[79] Whether the strangers are foreign or domestic, the economic message to big government is clear: no injudicious tampering; politicians and bureaucrats, mind your own business.

75. Smith, *Wealth of Nations*, 175–76.
76. D. Stewart, "Account of the Life," lxxix.
77. Letter to Abigail Adams, May 12, 1780.
78. "Most of the arts and professions in a state are of such a nature, that, while they promote the interests of the society, they are also useful or agreeable to some individuals; and, in that case, the constant rule of the magistrate, except, perhaps, on the first introduction of any art, is to leave the profession to itself, and trust its encouragement to those who reap the benefit of it. The artisans, finding their profits to rise by the favor of their customers, increase as much as possible their skill and industry; and as matters are not disturbed by any injudicious tampering, the commodity is always sure to be at all times nearly proportional to the demand" (H, 3:128).
79. T, 519; TM, 571.

In his essay "Of Commerce," Hume argued that "private men" are the key to the greatness of a state, and the state would do well to leave them to conduct their business affairs in an independent fashion.[80] Furthermore, intrusion by a king or legislator into commercial affairs is "contrary to the more natural and usual course of things."[81] Hume admonished sovereigns to "take mankind as they find them, and not pretend to introduce any violent change in their principles and ways of thinking." Even the legislator should cultivate these common principles, and "it is his best policy to comply with the common bent of mind."[82] When government steps in to arrange commercial affairs in an unnatural way, a "habit of sloth [will] naturally prevail." However, when government cultivates manufacturing and the mechanical arts in a natural way, commercial men will "redouble their industry and attention."[83]

Domestically, Hume believed that, left alone, common society would organize its affairs in order to promote prosperity without the intervening dictates of senseless politicians and government officials. To illustrate the iniquity of government regulation of commerce, Hume cited the following example from the reign of Henry VII:

> If we may judge by most of the laws enacted during his reign, trade and industry were rather hurt than promoted by the care and attention given to them . . . . It is needless to observe how unreasonable and iniquitous these laws, how impossible to be executed, and how hurtful to trade, if they could take place.[84]

And all this, Hume said, from a king whose "love of money naturally led him to encourage commerce"! Hume referred to one set of Henry's deleterious domestic laws concerning the archery and woolen industries, as well as labor wage control.[85] In other places, Hume attacked government market restrictions in farm commodities,[86] minimum wages,[87] and monopolies[88]—to name only a few of his condemnations of public interference in the private exchange of goods and services within the national borders.

80. E, 261; LF, 255.
81. E, 264; LF, 259.
82. E, 266; LF, 260.
83. E, 267; LF, 261.
84. H, 3:72.
85. H, 3:73.
86. H, 2:172.
87. H, 3:316–17.
88. H, 4:295, 336, 394, 417.

Furthermore, Hume argued against national debt. He give five disadvantages of public debt, two of which are of interest to us now: 1. "It is certain that national debts cause a might confluence of people and riches to the capital, by the great sums, levied in the province to pay the interest." 2. Holders of the debt are "men who have no connexions with the state, who can enjoy their revenue in any party of the globe in which they chuse to reside."[89]

Internationally, Hume held to the same trade philosophy: government that governs least, governs best. He argued in two essays, "Of the Balance of Trade" and "Of the Jealousy of Trade," that free trade among nations was salutary for all international and domestic economies and that government ought not to erect barriers in response to political pressure. In "Jealousy," Hume advocated that, rather than treating other nations with suspicion, rivalry, or jealousy, "sovereigns and ministers [should] adopt . . . enlarged and benevolent sentiments toward each other."[90] He asserted "that the encrease of riches and commerce in any one nation, instead of hurting, commonly promotes the riches and commerce of all its neighbors; and that a state can scarcely carry its trade and industry very far, where all the surrounding states are buried in ignorance, sloth and barbarism."[91]

Hume gave two reasons for this mutual prosperity: encouragement and cultural appropriation. "Every improvement, which we have since made, has arisen from our imitation of foreigners; and we ought so far to esteem it happy that they had previously made advances in arts and ingenuity."[92] Foreign trade is a prod to the national spirit of industry by encouraging the adoption of the "inventions and improvements of our neighbors" in order to stay competitive. Indeed, foreign competition serves to keep industry alive. If a nation loses out in the free trade marketplace, it is due, said Hume, to "their own idleness or bad government."[93] Nations cannot afford to have other trading nations "buried in ignorance, sloth and barbarism" where there is no commercial art or cultivation. If art or cultivation languish, in what can they trade? "They will have nothing to give in exchange."[94]

Hume's response to government's hand in all this international trading activity? The same response he gives to domestic interference: Stay out![95]

---

89. "Of Public Credit," LF, 354–57.
90. E, 338; LF, 331.
91. E, 334; LF, 328.
92. E, 335; LF, 328.
93. E, 336; LF, 330.
94. E, 335; LF, 329.
95. E, 338; LF, 331. See Rotwein, *David Hume,* and Stockton, "Economics."

Because Hume observed and described life as it is lived, he recognized that commerce and trade are not only good for society (public life), but also good for the individual (private life). Hume noted the edifying effects of trade on personal qualities, such as mental vigor, honesty, general morality, and industriousness.[96] That is, Hume saw that work (all caused by commercial trade) energizes the body, ennobles the human spirit, renews the creative talents, spurs mental imagination, and curtails human weakness; work is good, useful, and utilitarian. *Le bon David*[97] even praised the risk-taking entrepreneur when he opined, "Men must have profits proportionable to their expense and hazard."[98] Bonar reflects: "The equality of possessions is impractical, or at least it is destructive to society. The motives to industry would be gone and the resources of society would immediately decline."[99]

Correspondingly, Hume followed his five rules of property acquisition with a defense of the feudal concepts of entail and primogeniture.

Entail is the concept that real estate is bound up inalienably in grantees and then forever to their direct descendants, thus supporting landed aristocracy, because it serves to prevent the disintegration of large estates through divisible inheritance.

Primogeniture is the concept that the eldest son (and his descendants) are given preference in inheriting the estate of the deceased, thus keeping the landed estate intact and preserving the power and prestige of the aristocracy. Hume supported primogeniture in his essay "Of the Populousness of Ancient Nations": "The universal preference given to the elder by modern laws, though it encrease the inequality of fortunes, has, however, this good effect, that it accustoms men to the same idea in public succession, and cuts off all claim and pretension of the younger."[100] The idea of succession finds its defense in Hume's notion of association of ideas (what doesn't), since we naturally think of children when we think of parents—and who has the most natural claim on the deceased's property but the children? This conservative view of property has a strong Roman-feudal character; it was designed to protect the family (a key social institution), so that real estate would not come under the control of an individual or the government. In short, Hume believed the death tax would destabilize society.

96. E, 277; LF, 270.

97. "*Le bon David*" is the sobriquet given to Hume by a Parisian editor during the dispute with Rousseau in 1765 (M, 530).

98. "Of Commerce," E, 273; LF, 267.

99. Bonar, *Philosophy and Political Economy*, 126. Hume wrote, "Avarice, the spur of industry, is so obstinate a passion" ("Of Civil Liberty," E, 94; LF, 93); cf. Prov 14:23; 19:15; 2 Thess 3:10; 1 Tim 5:8.

100. E, 410; LF, 413.

DAVID HUME AND THE SACREDNESS OF COMMON LIFE

Hume held that the more disengaged persons were in political decisions of common life, the more dangerous they were to social tranquility. If people operated on a metaphysical/rationalistic basis, they would have no stake in orderly, systematic, gradual social change or alteration. They would be more interested in a wholesale demolishing of social norms and structures: "It may safely be averred, that the more sincere and the more disinterested they are, they only become the more ridiculous and the more odious."[101]

Obviously, there appears to be a contradiction in Hume's notion of disinterestedness in the political as opposed to the moral realm. But the contradiction is more apparent than real. Both in political science and in moral science, Hume sought stability. For instance, a disengaged political perspective serves to uproot one's commitment to the individual society in which one is placed—the person does not care, especially, what happens to the community immediately around him, such as his own family. But a disengaged, disinterested moral perspective does serve to provide a general framework for moral approbation, as opposed to a private and biased (particular) framework. Consequently, there can be commonly held social conventions of justice that will order social relationships.[102]

Furthermore, Hume believed that social stability and happiness depended on the immediate, local, and personal benefits of commerce and the arts. It would not be conducive to social harmony to have commercial prosperity too removed or abstracted from the local citizenry. Social justice and morality are, after all, based on experience.[103] While Hume did not believe in original sin, the Founding Fathers did, and their belief in Adam's fall made them susceptible to Hume's notion of government in small pieces (factions) and in checks and balances with each other. American Calvinism with a dose of Edinburgh skepticism at work in Philadelphia!

In order to temper the metaphysical excesses of Christianity, Hume held that it was better to have an established church (a social institution) which is influenced, if not controlled, by government (another social institution).[104] The more theologically apostate the church became, the more socially suitable it became, in Hume's opinion, because he thought it would

---

101. H, 5:364
102. T, 499; TM, 550.
103. "Of Commerce," E, 269; LF, 263.
104. H, 4:93

be less ideological and divisive.¹⁰⁵ Moreover, "of all the Sects, into which the Christians have been divided, the Church of England seems to have chosen the happy Medium."¹⁰⁶

The Church of England, however, was not the only ecclesiastical body to bear the appropriate interference of the state. Hume believed that the Scottish Presbyterians needed the same direction. In his essay "Idea of a Perfect Commonwealth," he opined that it was important that "Magistrates name rector or ministers to all the parishes . . . try, and depose or suspend any presbyter [and] . . . take any cause from this [ecclesiastical] court and determine it themselves."¹⁰⁷ Hume argued that the only clear benefit of an established church was that it would curb the pernicious and "interested diligence of the clergy." Mercy!

Hume's point here, as elsewhere, was that unless one was grounded and rooted in the common life, one had no basis for social criticism or action. If one failed to affirm that common life was normative for morality and social association, one's social judgments would be biased, arbitrary, and abstract. One must see common life in practice as the norm, then extract, from that flowing historical norm, principles to evaluate the common life in a practical way—emphasizing that common life is the only life we know and experience. Hume always moved from the concrete to the abstract, from the physical to the metaphysical, from the tangible to the intangible.

Social reform and progress, following Hume's theory of understanding, comes back to the notion that impressions (e.g., of social customs and conventions) must precede ideas (e.g., of social morality and structure). Otherwise, a proposed reform would have no foundation in reality.

A politically active overcoat without philosophic underpants leaves the politician buck naked.¹⁰⁸ Every political theory needs a speculative science to give it meaning. Hume wrote in his essay "Of the Original Contract": "No party, in the present age, can well support itself without a philosophical or speculative system of principles annexed to its political or practical one."¹⁰⁹

105. Hume's mention of the suitableness and historicity of the church's socially stable beliefs, both of which conform to his general philosophic principles.

106. Mossner, *Life of David Hume*, 307

107. E, 506; LF, 560.

108. Unfortunately, a favorite thinker of mine, Michael Oakeshott, perhaps the most respected intellectual spokesman for British conservatism in the last half of the twentieth century, has written against this claim: "Political philosophy cannot be expected to increase our ability to be successful in political activity; it will not help us to distinguish between good and bad political projects; it has no power to guide us in the enterprise of pursuing the intimations of our tradition" ("Political Education," in *Rationalism in Politics and Other Essays*, 65).

109. "And though a philosopher may live remote from business, the genius of

But reform must be done carefully, reflectively, and slowly, since the mere existence of a convention, a tradition, a prejudice is prima facie evidence of its importance, value, and meaning, indeed, of its cultural divinity. Social arrangements have, after all, a sacred, or reverential character about them.[110] Hume's reverential view of the past put him in direct cultural conflict with contemporary rationalistic Continental philosophers. Carl L. Becker, in his 1932 Storrs Lectures at Yale, noted that Hume's eighteenth-century colleagues often treated the future as a religious matter: "The thought of posterity was apt to elicit from eighteenth-century philosophers and revolutionary leaders a highly emotional, and essentially religious, response. Posterity, like nature, was often personified, reverently addressed as a divinity, and invoked in the accents of prayer."[111] In short, history is divine and has the authority of revealed Scripture. Historical precedents should govern our lives as if revealed from God, if there was such a being.

In yet another essay, "Of the Original Contract," Hume colorfully contrasted humans to silkworms and drew out the instability and unnaturalness of the biological flow from silkworms to butterflies to the more stable and natural flow of "one generation of men" giving social birth to another.[112]

Since, as we have seen, the future is speculative, our present actions must be based on the past. The past, however, is apprehended only through historical narrative of associations. So, for Hume, the only acceptable method of improving our social order was by deliberation and reflective

---

philosophy, if carefully cultivated by several, must gradually diffuse itself throughout the whole society, and bestow a similar correctness on every art and calling. The politician will acquire greater foresight and subtlety, in the subdividing and balancing of power" ("Of the Original Contract," EU, 10; P, 14. E, 452; LF, 465). This sounds a lot like Richard Weaver's thesis in his seminal conservative work *Ideas Have Consequences*.

110. E, 499; LF, 512–13.

111. Becker notes four representative figures: Maximilien Robespierre (1758–1794), "O posterity, sweet and tender hope of humanity, thou art not a stranger to us.... Make haste, O posterity, to bring to pass the hour of equality, of justice, of happiness"; Joseph Priestly (1733–1804), "What an inspiration if was to contemplate the progress of the species towards perfection. It requires but a few years to comprehend the whole preceding progress of any one art or science and the rest of a man's life, in which his faculties are the most perfect, may be given to the extension of it"; Johann Herder (1744–1803), "His philosophy is a strange compound of learning insight and mystical power. It sustained an oratorical exposition of the text that God realized himself in humanity, and that all good men, in working for the happiness of posterity, are furthering the divine purpose"; and Denis Diderot (1713–1784), "One evening in the year 1765, so we are told, in a corner by the fire, in the Rue Taranne, argued the question whether a regard for posterity inspired men to noble action and the creation of great works.... Posterity is for the philosopher what the other world is for the religious" (Becker, *Heavenly City*, 142–151).

112. E, 463; LF, 476–77.

commitment to maintain the past, with refining actions based on principles derived from an analysis of the common life of human society.[113]

With this approach in mind, it is easy to see that Hume indeed deified common life. For him it had a sacred, religious dimension. Hume's reading of Cicero influenced him at this point, for Cicero wrote, "I do not know whether, if our reverence for the gods were lost, we should not also see the end of good faith, of human brotherhood, and even of justice itself, which is the keystone of all the virtues."[114] Hume's reverence for a religious approach to common life thus corresponded to the classical view that piety is the strongest support of common morality. For Hume, there was a divine-like authority attached to social order.[115]

True religion, for Hume, was based in the common life of the social being of humanity. He advocated a kind of presidential Prayer Breakfast civil theology: as we live life together in society, we develop empirical regularity of custom, tradition, prejudices, and associations, which are justified in turn by our human nature, our human propensities, as being the product of a mind or intelligence. While this mind may not be a personal, salvific being (as in biblical Christianity), it nevertheless is a power that guides social arrangements and therefore deserves our worship. In the *Dialogues*, Hume had Cleanthes, the Greek philosopher (330–230 BC), state what appears to be a summary of his own views:

> The proper office of religion is to regulate the heart of men, humanize their conduct, infuse the spirit of temperance, order, and obedience; and as its operation is silent, and only enforces the motives of morality and justice, it is in danger of being overlooked, and confounded with these other motives. When it distinguishes itself, and acts as a separate principle over men, it has departed from its proper spheres, and has become only a cover to faction and ambition.[116]

Thus, true religion, for Hume, was one that is part and parcel of the common life, with no literal, otherworldly character about it. The established church is the ritualistic institution to sacralize society's value system.

---

113. Cf. Jer 6:16.

114. Cicero, *Nature of the Gods*, 70.

115. See Hume's essay "Of Parties in General" (E, 61; LF, p. 62). Sabine disagrees with this assessment: "In destroying reverence for the law of nature [Hume] felt no need to put a new reverence in its place, and a cult of society would not have appeared to him better than other cults" (Sabine, *History of Political Theory*, 619).

116. Flew, *Introduction to Western Philosophy*, 284.

In his essay "Of the Origin of Government," Hume wrote of the political and civil moral purposes of the church:

> We are, therefore, to look upon all the vast apparatus of our government, as having ultimately no other project or purpose but the distribution of justice.... Even the clergy, as their duty leads them to inculcate morality, may justly be thought, so far as regards this world, to have no other useful object of their institutions.[117]

True religion, the religion of the common life, is preeminently utilitarian. It does not rest on "separate principle over men" as Christianity does, but rather is "built entirely on public interest and convenience."[118] These undergirding principles of true religion that deserve our obeisance are known to us by "our experience of their reality" in our common life.[119] Hume warned against Christian philosophers, "these sublime theorists,"[120] having too great an influence in society.[121] In the first *Enquiry*, Hume made the charge that when popular religion makes common cause with rationalism, what one gets is an unholy marriage between superstition and philosophy, with the resulting offspring of intransigent dogmatism and bigotry,[122] leading to cruelty, injustice, and social insecurity. Only a political environment free from religious interference is conducive to the study and discussion of philosophic matters.[123] In the above citation, Hume was referring to ancient Athens. However, he failed to mention that the Athenians put Socrates to death, and that Aristotle had to flee Athens in order to avoid the same fate.

DAVID HUME AND REFORMING SOCIETY

In seeking to change the social order or the conventions of common life, we must move with a methodical and reverent attitude, because we are tampering with the very basis of understanding, knowledge, morality, and the

---

117. E, 35; LF, 37.

118. T, 525; TM, 577.

119. T, xxii; TM, 45.

120. Including Samuel Clarke (1675–1729), George Berkeley (1685–1753), and Joseph Butler (1692–1752).

121. EM, 193; OC, 26.

122. "This pertinacious bigotry [revealed religion], of which you complain, as so fatal to philosophy, is really her offspring, who, after allying with superstition, separates himself entirely from the interest of his parent, and becomes her most inveterate enemy and persecutor" (EU, 133; P, 121).

123. EU, 132; P, 120.

object of worship for humanity. Those who would turn society upside down for utopian perfection are not reformers, for they do not want to reform. They are revolutionaries, because they want to revolve or turn society over onto its head. This reminds me of the 2020 Democratic Party. In his essay "Of Moral Prejudices," Hume disdainfully wrote, "There is a set of men lately sprung up amongst us, who endeavor to distinguish themselves by ridiculing everything, that has hitherto appeared sacred and venerable in the eyes of mankind."[124] Hume's judgment of revolutionaries is echoed by F. L. Lucas in his chapter on Hume: "There is also the factor that an observant person tends, the longer he lives, to grow more and more convinced of the folly and hysteria of men, the obscurity and complexity of things. Most revolutionaries are minds not fully adult."[125] In his *History*, Hume wrote of the tension between those who would advocate liberty and civil perfection in social arrangements and those who would press for civil stability.[126]

In short, those who would press for the established character of government are in an inevitable state of tension with those who would press for its perfection. Hume claimed that the search for political perfection would lead to endless confusion, ineffectual government, and, probably, sedition.[127] In his *History*, he covered the death of Richard III in 1485. As he reflected on the changes in British government over the approximately one thousand years between the fall of the Roman rule and the death of Richard, Hume expressed his bias towards established rule: "In each of these successive alterations [of rulers], the only rule of government which is intelligible, or carries any authority with it, is the established practice of the age, and the maxims of administration which are at that time prevalent and universally assented to."[128] Thus, whatever the contemporary mores are should be reflected in governmental actions.[129]

It is the obligation of the wise magistrate to artfully guide this creative tension between competing factions for the established government, for such action will provide public well-being.[130]

124. E, 573; LF, 538.
125. Lucas, *Art of Living*, 57.
126. H, 4:365–66.
127. T, 555; TM, 606.
128. H, 2:514.

129. When he wrote of Elizabeth I (1533–1603), he noted his guide to political action: "In the particular exertions of power, the question ought never to be forgotten, what is best? But in the general distribution of power among the several members of a constitution, there can seldom be admitted any other question than, what is established?" (H, 4:344).

130. "Idea of a Perfect Commonwealth," E, 499; LF, 512–13.

In order to be applicable to society, any change must come from a grounding in the historical narrative of the past, because only history has meaning for the human. Any change that is extra-historical is vacuous and incoherent, since it does not make any sense in a tensed world. Therefore, rationalism's total rejection and scathing criticism of social arrangements, convention, traditions, and prejudices of common life was utterly nonsensical to Hume. It is not surprising that he did not miss the opportunity to challenge political rationalism at this point: "All plans of government, which suppose great reformation in the manners of mankind, are plainly imaginary."[131]

There are always limits that historical lessons force on social change. English philosopher Antony Flew cogently summarized this crucial Humean doctrine:

> Always Hume insists: both that the scope and potentialities of human reason are limited; and that we are, above all, creatures of habit. If we cannot even know that there are mind-independent realities in an External World, how absurd it is to think that we could form and execute some scheme of wholesale Utopian social engineering having all but only the benign consequences allegedly intended. As creatures of habit we must be forever liable to relapse into our former ways, while both resenting and struggling against the disappointment of long-cherished expectations. The burden of proof, therefore, must rest always on the would-be innovator.[132]

The Humean rules for justifying social reform are social beneficence, utility, and convenience. Laski calls Hume the real founder of utilitarianism.[133] But even if to some extent he was, his view, unlike that of classical utilitarians such as Jeremy Bentham (1748–1832) and John Stuart Mill (1806–1873), did not entail radical and abrupt change.[134] The circumstances

---

131. E, 500; LF, 514.

132. Flew, *David Hume*, 174.

133. Laski, *Political Thought*, 104. Albert Schweitzer shares Laski's view in *Philosophy of Civilization*, as does Plamenatz, *English Utilitarians*, 22.

134. Many think Laski wrong in his opinion. J. J. C. Smart did not think it advisable to even consider Hume a utilitarian, much less the real founder of utilitarianism: "David Hume is often classified as a utilitarian, but he used utility not as a normative or even as certain traits of character, he would point out that they are traits which either are useful or are immediately agreeable" (Smart, "Utilitarianism," 208). Copleston expresses the view of some that utilitarianism goes back at least to George Berkeley (1685–1753), who maintained in his treatise on *Passive Obedience* that it is "the general well-being of all men, of all nations, of all ages of the world; which God designs should be procured by the concurring actions of each individual" (cited in Copleston, *History*

continually confronting society force gradual changes to accommodate them. Human society must, indeed, change; it is a necessity of human society to adapt to circumstances. But the adaptation must proceed at a proper pace. This changing circumstantial basis for morals does, however, constitute an argument against set moral rules. Therefore, human action can be legislated, but internal moral feelings cannot: "The external performance has no merit [in itself]. We must look within to find the moral quality."[135] Hume's notion that it is the internal motive or feeling that is important in ethical considerations (out of the heart), rather than the external action, seems to argue against Hume being classified as the legitimate founder of utilitarianism.[136] This moral feeling approach favors what are essentially utilitarian-sanctioned principles, viz. the big three fundamental laws of nature: stability of possession, transference by consent, and performance of promises.[137]

Human conventions or rules emerge before any government action comes into focus. People unconsciously decide for themselves, initially, what is important to a stable society and community. While Hume denied the rational basis for social arrangements, he asserted rather the customary or natural basis for such arrangements.[138] Government, in its initial forms, simply responds and consents to codify the existing evolved social rules. This notion of traditions, customs, conventions, and social institutions preceding the formation of government is clearly biblical.[139] "Politics is downstream from culture," said Andrew Breitbart (1969–2012) in 2011.

The task of political science is to understand the relationship between individuals and society, gaining its understanding from history (the past) and observation (the present).[140] Hume applied his theory of causality to political science.[141] In order to arrive at an understanding of political behavior, the political scientist must look for corresponding rules by means of the experimental method.[142] Accordingly, Hume inferred that human

---

of Philosophy, 5:253–54). Furthermore, Berkeley speaks of "moral or practical truths being ever connected with universal benefit" (Copleston, *History of Philosophy*, 5:253).

135. T, 477; TM, 529.

136. T, 469; TM, 520–21.

137. T, 526; TM, 578.

138. T, 484; TM, 536.

139. T, 541; TM, 592; cf. 1 Sam 8, when government comes after family, church, guilds, etc.

140. "That Politics May Be Reduced to a Science," E, 14; LF, 16.

141. Four principles of that relationship are contiguity, conjunction, temporal priority, and resemblance (T, 173–74; TM, 223).

142. At the same time, Hume could write in his essay "Of the Original Contract"

nature was uniform regardless of time and place.¹⁴³ This conclusion did not preclude variety or change or difference in human conduct. For if human nature is basically the same everywhere, then the incidental variations are attributable to social conventions, which are the chief cause of actions. Two of Hume's rules by which to judge causes and effects are particularly applicable to politics:

> Rule 5. There is another principle, which hang upon this, viz. that where several different objects produce the same effect, it must be by means of some quality, which we discover to be common amongst them. For as like effects imply like causes, we must always ascribe the causation to the circumstance, wherein we discover the resemblance.
> Rule 6. The following principle is founded on the same reason. The difference in the effects of two resembling objects must proceed from that particular, in which they differ. For as like causes always produce like effects, when in any instance we find our expectations to be disappointed, we must conclude that this irregularity proceeds from some difference in the causes.¹⁴⁴

While general and certain effects may be predicted from various causes in civil society, political science depends upon observation of, and experiments with, human affairs in order to infer sound conclusions. Hence, Hume warned against feeling too certain in one's political judgments.¹⁴⁵

This is a straightforward political application of Hume's notion of mitigated skepticism, for he believed that a healthy dose of philosophic doubt was indispensable to a stable political process, in order to keep the politicians from taking themselves too seriously. Concerning Hume's science of politics, Frederick Whelan writes, "The common sense of human nature is the only available guide, but its soundness depends on an admixture of skepticism that tempers its tendency to credulity and its pretension to insight and teaches it its due limitations."¹⁴⁶ This Humean political skepticism keeps Hume from vigorously embracing any particular ideology, even democracy. In fact, he was purposefully vague and indifferent about political schemes:

> Thus, if we have reason to be more jealous of monarchy, because the danger is more imminent from that quarter; we have also

that "the scene of politics affords few rules, which will not admit of some exception, and which may not sometimes be controuled by fortune and accident" (LF, 477).

143. Cf. Gen 1.
144. T, 174; TM, 224.
145. E, 90; LF, 89; cf. Prov 16:18.
146. Whelan, *Order and Artifice*, 329.

reason to be more jealous of popular government, because that danger is more terrible. This may teach us a lesson of moderation in all our political controversies.[147]

Hume's political theory, then, does not consist of a defense of a set of principles. Still, one can find in Hume's political ideas the emphasis on observation,[148] probability, and uniformity that characterized his theory of understanding and his theory of morals; in fact, everything he wrote. British Anglican pastor John Stott points out that eyewitness testimony through observation indicates authoritative experience.[149]

Artificial virtues are to morals what social rules are to politics—rules provide stability, uniformity, and probability. Past observations are fundamental in predicting the future. Our human nature demands that this be the case. Human nature has a basic affinity to custom and order; therefore, any effective authority must rest with this natural affinity. Customary social rules control emotional impulse. Virtue is practiced because we accept, naturally, the discipline of such rules. Authority, for Hume, was embodied in rules rather than in rule, in institutions and common practices rather than in persons.[150] Government is to act as a facilitator, to use a present-day term, in order to coordinate, assist, and protect the independent center of power and authority resident in social institutions, which are the only valid expression of the human propensity for freedom, security, and happiness. Only from time to time will it be necessary for the government to exercise authority by passing laws. Usually, if left to themselves, people will create a more satisfactory society than one that government would impose on them.

It is this Humean emphasis on rules, order, the past, and limited government that should be esteemed by evangelical conservatives.

Institutions were seen by Hume to be a largely unreflective response to human experience, and thus were thought to be a natural guide to human corporate behavior. We humans just naturally like to socialize.

---

147. "Whether the British Government Inclines More to Absolute Monarchy, or to a Republic," E, 53; LF, 53.

148. Bauckman, *Jesus and the Eyewitnesses*. Cf. Luke 24:39, 48; John 1:34; 3:11, 32; Acts 1:8; 1 John 1:1; etc.

149. Stott, *Letters of John*, TNTC, 61–66 (*martyreisthai*, testifying, witnessing, in 1 John 1:1–4).

150. Hume, of course, discounts the rule of Adam over us in our natural inclination to sin.

DAVID HUME AND GOVERNMENT BY PUBLIC OPINION

Government is an important social institution because it helps to enforce observance of moral rules, and without such rules of conduct there would be no social stability. We observe these rules not only because observance is consistent with our natural propensity to sympathize with others and therefore demonstrate a benevolent attitude towards society but also because observance benefits us. Observance of social rules of conduct is good for everybody. Well, almost everybody. Ultimately, it is customary social interaction that fuels our approbation of government. Government provides law and order, which have in the past proved useful in living our lives. Hume's moral theory was consensus-based, that is, based on public opinion: "The general opinion of mankind has some authority in all cases."[151] Moreover, in order to be efficacious and supported by the public, "laws have, or ought to have, a constant reference to the constitution of government, the manners, the climate, the religion, the commerce, the situation of each society."[152] As Hume perspicuously observed in his essay "Of the First Principles of Government," government is supported only by the opinion of the governed.[153] First culture, then government. Laski notes that the importance of public opinion in relation to utility is a persuasive theme of Hume's political philosophy.[154]

In his essay "Idea of a Perfect Commonwealth," Hume advanced several notions for the structure of a large republic, and these notions depend on his view that public opinion is important for political and social stability. One such notion is modified federalism—a territorial separation of jurisdictions that is to be a separation of interaction and discussion, but not of legal autonomy (like Denmark/Greenland). He believed that there should be a national, indirectly elected body (a senate) that would make national laws and have veto power over territorial (county) laws made by the directly elected representatives of the people. These two bodies would need to interact with each other by reasonable discussion and debate. These bodies would substitute for a large gathering of people, which Hume believed would

---

151. T, 552; TM, 603.

152. EM, 196; OC, 30.

153. E, 29; LF, 32.

154. "His whole attitude is simply an insistence that utility is the touchstone of institutions, and he may claim to be the first thinker who attempted its application to the whole field of political science. He knows that opinion is the sovereign ruler of mankind, and that ideas of utility lie at the base of the thoughts which get accepted" (Laski, *Political Thought*, 97–98).

inevitably be a mob and therefore infectious, swayable, and unwieldy: "If the people debate, all is confusion."[155] Contrarily, smaller, territorial groups (i.e., provinces/states) of legislators could debate the issues in social harmony. "Divide the people into many separate bodies, and then they may debate with safety, and every inconvenience seems to be prevented."[156] Representative government and even state's rights.

Hume believed the general populace were too ignorant and unfit to hold office themselves, but they could choose representatives who had common sense (middling sense) to do their bidding: "And though every member [of the local legislatures] be only of middling sense, it is not probable, that anything but reason can prevail over the whole. Influence and example being removed, good sense will always get the better of bad among a number of people."[157] Debate and discussion, therefore, were critical for Hume in order to arrive at the most stable form of government. He even made provision for losers of elections to have "the power of accusing and appealing to the people."

Parliament should be a body of high debate and rationality, for in it laws are refined and accommodated to the public good: "When a popular bill has been debated in parliament, is brought to maturity, all its conveniences and inconveniences, weighted and balanced [it becomes] the unanimous desire of the people."[158] After laws are sent from the national senate to the local county assemblies, "a copy of the bill, and of the senate's reasons, must be sent to every representative eight days before the day appointed for the assembling, in order to deliberate concerning it."[159] Government, in short, is guided by public opinion, refined through legislative debate.[160] British federalism at work! No wonder he was for American independence from the British.

Good persons with good intentions did not, for Hume, a good society make. The greatest social goods, i.e., justice, peace, and liberty, are politically negative, in that they existed prior to government, and government must protect against personal and social evil (i.e., injury), as opposed to fostering these social goods. Indeed, Hume's concept of the artifacts of justice was that their purpose is to thwart undesirable tendencies in human nature and

---

155. E, 508–9; LF, 522–23.
156. E, 509; LF, 523.
157. E, 509; LF, 523.
158. E, 501; LF, 515.
159. E, 503; LF, 517.
160. E, 125; LF, 124.

not perfect that nature.¹⁶¹ While good individuals, acting as government officials, cannot ensure the flowering of these social goods, social institutions and conventions (i.e., club, churches, marriage, family, guilds, etc.) can do so, because they come from the people themselves. Indeed, institutions and conventions are the only thing that can give birth to and nurture the good.¹⁶² Hume, observing that the British constitution is a political/social convention, noted that "the constitution had . . . made it . . . the interest, even of bad men, to act for the public good."¹⁶³

This notion of institutional protection of individual liberties is a paramount political contribution to twenty-first century American social stability. I will discuss it further in the following chapter.

DAVID HUME AND SOCIAL INSTITUTIONS

Hume's rejection of reason as the ground of moral distinction led him to reject all forms of government other than those arising from custom, tradition, or association. In his essay "Of the Original Contract," he criticized the idea of a deliberate social compact, from which some political philosophers (e.g., Hobbes, Locke, Rousseau) trace the origin of government, in favor of the voluntary common, circumstantial need of organizing to meet the daily exigencies of life.¹⁶⁴ He argued, specifically, that it is the natural family that provides the ultimate basis for social arrangements.¹⁶⁵ As Skinner reminds us, sex is natural to humans: "Hume argued that 'there is in all men, both male and female, a desire and power of generation, more active than is ever universally exerted.'"¹⁶⁶ Furthermore, "the state of society without government is one of the most natural states of men, and must subsist with the conjunction of many families, and long after the first generation."¹⁶⁷ "Hence, we may give a plausible reason, among others, why all governments are at

161. Cf. Rom 13:1-4.
162. Cf. 1 Cor 5.
163. "That Politics May Be Reduced to a Science," E, 14; LF, 15-16.
164. E, 452-73; LF, 465-87.
165. "This necessity [the need to form a society] is no other than that natural appetite betwixt the sexes, which unites them together, and preserves their union, till a new tye takes place in their concern for their common offspring. This new concern becomes also a principle of union betwixt the parents and offspring and forms a more numerous society; where the parents govern by the advantage of their superior strength and wisdom, and at the same time are restraint in the exercise of their authority by that natural affection, which they bear their children" (T, 486; TM, 538); cf. Gal 3:26-29.
166. Skinner, "Hume's Principles," 397.
167. T, 541; TM, 592.

first monarchical, without any mixture and variety . . . . Camps are the true mothers of cities."[168]

Hume held that it was social institutions, created in the historical flow of common life, that had true political authority.[169] Note the importance of family tradition in civil virtue and of the family paradigm in civil arrangements.[170] Such historical institutions have the original authority, since they are a product of human sentiment over the course of time.

Hume continued his attack on the social contract (or original contract) by observing that "it is not justified by history or experience, in any age or country of the world."[171] Indeed, social peace and order preceded any written document, because we can trace the propensity for civil agreement to the "nature of man, and in the equality, or something approaching equality, which we find in all the individuals of that species."[172] Furthermore, if one were to preach that political contracts or connections are founded on voluntary consent or mutual promise, one would risk imprisonment by the civil authorities or commitment to an asylum by friends.[173] But if the civil magistrate would complain, "How is civil obedience possible when nothing is rationally agreed upon by the citizens?," Hume would answer, "Obedience or subjection becomes so familiar, that most men never make any enquiry about its origin or cause, more than about the principle of gravity, resistance, or the most universal laws of nature."[174]

Historical associations and customs show what common human nature deems moral. Therefore, history is infallible in determining the moral order—not the timeless, abstract, independent, metaphysical, judgmental authority of reason or rationality.[175] Hume's rejection of rationality, and his impressions of epistemological ideas, is not only an argument against the Hobbesian social contract[176] but also a body blow to the natural rights

---

168. T, 540–41; TM, 92.
169. "Of the Original Contract," E, 456; LF, 470.
170. Cf. Gen 1:28.
171. E, 457; LF, 471.
172. E, 454; LF, 468.
173. E, 456; LF, 470.
174. E, 456; LF, 470.
175. H, 6:346.
176. Thomas Hobbes (1588–1679) suggested in *Leviathan* that individuals in a prepolitical state are drawn together in accordance with laws of nature, which Hobbes defines as "precept[s], or general rule[s], found out by reason, by which a man is forbidden to do that which is destructive of his life or taketh away the means of preserving the same" (14). For Hobbes, the individual instinctively pursues self-preservation and security, and these laws of nature are rules which any reasonable individual would

theory of John Locke. Locke argued that all individuals are born with certain inalienable natural rights like life, liberty, property, and preservation of self.[177] Hume's view that behavior depends on the pursuit of pleasure or

---

pursue for his own advantage. In the *Leviathan,* there are nineteen such laws of nature, but only a couple are of interest to us. The first "general rule of reason" for Hobbesian society is "That every man ought to endeavor peace, as far as he has hope of obtaining it; and when he cannot obtain it, that he may seek and use all helps and advantages of war" (14). One of the helps of which the Hobbesian individual will take advantage is a contract with other individuals in which there is a "mutual transferring of rights" for personal defense by "every man saying to every man: 'I authorize and give up my right of governing myself to this man [sovereign], or to this assembly of men, on this condition; that thou give up thy right to him, and authorize all his actions in like manner.' This done, the multitude so united in one person is called a COMMONWEALTH; in Latin CIVITAS. This is the generation of the great LEVIATHAN" (17). A third natural law is that "men perform their covenant made" (15). Men will keep these covenants or contracts because, Hobbes argues, "all men agree on this, that peace is good, and therefore also the way or means of peace" (15). It must be noted that Hobbes was no sentimental rationalist. He knew the devious nature of the individual, for he also wrote that "covenants, without the sword, are but words and of no strength to secure a man at all" (17). In other words, the great Leviathan must carry weaponry to enforce the contract. Thus, a social contract is entered for mutual benefit by the purposeful reasoning of rational individuals, a contract which is subsequently enforced with the centralized power of weaponry. While Hume rejected the social covenant notion of Hobbes, he did agree with Hobbes that social justice is a matter of observing social conventions or rules which are of human invention and therefore are artificial, not natural, as Locke would maintain.

177. John Locke (1632–1704) argued in his "Essay Concerning Human Understanding": "Moral good and evil is only the conformity or disagreement of our voluntary actions to some law, whereby good or evil is drawn on us, from the will and the power of the lawgiver [God]" (229). Concerning the law, Locke distinguished three kinds: civil, opinion or reputation, and divine (230). It is Locke's notion of divine law that interests us here. Locke defined divine law as that "law which God has set to actions of men-whether promulgated to them by the light of nature [reason], or the voice of revelation" (230). Locke thought that by reasoning about the nature of God and man and their relationship, universal moral laws would become self-evident to the reasoner.

In his *Second Treatise of Government,* Locke wrote that all men are in a state of nature until they consent [and they always do] to join a "politic society" (28). He wrote of this pristine state of nature: "The state of nature has a law of nature to govern it, which obliges every one: and reason, which is that law, teaches all mankind, who will but consult it, that being all equal and independent, no one ought to harm another in his life, health, liberty or possessions" (26). Locke's natural divine law leads to natural rights, such as the natural right of "life, health, liberty and possessions." Of these natural rights, Locke gave most of his attention to possessions or property (30–36). In Locke's conception of property, God gave the world to "Adam and his heirs," in common (30). But it is the individual's labor, acting appropriately in God's economy, which gathers ownership to that individual, out of the common fold. Locke wrote, "Every man has a property in his own person: this nobody has any right to but himself. The labour of his body, and the work of his hands . . . are properly his. Whatsoever then he removes out of the state that nature hath provided, and left it in, he hath mixed his labour with and joined to it

avoidance of pain replaced the rational standard of inherent good that is fundamental to natural law theory. For Hume, there were no self-evident rights for the individual that would guarantee social harmony. Instead, social harmony was to be achieved through the utilitarian value of social institutions, behavior, and morality based on human feelings.

George Sabine offers a summative and critical paragraph on Hume's relation to natural law theory:

> If the premises of Hume's argument be granted, it can hardly be denied that he made a clean sweep of the whole rationalist philosophy of natural right, of self-evident truths, and of the laws of eternal and immutable morality which were supposed to guarantee the harmony of nature and the order of human society. In place of indefeasible rights or natural justice and liberty there remains merely utility, conceived in terms either of self-interest or social stability, and issuing in certain conventional standards of conduct which on the whole serve human purposes. Such conventions may, of course, be widespread among men and relatively permanent, because human motives are fairly uniform and in their general outlines change slowly, but in no other sense can they be called universal. They are always contingent upon some state of the facts, upon the causal relations of facts to human inclinations, and upon the formulation of workable rules to give scope to these inclinations. The conventions of society may be explained by history or psychology or anthropology, but they cannot claim validity in any but the relative sense of being generally convenient and in accord with men's estimate of utility. All the attempts to find in them an eternal fitness or rightness are merely confused ways of saying that they are useful; granted the principle of utility the whole system of natural right can be dispensed with.[178]

If there are no self-evident rights or truths, what will perform the function traditionally attributed to them? Hume's answer: common life in society, of course. Sentiment, tradition, prejudice, conventions—all are the bedrock of human rights and morality. The propensity of human nature for sympathy, and the moral codes and institutions that evolve out of human nature and associations, create society. Human conventions, traditions, etc.

---

something that is his own, and thereby makes it his property" (30). The point for our discussion here is that Locke's notion of natural rights insisted on a God who gave these timeless rights, naturally before government, to humankind as part of his creation of "Adam and his heirs." Hume rejects this view that God-given natural rights—justice, for instance—are part of the nature of things and therefore discernible by reason.

178. Sabine, *History of Political Theory*, 604.

are the repository of civilization, the source of religion, and the arbiter and only legitimate critic of reason itself. Moreover, manifestations of common life can appropriately be evaluated only in relation to other such manifestations but not in relation to any supposedly otherworldly norms.

In many respects, Hume and Burke agreed that social institutions are the carriage for the passenger of civilization along the path of history. Burke's virtual representation, which he defined in a 1792 letter to Sir Hercules Langrishe (1729–1811) as political representation "in which there is a communion of interests and a sympathy in feelings and desires between those who act in the name of any description of people,"[179] really is the political embodiment of Hume's concept of sympathy. Hume's institutions, like Burke's, form a vast network of observances, rights, practices, and terminology that have developed continuously over time and therefore warrant a certain religious type of reverence, because, as Sabine writes, social institutions are the keepers of our collective intelligence and civilization. Hume and Burke both believed that conventions arise from the habitual and prescriptive arrangements that form a body of individuals into a civil and humane society.

Strong, independent, and voluntary social institutions provide the bulwark against the intrusion of an all-powerful government into the lives of the citizens.[180] Hume held that rational and free state[181] political arrangements could lead to degeneracy[182] and maladministration[183] without the moderating influences of conventional institutions and associations that would naturally result in a mixed government.[184] The great danger of rationalistic political science is analogous to that of imposing a foreign social system on a native population. A rationalistic system tends to order all aspects of social life to reflect its grand design, which is above common life, thereby obliterating all opposition and counter-rational arrangements. Hume was convinced that the successful politician had to be like Antaeus, coming down to Earth to receive wisdom and strength in order to carry out his assigned responsibilities.[185]

179. As cited in Macpherson, *Burke*, 49.

180. See the persuasive work of sociologist Robert Nisbet, especially *The Quest for Community, The Making of Modern Society,* and *The Present Age: Progress and Anarchy in Modern America.*

181. "Of Civil Liberty," E, 91; LF, 89.

182. E, 96; LF, 95.

183. "That Politics May Be Reduced to a Science," E, 25; LF, 29.

184. "Of the Independency of Parliament," E, 43–45; LF, 45.

185. See Bulfinch, *Mythology*, 159, among many other collections of Greek mythology. Antaeus was the son of Poseidon (the sea god) and Gai or Terra (the earth

Hume's concern over the rise of the free state (or modern liberal state)[186] was that its metaphysical preoccupations would become sovereign over all of life, and common life would be erased. For the modern liberal state, there was to be no authority except itself. And what animated this tidal wave of coercive sovereignty in the modern state was the Lockean notion of natural rights and the Rousseauian notion of social contract, both leading to an absolutized set of individual rights. In short, individual liberty was to become the rallying cry of the modern liberal or free state, and Hume was the first authentic prophet against it.[187]

With Leviathan growing fat, Hume proposed Weight Watchers—social institutions and conventions to monitor it and resist. Twenty-first-century American government needs a healthy dose of Humean resistance.

Hume offers a unique contribution to American civil and social structure, and his ideas are relevant to a contemporary conservative cultural and political vision from which American evangelicals can profit.

---

goddess). He was a mighty and invincible giant if he stayed in touch with Mother Earth. Hercules strangled him by coaxing him into the air in a fight.

186. The term liberal attached to state has contemporary meaning which Hume did not foresee. What I mean by liberal state in this context is the seventeenth- and eighteenth-century belief in the freedom of the individual from external economic, political, and religious restraints, as in Locke's *Second Treatise of Government*. I believe Hume understood that the deep religious skepticism animating early liberal political writings would eventually lead to a destructive doubt of tradition, authority, things long established, belief in a constant human nature, man's power of moral choice, and his corresponding moral responsibility for his actions. Consequently, Hume advocated a national, established church with a social conscience.

187. See Bongie, *David Hume*.

5

David Hume for Conservative Evangelicals

"I am an American in my Principles and wish we would let them alone to govern or misgovern themselves as they think proper."[1]

WITH THESE POLITICALLY INCORRECT words, written in the turmoil of 1775, David Hume forever became an honorary American citizen and should become the Sage of Ninewells for all American conservative evangelical Christians.

Full disclosure here: I like David Hume. A value of Hume's thought is that it is a systematic treatment of understanding without the historical tendentiousness of an Edmund Burke (French Revolution) or a John Locke (Glorious Revolution of 1688).[2] Hume wrote reflectively, systematically, and widely, and therefore left a body of substantial work that effectively does combat with the age of rationalism from a secular vantage point. Hume's writings can provide guidance and direction for the implementation and sustenance of an American conservative and therefore stable society,

---

1. Baron William Mure of Caldwell had requested Hume to pen an appeal for greater discipline of the obstreperous American colonies by the British government. Hume responded to Mure in a letter written in 1775 (*Letters of David Hume*, 2:303).

2. While Hume did not write primarily in reaction to a particular event, he was profoundly a contextual philosopher, for he exalted tradition, custom, habit, human social conventions, and history. For more on this aspect of Hume, see Dees, "Hume and the Context of Politics."

conducive to the spread of the gospel of Jesus Christ. But he also had salutary ideas about a lot of important subjects on which I will touch in this chapter.

Clearly, Hume has had a remarkable influence in the shaping of American political society from its very codification,[3] and therefore we already are more Humean than we are apt to realize. A brief look at David Hume's Americana at our founding will set the stage for some final observations on David Hume's Americana in the twenty-first century as it applies to evangelical political conservatives.

THE SCOTS ARE COMING!

The political task for the framers of the new American republic was to foster prosperity and commerce and yet confine the popular vote to those who understood social arrangements (e.g., conventions, traditions, institutions, and customs). For Hume, Franklin, Dickinson, Wilson, Sherman, Madison, Hamilton, et al., experience was not just a personal guide; it was a political guide as well. Custom is king.[4]

Hume's theory of interests, factions, and influence,[5] had a profound impact on the American experiment in political science during the last half of the eighteenth century.[6] In one of his essays, Hume referred to governmental science as being almost as certain as mathematical science. He wrote, "So great is the force of laws, and of particular forms of government, and so little dependence have they on the humours and tempers of men, that consequences almost as general and certain may sometimes be deduced from them, as any which the mathematical sciences afford us."[7] This approximation to certitude helped inspire the leading colonial political thinkers who created the United States of America in the late eighteenth century.

Douglass Adair comments:

> In 1776—the year Hume died—a provincial notable named George Washington was starting on the career that was to justify

---

3. Adrienne Koch, in his book *The American Enlightenment*, which covers the shaping of the American experiment through the thoughts and selected writings of five of our major philosopher-statesmen (Franklin, Adams, Jefferson, Madison, and Hamilton), argues that the greatest figures of the so-called American Enlightenment included Hume, along with Voltaire and Rousseau (36).
4. Cf. 2 Thess 2:15 (*paradosis*, tradition).
5. "Of the Independency of Parliament," T, 534–39; TM, 585–90.
6. A helpful essay in this regard is Walton's "Hume and Jefferson."
7. "That Politics May Be Reduced to a Science," E, 14; LF, 16.

Hume's penetrating analysis of the unifying role of the great man in a large and variegated empire. Hume would have exulted at the discovery that his deductive leap into the future with a scientific prediction was correct: all great men who consolidated empires did not necessarily desire crowns.[8]

Also, in eighteenth-century America, Hume's seminal works were read by college students throughout the colonies. They also wrote in Humean phraseology, presumably to those who also understood Hume's thought.[9] Hume's notions of experience and skepticism,[10] the uniformity of human nature, commerce and culture, factions and interests, customs and social institutions, and most importantly, the science of politics,[11] were avidly studied, absorbed, and promulgated by the leading young colonial minds.[12]

Hume was read far more widely in America than was any other historian. His political writings fit the temper of the new Americans. He argued that the state never has been established by perfectly free contract among the majority of people—let alone by unanimous consent. What the Founding Fathers found attractive in Hume was Hume's Scottish common sense, his freedom from political and religious mysticism and fanatic convictions. Hume's powerful practical intellect resulted in political compromise and Trump's art of the deal. Jonathan Edwards (1703–1758) voraciously read Hume, all the while disagreeing with much of what he read. But both men attacked the "strutting Rationalism of the Enlightenment" (to use Russell Kirk's phrase). It is no paradox that Americans have always continued to have faith in their religion but skepticism in their politics. Skepticism is the rejection of easy, simplistic, and narrow approaches to life. Thus, Hume

---

8. Adair, *Fame and the Founding Fathers*, 140.

9. Adair, *Fame and the Founding Fathers*, 201.

10. There is a sense in which Hume's mitigated skepticism has its political application in the American civil experience, in that Americans are patriotically skeptical about their politics; it is the American custom to believe that there are no easy answers to social problems, there are no honest politicians, and there is no place in America for political ideologues.

11. "That Politics May Be Reduced to a Science."

12. Cf. Adair, "That Politics May Be Reduced to a Science: David Hume, James Madison, and the Tenth Federalist," in Livingston and King, eds., *Hume: A Re-Evaluation,* 406; McDonald, *Novus Ordo Seclorum,* 66; Kirk, *Roots of the American Order,* 358: "Hume was read far more widely in America than was any other historian of that age." McDonald notes that Hume was used often in Constitutional Convention debates: "[William] Paterson [of New Jersey] appealed to Hume's idea of a legislature 'refined by the mode of election' in support of his plan, and Gunning Bedford of Delaware supported the Paterson plan by applying a Humean theory of the passions to the states" (McDonald, *Novus Ordo Seclorum,* 234).l

continues to resonate with sincere Christians, even as we disagree with some of his conclusions.

THE COLONIALISTS ARE COMING!

David Hume and George Washington

I start with the greatest of the colonialists and the one who has left us with only a scanty amount of his ideas on Hume. Surveyor Washington focused his early attention on useful knowledge or practical wisdom that aided his vocation. But later in life he assembled a large library containing the works of Voltaire, Locke, Seneca, Addison, and, most suggestively, historians Gibbon and Macaulay. Chernow maintains that Washington was "a far more voracious reader than generally recognized."[13] Adair convincingly argues that the ideas of the Scottish Enlightenment permeated the ideas of the Founding Fathers. It is reasonable to think that, while we have little direct evidence that Washington read Hume, Washington was indirectly influenced by the Scotsman, since Hume was in the philosophic waters in which our first president swam.

David Hume and John Witherspoon

Scottish philosophy was a dominant source of inspiration among the Founding Fathers.[14] While Hume was preeminent, his good friend and casual acolyte Adam Ferguson (1723–1816) was also widely read. Ferguson, a teacher of Rev. John Witherspoon, who taught John Madison, wrote *Essay on the History of Civil Society*, which contained Humeian ideas. The *Essay* appeared in no less than 22 percent of the American library catalogues and bookseller's lists.[15] By the time Witherspoon left Scotland in 1768 to take up his position at Princeton College, he was thoroughly familiar with the writings of David Hume. He insisted that his students understand Hume and appreciate his writing style and ideas. As Elkins notes, "It was a working principle with Witherspoon that if persons suspected a thing of being pernicious, 'they ought to acquaint themselves with it; they must know what it is,

---

13. Chernow, *Washington: A Life*, 470.

14. Cf. Wills, *Explaining America*. Witherspoon was insulted that Hume's virtues included "wit, genius, health, taper legs and broad shoulders." This, unfortunately, is a deliberate misquote from Hume's *Treatise*, book 3, part 3, sect. 4, "Of Natural Abilities."

15. Hamowy, "Scottish Thought," 354–56.

if they mean to shew that it is false.'"[16] In his lectures on moral philosophy, the great Presbyterian cleric and educator thundered against Hume, calling him an infidel. Witherspoon insisted that his young students be completely familiar with Hume's ideas and writings. While torching Hume's religious views he, at the same time, called the Scotsman sagacious, with a "great reach and accuracy of judgment in matters of criticism."[17] Witherspoon taught Ashbel Green, who taught Charles Hodge, who taught J. Gresham Machen, who taught everybody.[18]

David Hume and Patrick Henry

It is recorded that the evangelical Patrick Henry (1736–1799) left a note in Thomas Jefferson's library, "Mr. J, I will take two volumes of Hume's *Essays*, and try to read them this winter." Thomas Randall continues, "But when Henry finally returned them, Jefferson remarked to a friend later, 'he had not been able to get half-way into one of them.'"[19] Henry and Jefferson were not the only prominent Founding Father readers of Hume. There existed a group of writers called the tractarians who read Hume (among others). They included such colonial activists as Robert Carter Nicholas (1728–1780), Dr. Arthur Lee (1740–1792), Thomson Mason (1733–1792), and John Randolph (1773–1833). These Virginia tractarians read widely and could recite from the great political philosophers and historians.[20]

David Hume and Benjamin Franklin

Benjamin Franklin (1706–1790), the pronounced deist, carried on an extensive correspondence with Hume covering topics from commerce[21] to lan-

---

16. Elkins and McKitrick, *Age of Federalism*, 85–86.

17. Witherspoon, *Early American Philosophers*, 203–5.

18. "David Hume has a scheme of morals that is peculiar to himself. He makes every thing that is agreeable and useful virtuous, and visa versa, by which he entirely annihilates the difference between natural and moral virtues as integrity and truth" (Witherspoon, *Lectures on Moral Philosophy*, lecture 4); "About this and some other ideas great stir has been made by some infidel writers particularly David Hume, who seems to have industriously endeavored to shake the certainty of our belief upon cause and effect, upon personal identity and the idea of power" (Witherspoon, *Lectures on Moral Philosophy*, lecture 6).

19. Randall, *Thomas Jefferson*, 58.

20. Randall, *Thomas Jefferson*, 201.

21. Franklin wrote to Hume in 1760, enthusiastic about Hume's essay "Of the Jealousy of Trade," calling it an excellent essay and a good argument for free trade.

guage to politics to religion. In 1761, Hume wrote Franklin, "America has sent us many good things, gold, silver, sugar, tobacco, indigo, etc.; but you are the first philosopher, and indeed the first great man of letters for whom we are beholden to her."[22] Ten years later, the deist Franklin wrote Scottish publisher William Strahan (1715–1785), "But that excellent Christian David Hume, agreeable to the precepts of the GOSPEL, has received the stranger, and I now live with him at his house in the new town most happily."[23] With this close friendship between these two great *belletrists,* it is no wonder that Franklin went to Hume's defense during the Edinburgh church trials in 1744.[24] Willard Randall notes that the Parisian *saloniste* Madame Marie Geoffrin (1699–1777) hosted Wednesday dinner parties at which Franklin, Hume, and British Prime Minister Sir Robert Walpole (1717–1797) would dine with French intellectuals.[25]

David Hume and John Adams

In 1814 John Adams (1735–1826), the second president of the United States, wrote to John Taylor of Caroline (1753–1824):

> By aristocracy I understand all those men who can command, influence, or procure more than an average of votes; by an aristocrat every man who can and will one man to vote besides himself. Few men will deny that there is a natural aristocracy of virtues and talents in every nation and in every party, in every city and village.[26]

Referenced in Beer, *To Make a Nation,* 154–55.

22. Van Doren, *Benjamin Franklin,* 290.
23. Van Doren, *Benjamin Franklin,* 391.
24. Van Doren, *Benjamin Franklin,* 464.
25. Randall, *Thomas Jefferson,* 389.
26. Adams, *Works of John Adams,* 6:451, 461–62. Taylor had written a tract, *Inquiry into the Principles and Policy of the Government of the United States,* which attacked Adams's view of government. In thirty-two letters, most of them running to several pages, Adams defended himself against Taylor's accusations of anti-republicanism, detailing what he meant by aristocracy and arguing for the importance of the Humean doctrine of political balance. But virtue alone, for Adams, was not enough: landed wealth must accompany virtue. He continued with Taylor, "Would Washington have ever been commander of the revolutionary army or president of the United States, if he had not married the rich widow of Mr. Custis? Would Jefferson ever have been president of the United States if he had not married the daughter of Mr. Wales?" (Howe, *Changing Political Thought,* 248). As Russell Kirk approvingly comments, "Talent tends to join itself to property, and out of that union comes aristocracy, which tends to perpetuate itself" (Kirk, *Roots of American Order,* 313).

Interestingly, Adams did not believe in an aristocratic or oligarchic type of government. He said such government deteriorated into despotism. Adams favored rather a mixed government of a strong executive, an independent judiciary, and a popularly elected legislature.[27] Hume argued for a somewhat similar mixed government structure in his essay "Of the Independency of Parliament."

As Joseph Ellis notes, Adams established his reputation as the premier political theorist in the colonies.[28] The quality of virtue for Adams was not some abstract concept he learned from reading Hume and others, but rather it was a principle of self-denial, of which he kept reminding himself. Adams was familiar with the writings of David Hume and sprinkled his own writings with citations from Hume. In his examination of governments down through the centuries (*Defense of the Constitutions of the United States*, 1787), the Bostonian made it clear that he knew Hume, for good and ill.[29]

David Hume and Thomas Jefferson

Thomas Jefferson (1743–1826) read and cited Hume's philosophic and historical writings throughout his own writings. Jefferson continued to recommend and even lend Hume's books to friends. In an 1815 letter to Horatio Spafford, the Whig Jefferson complained that Hume "was making Tories of all England and is making Tories of those young Americans whose native feelings of independence do not place them above the wily sophisticates of a Hume." As a bachelor attorney, Jefferson contemplated marriage and divorce and in 1773 argued a domestic divorce case, borrowing heavily from Hume. Echoing Hume's *Essay Concerning Human Understanding*, Jefferson argued that a marriage "made at first by mutual love but now dissolved by hatred was to chain a man to misery till death. Liberty of divorce prevents and cures domestic quarrels and preserves liberty of affection which is a natural right." And on he went. The importance of this case is that it contained the roots of Jefferson's ideas on the great divorce between the colonies and Great Britain.

---

27. Ellis, *Passionate Sage*, 149.
28. Ellis, *Passionate Sage*, 47.
29. Cf. McCullough, *John Adams*. 121, 376–77.

David Hume and Roger Sherman

Roger Sherman (1721–1793), the devout Puritan, used Hume's ideas in his brilliant Connecticut Plan in the Constitutional Convention of 1787, providing a very practical example of the influence of Hume's political theory. Sherman, a Connecticut delegate to the Convention, devised his brilliant Connecticut Compromise, which broke a unity-threatening deadlock at the convention. Initially, the Virginia Plan had called for a strictly proportional representation in congressional formation. Smaller states objected and refused to proceed to ratification if this plan was adopted. The Sherman compromise was a balance of interest between large and small geographical territories. Humean in design,[30] the compromise was a balance of interest between large and small geographical territories in framing a national legislature.[31] Sherman's plan made membership in the lower house (House of Representatives) proportional to population, but decreed that each state, regardless of size, would have an equal number (originally one, later two) in the upper house (Senate). The plan, embodied in Article IV and the 10th Amendment of the U. S. Constitution, continues to frame policy debates and decisions in the United States.

David Hume and John Dickinson

John Dickinson (1732–1808), the pious Quaker of Philadelphia, author of the most widely read tract in the Revolutionary period ("Letters from a Farmer in Pennsylvania") prior to Thomas Paine's *Common Sense* (1776), was a Pennsylvania delegate to the Constitutional Convention. This was pure Hume. Dickinson was a law partner of the Christian heterodox James Wilson, who had studied in Scotland and bore "the unmistakable marks of that great mind [of David Hume]."[32] Wilson later became one of the original justices of the U. S. Supreme Court as a George Washington appointee. Philadelphia attorney Dickinson wrote about Hume: "Experience must be our only guide for Reason may mislead us."[33] Dickinson authored the separation

---

30. E, 509; LF, 523.

31. Hume wrote, "The *balance of power* is a secret in politics, fully known only to the present age" (E, 94; LF, 93). Farrand records Sherman as stating during the Convention debates that each state, "like an individual" had its "peculiar habits, usages and manners." Therefore, it was important to isolate diverse interests from each other for the sake of national harmony (Farrand, *Records of the Federal Convention*, 1:353 [June 20, 1788]).

32. Beer, *To Make a Nation*, 361.

33. Farrand, *Records of the Federal Convention*, 2:278 (Aug. 13, 1788). More recently,

of powers articles of the Constitution, based in part, no doubt, on Hume's theory of contending power parties.[34] Dickinson, like all of the colonial leaders, had read Hume and was a law partner of Wilson (1742–1798), who was also a Pennsylvania delegate to the Convention.

David Hume and Alexander Hamilton

Alexander Hamilton's (1755–1804) evangelical Christian faith is seldom mentioned, but was, ironically, the rage of New York liberals then and now. Elkins and McKitrick argue that Hamilton read Hume early in his life and "the affinity of his thoughts paragraph by paragraph to those of Hume is striking."[35] Hamilton described Hume in the "Eighty-Fifth Federalist" as "a writer equally solid and judicious." Famously, Hume argued that politically men must be treated as knaves, but individually, alone, this is not the case. Rather, "honour is a great check upon mankind."[36] This sentiment became a Hamilton staple. Hamilton advanced the Humean idea of an electoral college as a barrier to mass disorder. Farrand's *Records* show that Hamilton also endorsed Hume's notion of the good-old-boy system as a favored method of stabilizing government operations.[37] Wills suggests, "Of Hamilton it can be said symbolically, as of Madison it was said literally, that he spoke his French with a Scottish accent."[38] With the current fawning popularity over the historically challenged musical *Hamilton*, Hume should be required reading for the smart set as background.

Anthony Harrigan writes in his article "The Making of American Conservatism": "If one's conservatism isn't based on personal experience of some kind, it is likely to be an ideology and ideology is the opposite of conservatism. The authentic conservative must respect differences of opinion and reject thought control in any form. Conservatism involves a human response and never legitimately appears in the form of a blueprint" (30).

34. "Of the Parties of Great Britain."
35. Elkins and McKitrick, *Age of Federalism*, 107.
36. "Of the Independency of Parliament."
37. Hamilton's speech to the Continental Convention (June 22, 1787): "We must take man as we find him, and if we expect him to serve the public must interest his passions in doing so. A reliance on pure patriotism had been the source of many of our errors.... It was known that [one] of the ablest politicians (Mr. Hume) had pronounced all that influence on the side of the crown, which went under the name of corruption, an essential part of the weight which maintained the equilibrium of the Constitution" (Farrand, *Records of the Federal Convention*, 1:376).
38. Wills, *Explaining America*, 71.

Hamilton of New York quoted and paraphrased Hume throughout the Constitutional Convention.[39] In his "Eighty-Fifth Federalist," Hamilton called Hume solid, ingenious, judicious, and moderate. Then he quoted from Hume's essay "The Rise of Arts and Sciences":

> To balance a large state or society, whether monarchical or republican, on general laws, is a work of so great difficulty, that no human genius, however comprehensive, is able, by the mere dint of reason and reflection, to effect it. The judgments of many must unite in this work: Experience must guide their labour: Time must bring it to perfection. And the feeling of inconvenience must correct the mistakes, which they inevitably fall into, in their first trials and experiments.[40]

Hamilton (along with many other colonial leaders) also shared Hume's distaste for radical democracy, in which the citizenry had direct participation in the determination of public policy. Hamilton wrote his germinal "Sixty-Eighth Federalist," in which he advanced the Humean idea of an aristocratic body and a popularly elected body, which the colonialists developed into our electoral college as a barrier to mass disorder:

> It is also peculiarly desirable to afford as little opportunity as possible to tumult and disorder.... And as the electors chosen in each State in which they are chosen, this detached and divided situation will expose them much less to heats and deferments, which might be communicated from them to the people, than if they were all to be convened at one time in one place.[41]

Elkins and McKitrick state that "Hamilton's use of Hume foreshadows the Publius who would take it for granted that no successful constitution of government was contrivable that did not provide for the harnessing of

---

39. It is recorded in Farrand's *Records* that during the convention (June 22, 1787), Hamilton stated, "Take mankind as they are, and what are they governed by? Their passions. There may be in every government a few choice spirits, who may act from more worthy motives. One great error, however, is that we suppose mankind more honest than they are. Our prevailing passions are ambition and interest; and it will ever be the duty of a wise government to avail itself of those passions, in order to make them subservient to the public good" (1:381). In the preceding sentence to the above referenced statement, Hamilton is quoted as saying, "Hume's opinion of the British constitution confirms the remark, that there is always a body of firm patriots, who often shake a corrupt administration."

40. E, 125; LF, 124. "Eighty-Fifth Federalist," in Hutchins, *Federalist*, 258.

41. "Sixty-Eighth Federalist," in Hutchins, *Federalist*, 205.

private interests in order to promote the public good."[42] Needless to say, the electoral college is still a break on national mob power.

To sum up Hume's contribution to the thought of Dickinson and Hamilton, Clinton Rossiter writes, "David Hume was treated with some respect, especially by young Alexander Hamilton and conservative John Dickinson."[43]

David Hume and James Madison

But perhaps the greatest colonial disciple of Hume was the Constitution's chief designer, the future fourth president of the United States, a conflicted evangelical Christian, the man from Montpelier, James Madison (1751–1836).[44] Madison embraced Hume's notion that social stability for a large state could be attained by the deft balancing of faction against faction, ambition against ambition, interest against interest, class against class. Borrowing from Hume, Madison held that the deliberative legal process in civil society was only a refining of interests already existing in the public sphere. Madison was a realist about human nature, so he devised a governmental structure for ordinary men and who they really were, not for the virtuous and righteous.

Adair summarizes the importance of the language of Hume's political science for the budding future president:

> In the debates in the Philadelphia Convention, the speakers were making a genuine "scientific" attempt to discover "the constant and universal principles" of any republican government regarding liberty, justice, and stability. The most creative and philosophical disciple of the Scottish system in the Philadelphia Convention was James Madison [from Virginia].[45]

---

42. Elkins and McKitrick, *Age of Federalism*, 97.

43. Rossiter, *Political Thought*, 67.

44. See the indispensable essay on Hume's influence on Madison in Adair's classic essay "That Politics May Be Reduced to a Science," first in the *Huntington Library Quarterly* (1957) and then in Adair's collected works, *Fame and the Founding Fathers* (1974). R. G. Frey downplays Hume's influence over the founding Federalists ("Moral Sense Theory and the Appeal to Natural Rights in the American Founding," in Womersley, *Liberty and American Experience*, 276ff).

45. Adair, *Fame and the Founding Fathers*, 407. Ellis connects Madison and Hume to yet another great colonial leader when he writes, "Just as James Madison established a reputation as 'Father of the Constitution' because of his leading role in the Constitutional Convention in 1787, [John] Adams established his reputation as the premier political theorist of the American Revolution because of his leadership in the Continental

With even a brief examination of Madison's masterful "Tenth Federalist" essay, the borrowing from Hume is evident in the following political science tennis match. If only the two men could have engaged each other personally in an epistolary interchange! But my selections are chosen to highlight the contrasts and similarities in the thinking of these two contemporary political thinkers.

Two of Hume's essays, "Idea of a Perfect Commonwealth"[46] and "Of Parties in General," are represented in Madison's thought. For instance, Hume wrote in "Of Parties in General": "Men have such a propensity to divide into personal factions that the smallest appearance of real difference will produce them." And, "if mankind had not a strong propensity to such divisions, the indifference of the rest of the community must have suppressed this foolish animosity [between two tribes], that had not any aliment of new benefits and injuries."[47]

Correspondingly, Madison aphorized,

> Liberty is to faction what air is to fire, an aliment without which it instantly expires.[48]

In Hume we read:

> Parties from principle, especially abstract speculative principle, are known only to modern times, and are perhaps, the most extraordinary and unaccountable phenomenon that has yet appeared in human affairs.

That is, political parties emerging from rational and abstract principles not rooted in the experience of the common man are modern inventions and dangerous to social harmony.[49]

Congress. But if Madison is the master sociologist of American political theory, Adams is the master psychologist. Virtue was not an abstract concept he learned about simply by reading Montesquieu, [or] David Hume . . . . A state constitution was not just an agreed-upon framework of social customs and laws. It was a public replica of one's internal order or constitution"(Ellis, *Passionate Sage*, 47). This was essentially Plato's view in the *Republic* (esp. book 4, sect. 12, 13).

46. Beer summarizes Madison's indebtedness to this Humean essay: "It seems almost certain that Madison read and was influenced by Hume's famous essay [i. e., "Idea of a Perfect Commonwealth"]. The similarity of their arguments—the premise of the big republic, the breadth of the franchise, the commitment to government by discussion, the presumption of a strong, active central government, the central legislative veto over local laws, the federal character of the institutions—would support this inference" (Beer, *To Make A Nation*, 269).

47. "Of Parties in General," E, 56; LF, 58.

48. "Tenth Federalist," in Hutchins, *Federalist*, 50.

49. More of the same: "The same principles of priestly government continuing, after

Madison wrote,

> The latent causes of faction are thus sown in the nature of man; and we see them everywhere brought into different degrees of activity, according to the different circumstances of civil society. A zeal for different opinions concerning religion, concerning government, and many other points, as well of speculation as of practice.[50]

Back to Hume:

> Factions may be divided into Personal and Real; that is, into factions founded on personal friendship or animosity among such as compose the contending parties .... In those factions, which are founded on the most real and most material differences, there is always observed a great deal of personal animosity or affection.[51]

And now to Madison,

> A latent cause of faction [is] a zeal for an attachment to different leaders ambitiously contending for pre-eminence and power.[52]

Hume asserted,

> By parties from affection, I understand those which are founded on the different attachments of men towards particular families and persons whom they desire to rule over them. These factions are often very violent; though, I must own, it may seem unaccountable that men should attach themselves so strongly to persons with whom they are nowise acquainted.[53]

Madison claimed,

> A latent cause of faction is a zeal to persons of other descriptions whose fortunes have been interesting to the human passions, have, in turn, divided mankind into parties, inflamed them with

---

Christianity became the established religion, they have engineered a spirit of persecution, which has ever since been the poison of human society, and the source of the most inveterate factions in every government. Such divisions, therefore, on the part of the people, may justly be esteemed factions of principle; but, on the part of the priest, who are the prime movers, they are really factions of interest" ("Of Parties in General," E, 60–61; LF, 62).

50. "Tenth Federalist," in Hutchins, *Federalist*, 51.
51. "Of Parties in General," E, 55–56; LF, 56.
52. "Tenth Federalist," in Hutchins, *Federalist*, 50.
53. "Of Parties in General," E, 61–62; LF, 63.

mutual animosity, and rendered them much more disposed to vex and oppress each other than to cooperate for their common good.[54]

Hume again,

> Of all factions, the first [those factions formed by common interest] are the most reasonable, and the most excusable. Where two orders of men, such as the nobles and people, have a distinct authority in a government, not very accurately balanced and modelled, they naturally follow a distinct interest; nor can we reasonably expect a different conduct considering that degree of selfishness implanted in human nature. It requires great skill in a legislator to prevent such parties; and many philosophers are of the opinion, that this secret, like the grand elixir, or perpetual motion, may amuse men in theory, but can never possibly be reduced to practice.[55]

Correspondingly, Madison:

> Those who hold and those who are without property, have ever formed distinct interests in society. Those who are creditors, and those who are debtors, fall under a like discrimination. A landed interest, a manufacturing interest, a mercantile interest, a moneyed interest, with many lesser interests, grow up of necessity in civilized nations, and divided them into different classes actuated by different sentiments and views.[56]

In sum, Hume's notion that social stability for a large state could be attained by the deft balancing of faction against faction and class against class, even by playing them off against each other, was widely accepted by the original American political architects of the new republic's constitution, particularly James Madison.[57] It might have been difficult to first organize this large, uncivilized country with all its competing interests, but with wise and judicious arranging it could have been made even more stable than a

---

54. "Tenth Federalist," in Hutchins, *Federalist*, 50.
55. "Of Parties in General," E, 58; LF, 59.
56. "Tenth Federalist," in Hutchins, *Federalist*, 50.
57. Gordon Wood argues that Madison believed that in order to sort out conflicting interests there needed to be "men whose enlightened views and virtuous sentiments render them superior to local prejudices, and to schemes of injustice—to decide question of the public good in a disinterested adjudicatory manner" (see "Tenth Federalist," in Hutchins, *Federalist*); Wood, "Is There a 'James Madison' Problem," in Womersley, *Liberty and American Experience*, 438). Moses the adjudicator comes to Philadelphia (Exod 18)!

small, personal European state. Madison, taking from Hume, held that the deliberative legal process in civil society was only a refining of interests already existing in the public sphere. Those public interests are known and felt by the leaders, and so the legislative process is inductive; it is not deductively driven from a superior base of rationally derived knowledge, on the part of the legislators, for the supposed common good. Madison wrote in the "Fifty-First Federalist,"

> Ambition must be made to counteract ambition. The interest of the man must be connected with the constitutional rights of the place. It may be a reflection on human nature that such devices should be necessary to control the abuses of government. But what is government itself but the greatest of all reflections on human nature? If men were angels, no government would be necessary.[58]

In some respects, it did not make any difference to the American constitutionalists which faction was most prominent. To them, all factions held a danger of destroying the new republic, and so checks and balances, limited voting rights, a strong executive, and a detailed written constitution were seen to be safeguards against what Hume had clearly—and to the colonials correctly—observed in the affairs of man. Madison, following some germane ideas contained in Hume's essay "Idea of a Perfect Commonwealth,"[59] wrote in the "Forty-Ninth Federalist": "But it is the reason, alone, of the public that ought to control and regulate the government. The passions ought to be controlled and regulated by the government."[60] Charles Murray adds a comment at this point: "It is important to emphasize that factions were an inevitable result of man acting in a public setting, not a reflection of an intrinsically deficient human nature."[61]

The current importance of Hume's warning against factions and interest groups in a society is evidenced by the tribalizing effect of the "cult of victimization"[62] in America, which divides people into factions based on self-perceived victimized status. It is the destruction of coherent American

---

58. "Fifty-First Federalist," in Hutchins, *Federalist*, 163.

59. Hume: "Separate this great body [parliament]; and though every member be only of middling sense, it is not probable, that anything but reason can prevail over the whole. Influence and example being removed, good sense will always get the better of bad among a number of people" (LF, 523).

60. Hamilton et al., *Federalist Papers*, 161.

61. Murray, *In Pursuit of Happiness*, 174.

62. See Sykes, *A Nation of Victims*. Schlesinger Jr., a scholar with impeccable liberal credentials, writes in the same vein with his book *The Disuniting of America*.

society by the hyphen. Daniel J. Boorstin (1914–2004) has been quoted as stating, "The menace to America today is in the emphasis on what separates us rather than on what brings us together-the separations of race, of religious dogma, of religious practice, of origins, of language."[63]

Hume saw political power blocks or interest groups in England during the eighteenth century as being focused with the king and the lords (court party) as one block and the House of Commons (country party) as the other block.[64] Civility, compromise, and consensus building was required from both factions in order for there to be a smooth, orderly, stable, moderate, and prosperous functioning of government and society. Madison received Humean intellectual support for his federalist construction of the American constitution from his essay "Liberty of the Press." The doctrine of states' rights, a form of geographical, interest-bound checks and balances, was clearly stated by Hume.[65]

So, the political task for the framers of the American republic was to foster prosperity and commerce and yet confine the popular vote to those who understood social arrangements (e.g., conventions, traditions, institutions, customs). For Hume and the American founders (e.g., Dickinson, Sherman, Madison, Hamilton, et al.), experience was not just a personal guide; it was a social guide as well. Moral and intellectual development is a process that is both personal and interpersonal. Custom is king. The founders of the American republic knew and quoted Hume and incorporated his teachings into the new American constitution.

Both Hamilton and Madison and Hume aspired to the fame and honor of the Roman legislator, public man, or illustrious citizen.[66] This idea that a community is best served by distinguished leaders (great man theory) and men of noble life is an echo of the structure of the church and particularly

63. Tad Szulc, "Greatest Danger We Face," 4.

64. See "Of the Parties of Great Britain."

65. "As the republican part of the government prevails in ENGLAND, though with a great mixture of monarchy, it is obliged, for its own preservation, to maintain a watchful jealousy over the magistrates, to remove all discretionary powers, and to secure every one's life and fortune by general and inflexible laws. . . . From these causes it proceeds, that there is as much liberty, and even, perhaps, licentiousness in GREAT BRITAIN, as there were formerly slavery and tyranny in ROME" (E, 10; LF, 12). Beer would have us believe that Hume's contribution to James Madison's federalism did not warrant a strict, autonomous separation of states' rights in the federal Constitution (Beer, *To Make a Nation*, 268–69).

66. They had to read no further than Hume to find an echo of this classical political glory, for Hume began his essay "Of Parties in General" by stating, "Of all men, that distinguish themselves by memorable achievements, the first place of honour seems due to LEGISLATORS and founders of states, who transmit a system of laws and institutions to secure the peace, happiness, and liberty of future generations" (LF, 54).

the Scottish Presbyterian Church, which rewarded its spiritual leaders with respect and honor.[67]

Hamilton, following suit, wrote in his "Seventy-Second Federalist":

> [The public man] is prompted to plan and undertake extensive and arduous enterprises for the public benefit, the love of fame, [and for] the ruling passion of the noblest minds.[68]

Madison reiterated in his "Thirty-Eighth Federalist":

> the task of framing . . . government . . . has been performed by some individual citizen of pre-eminent wisdom and approved integrity, whom Madison likened to the Spartan Lycurgus. He called such a framer, an "illustrious citizen."[69]

For Hume, political rationalism is to be rejected as dangerous and noxious, in favor of political public opinion. His essay "Of the First Principles of Government" was used to advantage by the American federalists to make this political argument. University of Alabama historian Forrest McDonald opines that the word opinion was used in the eighteenth century to signify confidence, esteem, high regard. Following a 1794 essay of Hume, "Of the First Principles of Government," Alexander Hamilton indicated in the Constitutional Convention that he used opinion in this sense. In other words, Hamilton was saying that it was not important to be well-regarded by rabble-rousers—or, to phrase it differently, that statesmanship is not a popularity contest.[70]

Hamilton, of course, was arguing for a Tory-type political aristocracy in American political life. But Madison, in his "Forty-Ninth Federalist," wrote contrarily about the value of democratic, opinion-based government.[71]

Both Hamilton and Madison sought support from Hume for their differing political visions. I believe each found it.

For Hume, social arrangements (i.e., institutions) become customary or habitual through usage. The conservative would look to the government,

---

67. Cf. Heb 13:7, "Remember your leaders [*hegeomai*, those that have rule], who spoke the word of God to you. Consider the outcome of their way of life and imitate their faith." See also Acts 7:10 (*hegeomai*, ruler over Egypt).

68. "Seventy-Second Federalist," in Hutchins, *Federalist*, 217.

69. "Thirty-Eighth Federalist," in Hutchins, *Federalist*, 121.

70. McDonald, "Rhetoric of Alexander Hamilton," 322.

71. "If it be true that all governments rest on opinion, it is no less true that the strength of opinion in each individual, and its practical influence on his conduct, depend much on the number which he supposes to have entertained the same opinion" (Madison, in Hamilton et al., *Federalist Papers*, 160).

hoping it would strengthen and preserve these social institutions since, by virtue of their custom and historicity, they are better adapted than anything else to provide satisfaction for the individual member of society. Therefore, they are natural and reasonable. T. S. Eliot calls this political source pre-political, and Andrew Breitbart calls it culture. Eliot describes this pre-political source as a "stratum down to which any sound political thinking must push its roots and from which it must derive nourishment."[72] It is this stratum that is created over a considerable period of time by a diversity of people in a diversity of professions.[73]

Sociologist Robert Nisbet (1913–1996) has forcefully argued that as individual rights have grown, they have not grown at the expense of the free state (which would have been preferable), but rather at the expense of other intermediate social associations, arrangements and institutions. Nisbet maintains that there must be social institutions between the government and the people to provide human values to relationships."[74]

Emile Durkheim (1858–1917), the French nineteenth-century pioneering social theorist, had a Humean concern that local social institutions (Durkheim called these institutions "secondary groups") would lose in a fight against a centralized government, and the ensuing loss would be devastating for the general social fabric and the specific individual moral consciousness.[75]

---

72. Eliot, *Literature of Politics*. See also Brunner, *Christianity and Civilization*.

73. George Will writes: "Society's institutions are concrete embodiments of social values which can claim precedence over the desire of the individual or even the collective will of the moment. No one disputes that a social order embodies certain values, or that law intimates purposes beyond itself. . . . Law counteracts the diversities of a people, requiring at least the minimal harmony required for social peace. But those diversities which necessitate law also necessitate law concerned with values as well as action. . . . They necessitate law as a ratifier and stigmatizer, in which role law is a tutor" (Will, *Statecraft as Soulcraft*, 76–77).

74. In Humean language, Nisbet writes, "More than liberalism and socialism [the philosophy of conservatism] took to its bosom the rights of the church, social class, family and property against the claims of natural rights theory and of the . . . national, increasingly democratic state on the other. In every one of the specific areas of conservative faith . . . the constant premise is the right—grown out of history and social development—of the whole intermediate structure of the nation to survival against the tide of both individualism and nationalism" (Nisbet, *Conservatism*, 22).

75. "Collective activity is always too complex to be able to be expressed through the state. Moreover, the State is too remote from individuals; its relations with them too external and intermittent to penetrate deeply into individual consciences and socialize them within. Where the State is the only environment in which men can live communal lives, they inevitably lose contact, become detached, and thus society disintegrates. A nation can be maintained only if, between the State and the individual, there is intercalated a whole series of secondary groups near enough to the individuals to attract them

In an important and very Humean book, Robert Bellah (1927–2013) has more recently written that "we live through our institutions." Human institutions are "patterned ways of living together," and social institutions afford "the necessary context within which we become individuals." Furthermore, institutions do not restrain us, but rather enable us to form our individual and corporate characters. Indeed, institutions are an "indispensable source" for character building.[76]

I now direct my attention to several key social institutions addressed by Hume and his American conservative counterparts, primarily theorists of the twentieth and twenty-first centuries.

THE GOVERNMENT AS AN INSTITUTION

Robert Nisbet explains how the modern democratic state has abrogated the authority of the church, family, and voluntary associations. The modern state tends to annul the rights of every institution and association, except individual rights, because it cannot abide divided loyalties of the citizenry.

Concerning the coercive and thus frightening power of the administrative state, Mark Henrie of the Arthur N. Rupe Foundation writes perceptively:

> With the weakening of alternative authorities, the individual has nowhere to stand to articulate a perspective differing from that of the liberal polity and culture. Claiming the sanction of universal Reason, liberal sovereignty rules out any fundamental critique of itself as a matter of principle.[77]

This Humean fear of the rationalized state has been given modern justification by the iconic 1992 book of Francis Fukuyama, *The End of History and the Last Man*.[78] Throughout his book, Fukuyama refers to "the

---

strongly in their sphere of action and drag them, in this way, into the general torrent of social life" (Durkheim, *Division of Labor*, 28).

76. Bellah, et al., *Good Society*, 3–4, 6. Interestingly, Bellah, in his paean to social institutions, does not reference Hume once, while referencing Locke, Adam Smith, and Tocqueville, among many others.

77. Henrie, "Rethinking American Conservatism," 10. Henrie seems to be borrowing from Tocqueville, who wrote of the value of provincial institutions, aristocracy, and localized government in 1835.

78. The title of this important book comes from the author's notion that since human history is nothing more than a history of social/political evolution, since liberal democracy (patterned after the French Revolution model) has conquered all rival forms of political ideology, since liberal democracy is free from any "fundamental internal contradictions," and since it provides complete human political satisfaction, it therefore

modern universal and homogeneous state," a phrase he borrows from the idiosyncratic French philosopher Alexandre Kojeve (1902–1968). Fukuyama defines this modern universal and homogeneous state in the following manner:

> The liberal state must be universal, that is, grant recognition to all citizens because they are human beings, and not because they are members of some particular national, ethnic, or racial group. And it must be homogeneous insofar as it creates a classless society based on the abolition of the distinction between masters and slaves.[79]

Fukuyama nowhere refers to Hume, and his extensive bibliography (over 250 titles) does not include Hume. References to John Locke and Jean-Jacques Rousseau abound, however. (Interestingly, Nisbet's above-quoted 1986 book, *Conservatism: Dreams and Reality*, includes no reference to Hume, either.)

Fukuyama's modern universal and homogeneous state is Hume's nemesis, for the state levels, blends, and regulates society to accomplish rational goals of efficiency at the expense of human traditions, prejudices, customs, conventions, and institutions. Fukuyama clearly states his political philosophic bias early in his book when he ties the principles of his universal and homogeneous state to the concepts of liberty and equality that emerged from the French Revolution.[80] This view is based on what Fukuyama optimistically calls the ideals of the French Revolution, which "vanquish the world's tyrants, autocrats, and superstitious priests. Blind obedience to authority would be replaced by rational self-government, in which all men, free and equal, would have to obey no masters but themselves."[81]

Humean conservatism implies that freedom and equality are incompatible. The chief purpose of liberty is the protection of individual and family property, both material and immaterial, whereas the chief purposes of

---

constitutes the end of history. Fukuyama's Hegelian last man is that individual who is completely satisfied by nothing more than universal and equal recognition in the universal and homogeneous liberal democratic state.

79. "The authority of the state does not arise out of age-old tradition or from the murky depths of religious faith, but as a result of a public debate in which the citizens of the state agree amongst one another on the explicit terms under which they will live together" (Fukuyama, *End of History*, 202).

80. "The twin crises of authoritarianism and socialist central planning have left only one competitor standing in the ring as an ideology of potentially universal validity: liberal democracy, the doctrine of individual freedom and popular sovereignty" (Fukuyama, *End of History*, 42).

81. Fukuyama, *End of History*, 4.

equality are redistribution of unequally gathered property and juridical leveling of diverse contributions, which cripple the liberties of society's most productive and brightest members. Nisbet quotes from the French Revolution's leading body, the Committee of Public Safety: "You must entirely refashion a people whom you wish to make free, to destroy its prejudices, alter its habits, limit its necessities, root up its vices, purify its desire."[82] In short, the Committee wanted the individualization of society and the rationalization of everything from money to property, education, religion, and government. So, rather than embracing the ideals of the French Revolution, secure, stable, and humane societies ought to be eschewing those unsettling chimeras, like modern-day China.

Furthermore, if it is true that the essence of social conservatism is "the preservation of the ancient moral tradition of humanity,"[83] then the modern state is the enemy to Humean conservatives, because it seeks, through its homogenizing force, to dehumanize its citizens.[84] Any society that fosters Humean customs and conventions also fosters traditions of artistic creativity, intellectual genius, and religious worship—all of which, in turn, can be expected to breed contempt and rejection for a soulless, homogenizing approach to social arrangements. Hume's society can be one that celebrates life that "arises out of the age-old traditions or the murky depths of religious faith," a society that celebrates idiosyncrasy, eccentricity, and non-conformity within the social conventionality of voluntary associations. A state church (Hume was thinking about the Church of England and Scotland, but not the "superstitious" Roman Catholic Church) that celebrates and deifies social and civil conventions and institutions would help keep social perversions at bay and provide a counter to the arms-bearing government.[85] Clearly, Hume was writing in a Christian culture when social perversions had common definitions. But the point is taken: the church provides a bulwark against social engineering by the state.

One of the features of a growing rational state is political and economic efficiency. With the rationalist at the helm, the state moves to organize the political life into democracy and to organize the economic life into a market economy—both dependent on the atomized individual with inalienable rights emanating from an unstated somewhere or someone—the rationalist doesn't know or care. Persons and property are rationalized, and

---

82. Nisbet, *Conservatism*, 10.
83. Kirk, *Conservative Mind*, 8.
84. Cf. Henrie, "Rethinking American Conservatism."
85. Nevertheless, nothing can guarantee against all evil aberrations and sociopathic behavior and alliances.

the human soul and its uniqueness are sacrificed for efficiency, productivity, uniformity, and conformity. A witless liberal dream state! Indeed, the weakening or dissolution of such conventional bonds as family, church, union, neighborhood, club has not liberated the individual. Rather, this dissolution has produced alienation, isolation, and the growth of Ortega y Gasset's (1883–1955) mass man.[86]

Social conventions and provide the best counterforce to the hyper-individualism of the rights talk[87] emphasis fostered by the rational liberal state. This individualism threatens to tear society apart as atomized individual rights collide without the buffer of traditional social conventions, customs, and institutions. Hume's notion of institutional, historical stability promotes citizen associations, networking alliances, and customs, thus supplying the fabric for the cloth of a national, stable, quilted culture. Indeed, relying on the past for social inspiration and models in a conservative tradition readily brings the politically liberal reproach of reactionary and the charge that conservatives, political and ecclesiastical, will return our society to the dark ages of bigotry, oppression, racism, and homophobia. However, the term reactionary is fitting because it is out of the rich history of human associations that conservatives, like Hume, point us to a current fashioning of our society into social institutions that resist the tide of either soulless, rampant individualism or a world order. Indeed, thoughtful conservatives should embrace the term reactionary as an approbation, for we do rightly react, resist, and revel in our historical stream of human experience and relations. Conservatives, of course, reject the negative and prejudicial portrayal of reactionaries. We do need to redeem that term. Conservatives should be the most active of all citizens, since we believe in the unique efficacy of evolving social institutions and conventions to promote a beneficent society.

Social institutions other than government are also structures of authority and should have implicit freedom, based on their historical priority, to carry on their functions without governmental interference. Hume argued

---

86. Gasset's mass man is not just an ordinary man, and he is not associated with any particular class. He is, rather, a product of European historical development, a kind of human being born for the first time in the nineteenth century. The mass man lives without any discipline. The mass man "possesses no quality of excellence." He demands more and more, as if it were his natural right, without realizing that what he wants was the privilege of a tiny group in the nineteenth century. He does not understand that technological wonders are the product of an intricate cultural process for which he should be grateful. "What before would have been considered one of fortune's gifts, inspiring humble gratitude toward destiny, was converted into a right, not to be grateful for, but to be insisted on" (Gasset, *Revolt of the Masses*, 55).

87. See a significant book written by Harvard Law School professor Mary Ann Glendon, *Rights Talk*.

in his *History* that commercial activity of all sorts "ought always to be left free and be entrusted to the common course of business and commerce." Institutions must battle with other voluntary institutions for citizen loyalty and commitment, but nobody has the sword. Putting it plainly, the claims of the family, church, academy, commercial association, trade union, village, and civic group all have a degree of autonomy to pursue their function and purpose within human society because human arrangements existed first.[88] There is a degree of feudal synthesis of authority and freedom, as well as separation, localization, and competition, in this notion of a Humean/conservative national community. It is at the point of institutional competition that national laws can help provide an ameliorating mediation. However, the burden is on institutions and the public to maintain civility between and among themselves amid the great strain in an age of social media.

THE CHURCH AS A SOCIAL INSTITUTION

One social institution for which the evangelical conservative could make a Humean defense would be a robust national church—not an established state-sponsored church!—in that not only would the church confer a certain sacredness on social life in general, but it would also act as a check on the power of the state.[89] (Edmund Burke argued for an established church for these very reasons.) With a powerful national church, like the Roman Catholic Church or Church of Jesus Christ of Latter-Day Saints, religion becomes a civic affair, and the Protestant conservative could argue that all societies then have a common essence of value that manifests itself in civic/religious holidays, such as the American Thanksgiving, Memorial Day, Independence Day, Labor Day, etc.[90] Every society has a dominant religious

---

88. One can profitably read Herman Dooyeweerd (if one can profitably understand Dooyeweerd) for his concept of cultural sphere sovereignty. His book *Roots of Western Culture* is a handy and accessible work on his philosophy. For those more ambitious, his multi-volume opus *A New Critique of Theoretical Thought* is available for perusal.

89. Dante wrote in *The Purgatorio*, concerning the positive value of a church-state standoff: "Now one declining sun puts out the other. The sword and crook are one, and only evil can follow from them when they are together; for neither fears the other, being one" (canto 16). Although there is no evidence of Hume quoting Dante, his love for Virgil would suggest, possibly, that the great Florentine poet did not escape his notice, hence, perhaps influencing him.

90. Bellah writes, "Religions at their best help us focus that urge to celebrate [the joy and mystery of life] so that it will include all the meanings we can encompass. The impulse toward larger meaning, thankfulness, and celebration has to have an institutional form, like all the other central organizing tendencies in our lives, so that we do not dissipate it in purely private sentiment" (Bellah, et al., *Good Society*, 285).

culture with its attendant value system. Minor cultures within that dominant culture should expect to exist freely but not to assume a position of power unless and until Humean cultural evolution eventually brings about that condition. The oppressive dominant cultures (Muslim) of the world will eventually reform themselves out of necessity and become more pluralistic and thus free.[91] Many leading conservatives share Hume's distrust of Christians who rely on revelation for guidance, since such enthusiasts inject personal evangelical religious convictions into the public policy debate. As I have indicated elsewhere, this is a secular conservative fear that I would argue should be ill-founded, but it does point out Hume's extreme relevance to conservative political theory in the twenty-first century.

Mark Henrie, president of the Arthur N. Rupe Foundation, has pointed out the reticence many conservative thinkers have in opposing the modern state, with its orientation towards individual efficiency and productivity to supply human goods and services. He writes, "The conservative must oppose efficiency when it conflicts with the human scale of life [which] he seeks."[92] It is this fear of the industrialization-mechanization-economization of modernity that should cause conservatives to pause in their embrace of the commercialization of American life through strip malls, mega malls, housing subdivisions, and Walmarts.[93] It is not just the economy. The conservatives' loving embrace of corporate America must be sprinkled with cold water, because as modern America substitutes its agriculture for an urban culture, more is being destroyed than just inefficient family farms and unenlightened rural life. Conservatives need to be wary of commercial progress lest they sell their birthright of tradition for the bowl of consumer porridge.[94]

91. See Mustafa Akyol, "The Islamic World Doesn't Need a Reformation" (*Atlantic*, Oct. 31, 2017); Thomas Friedman, "An Islamic Reformation" (*New York Times*, Dec. 4, 2002); Raza Rumi, "Islam Needs a Reformation from within" (*Huffington Post*, May 18, 2015); and Ayaan Hirsi, *Heretics: Why Islam Needs a Reformation Now* (New York: Harper, 2015).

92. Henrie, "Rethinking American Conservatism," 12.

93. A strip mall is a neighborhood shopping center of about 50,000 sq. ft. of shopping area. It occupies about three acres, offers parking and a covered pedestrian walk, and usually has a supermarket as an anchor tenant. It serves up to 40,000 people. A mega mall has more than 1,000,000 sq. ft. of shopping area. It can occupy one hundred acres, offers complete shopping selection, and serves at least 500,000 people. Large mega malls can be self-contained cities with hospitality accommodations. Housing subdivisions are blocks of homes covering many acres with hundreds of homes, all from a few basic floor plans. Walmart is the largest retailer in the United States with 4800 stores. The newest "super center" stores exceed 200,000 sq. ft. of retail area, plus parking. By the mid-1990s, Walmart was opening a store every other day.

94. See the Southern Agrarians' manifesto, *I Take My Stand* (1930). This important

There is more to satisfied life than a healthy 401(k).

We have seen that Hume favored a hierarchical society with an aristocracy at the top. A society thus structured was orderly, secure, and prosperous. One of the aftermaths of the Enlightenment was the destruction of the aristocracy and the emergence of what Burke called "political men of letters"[95] and "political theologians and theological politicians"[96]—in France, Rousseau; in America, Thomas Paine (1737–1809); and in England, Richard Price (1723–1791).[97]

Burke's formulation of a nascent sociology of the intellectual class continues to resonate through conservative thought.[98] He suggested that with the breakdown of social institutions and distinctions and a corresponding rise of a new economic class, there came to be a great deal more social fluidity than before. The intellectual class, heretofore connected to either the church or the crown (i.e., aristocracy), was now free to move around: "What [the intellectuals] lost in the old court protection, they endeavored to make up by joining in a sort of incorporation of their own," i.e., the secularized universities.[99] Burke argued that the main enemies of this new aristocracy were the old institutions, i.e., the church and the crown (e.g., political aristocracy).[100] This new class of intellectuals had no stake in society, were very mobile ("have degree, will travel"), were bright, witty, engaging, and adversarial to all who disagreed with them. They were society's new militant nobility.[101]

---

work contains such southern thinkers as Donald Davidson, Stark Young, Robert Penn Warren, and John Crowe Ransom, among others. This volume served as a rebuke to materialism, a corrective to the worship of progress, and a reaffirmation of man's aesthetic and spiritual needs.

95. Burke, *Reflections on the Revolution*, 114.

96. Burke, *Reflections on the Revolution*, 15.

97. See the pro-American Price's essay "Observations on the Nature of Civil Liberty: The Principle of Government and the Justice and Policy of War with America" (1776).

98. Note Hollander's books *Political Pilgrims* and *Anti-Americanism*.

99. Burke, *Reflections on the Revolution*, 115.

100. "These writers, like the propagators of all novelties, pretended to a great zeal for the poor, and the lower orders, whilst in their satires they rendered hateful, by every exaggeration, the faults of courts, of nobility, and of priesthood" (Burke, *Reflections on the Revolution*, 116).

101. Hollander explores this concept as it has come to be manifested in contemporary Western society. Hollander's basic premise is that many academic and literary intellectuals are anti-American, i.e., they have a deep-seated biased predisposition against American (and, in some cases, all Western) society, culture, political institutions, and foreign policy, which is comparable to sexism, racism, and antisemitism. He maintains that academic and literary intellectual, left-leaning clergy and people associated with the mass media use a double standard. Furthermore, the direction of their

I have noted elsewhere that Hume warned against the dangers of undoing the traditions and customs of property in the name of early democratic reform. He warned us against the social ramifications of the abrogation of entail and primogeniture. If Hume's advice had been taken more to heart, America perhaps would have the social and economic structures to provide an orderly framework from which to make changes and modifications.[102]

Robert Nisbet holds that the "reforms" outlawing entail and primogeniture inaugurated modernity in the Western world, for they elevated the individual over the social group of the family.[103] Additionally, as families became separated from the source of wealth (the land), they were—to use Samuel Johnson's (1709–1784) colorful phrase—"hanging loose upon society." They had no commitment to the present state of things, much less to future generations. With the loss of the landed gentry, Western society became liquefied, amorphous, chaotic. Individuals no longer knew their place, their station, or role in society. There was social freedom without social form, and therefore there was social license.

James Fenimore Cooper (1789–1851) wrote a political tract, *The American Democrat*, in which he examined and set forth the defects and dangers of democracy as it flourished in America in his century. At one point, Cooper wrote:

> The word "gentleman" [derived from the French *gentilhomme*, which originally signified one of noble birth] has a positive and limited signification. It means one elevated above the mass of society by his birth, manners, attainments, character, and social condition. As no civilized society can exist without these social differences, nothing is gained by denying the use of the term.[104]

---

moral indignation and compassion is set and guided by their ideologies and partisan commitments (Hollander, *Political Pilgrims* and *Anti-Americanism*).

102. As Alexis de Tocqueville (1805–1859) observed: "In an aristocracy, order can always be maintained in the midst of liberty; and as the rulers have a great deal to lose, order is to them a matter of great interest. In like manner, an aristocracy protects the people from the excesses of despotism because it always possesses an organized power ready to resist a despot. But a democracy without provincial institutions has no security against these evils. How can a populace, unaccustomed to freedom in small concerns, learn to use it temperately in great affairs? What resistance can be offered to tyranny in a country where each individual is weak, and where the citizens are not united by any common interest? Those who dread the license of the mob, and those who fear absolute power, ought alike to desire the gradual development of provincial liberties" (Tocqueville, *Democracy in America*, 1:106).

103. Nisbet, *Conservatism*, 57.

104. Cooper, *American Democrat*, 112. I am indebted to Kirk for bringing this volume to my attention.

Hume and Hamilton would have agreed with Cooper that civilized society needs a hierarchical, aristocratic order to provide a sense of place and station for the citizenry. Indeed, Thomas Jefferson (1743–1826) complained in a March 1814 letter to Horatio Gates Spafford (1778–1832) that David Hume, the Tory propagandist, was making "Tories of all England and [is] making Tories of those young Americans whose native feelings of independence do not place them above [his] wily sophistries."[105] For Jefferson, Hume's writings were dulling the fervor of American youth for democratic political institutions.

THE FAMILY AS A SOCIAL INSTITUTION

In concert with Hume's opinion that the natural or conjugal family (as Albert Mohler would say) is the primary social institution, Russell Kirk has written,

> The first form of human association is the little family group. To defend themselves from enemies, such groups league together, and the political state grows slowly out of their military necessity.... At first, then, people are moved by self-interest to join in a larger community, obtaining the benefits of a rude government's protection. Later, a sense of obligation arises among the members of a commonwealth, and habit accustoms them to loyal obedience to the laws.[106]

In 1949, Yale University's George Peter Murdock issued his classic study on cultural institutions, entitled *Social Structure*. In the first chapter, "The Nuclear Family," Murdock states, "The nuclear family is a universal human social grouping. Either as the sole prevailing form of the family or as the basic unit from which more complex familial forms are compounded, it exists as a distinct and strongly functional group in every known society."[107] Since 1949, Murdock's work has been evaluated and his study has undergone several re-issues, yet the basic conclusions have not been overturned or defeated in the face of changing cultural patterns in modern society.[108]

---

105. Randall, *Thomas Jefferson*, 56.
106. Kirk, *Roots of the American Order*, 363.
107. Murdock, *Social Structure*, 2.
108. There are, of course, those who dispute this positive view of the importance of the natural family. Coontz, *Way We Never Were*, is representative of such contrary views. To her, the traditional family is a social institution that has perpetuated subjugation, abuse, and bigotry. Indeed, to Coontz, the strength of the traditional family is a debilitating social myth.

Murdock, while neglecting Hume, nevertheless gives a Humean interpretation on the value and origination of the family when he writes,

> This universal social structure [family], produced through cultural evolution in every human society as presumably the only feasible adjustment to a series of basic needs, forms a crucial part of the environment in which every individual grows to maturity.[109]

Habituation, conventions, custom, association—Hume would have been pleased with Murdock's sentiments on the family.[110]

In his book *Culture Wars: The Struggle to Define America,* University of Virginia sociologist James Davison Hunter notes the cultural importance of the American family: "In the final analysis there may be much more to the contemporary culture war than the struggle for the family, yet there is little doubt that the issues contested in the realm of family life are central to the larger struggle and are perhaps fateful for other battles being waged."[111] It is apparent that as America debates the importance and meaning of so-called family values and even the definition of family, Hume's ideas have a place in this very personal debate. Hume defended the institution of the natural or conjugal family of one man and one woman as the cornerstone in a stable and just society. It all begins at home with dad and mom.[112]

---

109. Murdock, *Social Structure*, 11.

110. University of Chicago scholar Allan Bloom (1930–1992) nicely captured a contemporary Humean view of the family: "Individualism, endemic to our regime, has been reinforced by another unintended and unexpected development, the decline of the family, which was the intermediary between individual and society, providing quasi-natural attachments beyond the individual, that gave men and women unqualified concern for at least some others and created an entirely different relation to society from that which the isolated individual has. . . . [Families] provide a material stake in [the community's] future . . . . It is a gentle form of patriotism. . . . The decay of the family means that community would require extreme self-abnegation in an era when there is no good reason for anything but self-indulgence" (Bloom, *Closing of the American Mind*, 86).

111. Hunter, *Culture Wars*, 176.

112. "In general, it may be affirm'd, that there is no such passion in human minds, as the love of mankind, merely as such, independent of personal qualities, of services, or of relation to ourself. . . . An affection betwixt the sexes is a passion evidently implanted in human nature; and this passion not only appears in its peculiar symptoms, but also in inflaming every other principle of affection, and raising a stronger love from beauty, wit, kindness, than what wou'd otherwise flow from them. . . . A man naturally loves his children better than his nephews, his nephews better than his cousins, his cousins better than strangers, where every thing else is equal. Hence arise our common measures of duty, in preferring the one to the other. Our sense of duty always follows the common and natural course of our passions. . . . I am of the opinion that tho' it be

A common axiom of all varieties of political and cultural conservatism is opposition to the forceful invasion of rationalism into political and social life. The English economist Harold Laski (1893–1950) credits David Hume with being the conservative morning star:

> The metaphysics of Burke, so far as one may use a term he would himself have repudiated, are largely those of Hume.[113]

Livingston holds that since Hume was such an ardent and systematic opponent of rationalistic metaphysics,[114] he should be "considered part of the conservative intellectual tradition."[115] Indeed, Livingston argues that Hume should be thought of as the first conservative philosopher.[116]

The English political philosopher H. B. Acton (1908–1974) has written of Hume's influence on Burke:

> From Hume to Edmund Burke the transition is smooth and easy. There is a common repudiation of abstract reason in politics, a common emphasis on nuances and gradual transitions, and a common insistence on prescription. Even Burke's support of "prejudice" is continuous with Hume's support of "'the most useful Byassas and Instincts.'"[117]

---

rare to meet with one, who loves any single person better than himself; yet 'tis as rare to meet with one, in whom all the kind affections, taken together, to not overbalance all the selfish. Consult common experience: Do you not see that tho' the whole expense of the family be generally under the direction of the master of it, yet there are few that do not bestow the largest part of their fortunes on the pleasures of their wives, and the education of their children, reserving the smallest portion for their own proper use and entertainment. This is what we may observe concerning such as have those endearing ties; and may presume, that the case would be the same with others, were they plac'd in like situation. . . . Now as 'tis by establishing the rule for the stability of possession, that this passion restrains itself . . . nothing can be more simple and obvious than that rule: that every parent in order to preserve peace among his children, must establish it; and that these first rudiments of justice must every day be improved, as the society enlarges" (T, 3, 1–2, 529–44).

113. Laski, *Political Thought in England*, 105.

114. A metaphysical rationalist is someone who endorses the Principle of Sufficient Reason (PSR), the principle that everything has an explanation. The PSR can be understood in a number of different ways, so metaphysical rationalists come in many different stripes. But every rationalist thinks that in some interesting sense there is an explanation (or reason) for everything. Metaphysical rationalism is defined as being metaphysical to distinguish it from other rationalisms (such as epistemic rationalism of Descartes, Spinoza, Leibniz, etc.).

115. Livingston, *Hume's Philosophy*, 309.

116. Livingston, *Hume's Philosophy*, 310.

117. As cited in Canavan, *Political Reason*, 42. The Humean quote is from "Of Moral Prejudices," E, 573; LF, 539.

George H. Sabine, however, disagrees with Livingston's view, holding that Edmund Burke is "rightly regarded as the founder of self-conscious political conservatism"; yet he does say that "in a sense Burke accepted Hume's negations of reason and the law of nature."[118]

Russell Kirk (1918–1994), one of the most influential American conservative thinkers in the last half of the twentieth century, agrees with Sabine. Kirk has written, "In any practical sense, Burke is the founder of our conservatism."[119] Even by Kirk's own criteria, Hume is as worthy of conservative esteem as Burke, given the current state of our post-Christian culture in America. As I noted earlier, Russell Kirk, in his magnum opus *The Conservative Mind*, has offered the following six canons of conservative thought:

1) "Belief in a transcendent order, or body of natural law, which rules society as well as conscience." That is, political problems are basically religious and moral problems.

2) "Affection for the proliferating variety and mystery of human existence." That is, the uniformity and egalitarianism of rationalistic systems are stultifying.

3) "Conviction that civilized society requires orders and classes, as against the notion of a Classless society." That is, a social aristocracy of merit, property, and talent prevents totalitarianism or anarchy.

4) "Persuasion that freedom and property are closely linked." That is, if one separates property from private possessions, Leviathan becomes master.

5) "Distrust of 'sophisters, calculators, and economists' who would reconstruct society upon abstract designs." That is, habit, custom, and convention, along with social associations and institutions, are checks upon social anarchy or political oligarchy.

6) "Recognition that change may not be salutary reform; hasty innovation may be a devouring conflagration, rather than a torch of progress." That is, society must evolve, but the change should be incremental, gradual, evolutionary, and consistent with human nature and aspirations.[120]

118. Sabine, *History of Political Theory*, 617, 607.

119. Kirk, *Conservative Mind*, 6.

120. Kirk, *Conservative Mind*, 8–9. In a 1993 book, *Politics of Prudence*, Kirk expands his conservative principles to ten. Noel O'Sullivan, British editor of the most influential American periodical of conservative thought, was recently quoted as stating that the imperatives of the American conservative political culture were threefold: 1) a strong but decent patriotic sentiment, 2) a belief in the free market, and 3) a traditional

Hume's writings embrace a ringing postulation of each of these conservative canons of Kirk's (except, perhaps, the metaphysical first). Hume might have insisted on an innate moral human nature from somewhere rather than a morality coming from a supreme being. As regards metaphysics, while Hume did not fully or correctly appreciate the contribution of historic, revealed Christian thought, he did have an appreciation for evangelical Calvinism[121] and the need for a transcendental perspective in human social life, since that is the religious ocean in which Hume swam as a young man.[122]

British scholar Noel O'Sullivan would ultimately choose one phrase, "politics of imperfection," to sum up conservatism, and he argues that David Hume is "the best representative of this school of thought."[123] Reason has its limits, and perfection, in any form, is unattainable. Moderation is thus the

---

morality that shapes citizens capable of living independently in a democratic society (Bridges, "Continent Not Cut Off"). O'Sullivan's remarks were made at the 1993 Philadelphia Society's annual meeting.

121. During 1749, Hume went to hear George Whitefield preach in the open air. Hume writes, "Mr. Whitefield is the most ingenious preacher I ever heard; it is worth going twenty miles to hear him. After a solemn pause, Mr. Whitefield thus addressed his numerous auditory: 'The attendant angel is just about to leave the threshold of this sanctuary and ascend to heaven. Shall he ascend and not bear with him the news of one sinner among all this multitude reclaimed from the errors of his way?' To give greater effect to this exclamation he stamped with his foot, lifted his hands and eyes to heaven, and gushing with tears, cried aloud, 'Stop Gabriel! Stop Gabriel! Stop, ere you enter the sacred portals and yet carry with you this news of one sinner converted to God!' He then, in the most simple but energetic language described what he called the Saviour's dying love to sinful man, so that almost the whole assembly was melted into tears. This address was accompanied with such animated yet natural action that it surpassed anything I ever saw or heard in any preacher" (Dallimore, *George Whitefield*, 2:274).

122. In fairness to Hume, note must be made of the view of Hume's Christian convictions by the great orthodox Scots divine John Cairns (1818–1892), who wrote in 1881: "But while so much of the career of this great thinker, in thought so clear, in heart so kindly, is on its spiritual side a darkness and a grief to Christian minds, let us remember the undoubted evidence of reaction and recoil from the gloom of doubt which no one has more eloquently expressed, and let us give as much acceptance as we can to the words uttered amidst the shock of his mother's death, and uttered as a reply to the charge of having broken with all Christian hope—Though I throw out my speculations to entertain the learned and metaphysical world, yet in other things I do not think so differently from the rest of the world as you imagine" (Cairns, *Unbelief in the Eighteenth Century*, 82). Scottish Enlightenment boasted world-class scholars who occupied the Scottish universities. These universities were dominated by Presbyterians who were determined to combine orthodox Calvinism with current ideological and cultural developments. Hume, while not a Calvinist and not a university habitué, nevertheless corresponded with these Presbyterian worthies.

123. O'Sullivan, *Conservatism*, 27.

key to individual happiness and social good. The Scriptures teach the same thing with their emphasis on the noetic effects of sin.[124]

It is left to George Will, the American secular conservative, to define conservatism politically and not philosophically, mainly that conservatives "seek to conserve the American Founding." By that, he means we conservatives are "the custodians of the classical liberal tradition." And by that, he means "the expansion and protection of individual liberty." And by that, he means American conservatives hold to the idea of American exceptionalism, which he defines as:

1. We are exceptionally free from entrenched aristocracy.
2. We are exceptionally receptive to intellectual pluralism.
3. We are exceptionally free to choose our happiness.
4. We are governed by an exceptional constitution.
5. We are exceptionally impervious to modern impersonal forces.
6. We are exceptionally free from discretionary political powers.
7. We are exceptionally guaranteed a zone of personal autonomy.[125]

It is not profitable for the intellectual conservative movement in the United States to neglect Hume's contribution to an articulated philosophic and political conservatism that opposes the rationalized state, since Hume was so helpful in so many ways in defending a biblical view of government and society.[126] The British constitutional theorist Geoffrey Marshall, commenting on Hume's skepticism, writes:

> Between *philosophical* skepticism and the conservative attitude to change, there is no necessary connection at all. Such skepticism has none of the consequences for social theory which are sometimes imputed to it. What undoubtedly does have these consequences is the *practical* skepticism and empirical caution

---

124. Cf. Ps 14; Acts 17:22–34; Rom 1:18–23.

125. Will, *Conservative Sensibility*, xxvii.

126. The term rationalized state is used to convey the set of abstract beliefs that modern government structures itself with a presumption that it speaks for the collection of individuals brought together under a juridical sovereignty by a social contract of mutual advantage. The state holds that this contract has been discussed, debated, and agreed upon by all citizens and therefore has sovereignty over all of life. Rational discourse would dictate that all opposition to the good life brought about by cooperation with the state should be stamped out as dangerous. The people know what is best for them, and their representatives have the authority to weed out the enemies of the state. Francis Fukuyama's *The End of History and the Last Man* is an excellent defense of the rationalized state.

of the Hume who mistrusted miracles whether they might be theological or political.[127]

Scholars such as David Miller,[128] Donald Livingston, Anthony Quinton, Frederick Whelan, Douglass Adair, Quinton Hogg, Sheldon Wolin, Constant N. Stockton, Michael Oakeshott, F. A. Hayek,[129] Christopher Berry, Jerry Muller, Noel O'Sullivan, James Q. Wilson, and Edmund Fawcett have noted Hume's conservative credentials, but all from a secular, skeptical vantage point. That is, they find in Hume four basic secular conservative philosophic tenets: 1) epistemological skepticism, 2) subordination of reason to sentiment (passion), 3) emphasis on the role of custom in human affairs, and 4) reticence to change existing social conventions.[130] My purpose has been to coalesce the chief points of these scholars and to argue that Hume can be of service to evangelical Christian conservatives as well, since he presents ideas that are consistent with much biblical teaching.

Hume's emphasis on the value of convention and custom, expressed in social institutions that convey the social arrangement that arises from human nature, is important, because it is only through felicitous social arrangements that the individual's rights can be preserved.[131] When conservatives stress Lockean individual and autonomous rights, they play into the statists' hand by eviscerating the protection that these agreeable social arrangements provide for the individual in the face of an all-powerful, aggrandizing social institution—the modern rational Leviathan, the ultra-Hobbesian state, the armed federal and state government. It is only as individuals, through customs and habits, voluntarily and habitually bond with other individuals in appropriate social and cultural institutions that the individual's rights will be protected. As Frederick Whelan has written, "Hume's skeptical denial

---

127. Marshall, "David Hume and Political Scepticism," 252.

128. Miller's *Philosophy and Ideology* is a particularly insightful and helpful discussion of Hume's political philosophy.

129. Hayek makes note of the fact that Hume has not been appreciated as a political and legal theorist: "Hume gives us probably the only comprehensive statement of the legal and political philosophy which later became known as liberalism" (Hayek, "Legal and Political Philosophy," 340). For Hayek, one of the great conservative thinkers of the last half of the twentieth century, liberalism is the doctrine of personal liberty against the claims of a totalitarian institution.

130. See Robertson, "A Changed Britain."

131. Hume was not the only thinker in the eighteenth century whose political philosophy rested on the importance of human convention. I refer, of course, to Rousseau, who likewise argued that all legitimate political authority was founded and rested on convention: "Since no man has a natural authority over his fellow men, and since force is not the source of right, conventions remain as the basis of all legitimate authority among men" (Rousseau, *Of the Social Contract*, 8).

of ultimate rational justification for any particular institutions leads him to recommend caution and diffidence—and a presumption of utility in established practices—as the most reasonable attitudes to bring to the active affairs of political life."[132]

Hume's conservatism might well be called empirical conservatism. For him, it was a Darwinian matter of one social institution versus another social institution in the political and cultural arena, with a conviction that the more useful would survive. For political conservatives, the need for strong intermediate social institutions (e.g., families, churches, schools, unions, trade associations, clubs) is great, because they are the only things that can stand with cultural authority, loyalty, and autonomy against the presence of a strong, centralized, rationalized, jealous, and sinful government.[133] Even with the breakdown of so many of our traditional social institutions, Hume gives us the secular philosophic structure for such social protection for the individual.

---

132. Whelan, *Order and Artifice*, 30.
133. Cf. 1 Sam 8.

A Concluding Observation

SOCIETY AT LARGE AND communities are held together by the glue of conventions. Social associations and institutions are important and effective because they have a history of habituation, familiarity, and respect. Any change will properly encounter resistance unless and until the proposed innovation has accumulated a similar body of habit and sentiment. It is, in short, custom, tradition, membership in a society that gives a moral quality to human life. It is not abstract reason. Sabine writes:

> Society and the social tradition are the guardian of all that the race has created, its moral ideals, its art, its science and learning. Membership means access to all the stores of culture, to all that makes the difference between savagery and civilization. It is not a burden, but an open door to human liberation.[1]

Hume's insistence that personal identity is formed in the crucible of personal history, that we know ourselves as we experience the world around us and our reaction to that world, can be a non-revealed basis for the conservative view that we are what history makes us. The humanness of our condition can be understood and appreciated only in the environment of the common life of the individual person. Hume showed a great deal of sympathy for the common problems and relationships in the everyday life of the citizen, realizing that a structuring of society must consider the historical development of its citizenry in order to be legitimate.

I believe, as I have already indicated, that conservatives are right to criticize abstract rationalists for subverting social habits, traditions, and institutions. In order to sustain civilization, we must be able not only to distinguish between good and bad, but also to cultivate a disposition to do good rather than bad. While many conservatives properly look to Judeo-Christian teaching for that guidance, they ought, in an increasingly secular

---

1. Sabine, *History of Political Theory*, 615.

age, to leave open the option of looking elsewhere as well. David Hume becomes relevant at this point, because he stressed human historical experience as it accrues through custom, habit, and convention. In sum, he gives us a coherent philosophy of the traditional common life—one which might indeed help us fashion a stable and free society in which to flourish as a human race, even in our changing world.

Bibliography

Adair, Douglass G. *Fame and the Founding Fathers*. Indianapolis: Liberty Fund, 1998.
Adams, Charles Francis, ed. *The Works of John Adams*. 10 vols. Boston: Little, Brown, 1851.
Agutter, William. "On the Difference between the Deaths of the Righteous and the Wicked, Illustrated in the Instance of Dr. Samuel Johnson and David Hume, Esq." New York: Ecco, n.d.
Ahlstrom, Sydney. "The Radical Turn in Theology and Ethics." *The Annals* (Jan. 1970) 1–13.
Allen, Diogenes. *Philosophy for Understanding Theology*. Atlanta: John Knox, 1985.
Anderson, James N. *David Hume*. Phillipsburg, NJ: P & R, 2019.
Anderson, John. *A Defense of the Church-Government, Faith, Worship and Spirit of the Presbyterians*. Reprint, Edinburgh: Palala, 2015.
Aquinas, Thomas. *On Kingship to the King of Cyprus*. Toronto: Pontifical Institute, 1949.
Ardal, Pall S. "Convention and Value." *David Hume: Bicentenary Papers*, edited by G. P. Morice. Austin: University of Texas Press, 1977.
Arnold, Matthew. *Culture and Anarchy: An Essay in Political and Social Criticism*. Cambridge Library Collection. Cambridge, UK: Cambridge University Press, 2003.
Ayer, A.J. "Hume." In *The British Empiricists*, by John Dunn et al., 179–280. Oxford: Oxford University Press, 1992.
———. *Hume*. New York: Hill and Wang, 1980.
Ayling, Stanley Edward. *Edmund Burke: His Life and Opinions*. New York: St. Martin, 1988.
Bacon, Francis. *On the Dignity and Advancement of Learning*. London: Colonial, 1900.
Bahnsen, Greg L. *Van Til's Apologetic: Readings and Analysis*. Phillipsburg, NJ: P & R, 1998.
Baird, James William. *Thunder Over Scotland: The Life of George Wishart, Scottish Reformer, 1513-1546*. Campbell, CA: Green Leaf, 1982.
Barker, William. "The Social Views of Charles Hodge: A Study in Nineteenth Century Calvinism and Conservatism." *Presbyterion* 1 (Spring 1975) 1–22.
Bauckman, Richard. *Jesus and the Eyewitnesses: The Gospels as Eyewitness Testimony*. Grand Rapids: Eerdmans, 2006.
Bavinck, Herman. *Reformed Dogmatics*. 4 vols. Grand Rapids: Baker, 2011.
Beattie, James. *An Essay on the Nature and Immutability of Truth, in Opposition to Sophistry and Scepticism*. Reprint, Los Angeles: HardPress, 2013.

Becker, Carl L. *The Heavenly City of the Eighteen-Century Philosophers*. New Haven, CT: Yale University Press, 1932.
Beer, Samuel H. *To Make a Nation: The Rediscovery of American Federalism*. Cambridge, MA: Harvard University Press, 1993.
Bellah, Robert N., et al. *The Good Society*. New York: Vintage Books, 1992.
Bennett, Jonathan. *Locke, Berkeley, Hume: Central Themes*. Oxford: Clarendon, 1971.
Berger, Peter L. *The Sacred Canopy: Elements of a Sociological Theory of Religion*. Garden City, NY: Doubleday & Co, 1969.
Berkeley, George. *Alciphron*. Cambridge Companion to Berkeley. Cambridge, UK: Cambridge University Press, 2005.
———. *Principles, Dialogues, and Correspondence*. Edited by Colin Murray Turbayne. Library of Liberal Arts. New York: Bobbs-Merrill, 1965.
Berkhof, Louis. *Systematic Theology*. Grand Rapids: Eerdmans, 1972.
Bernal, Martin. *The Fabrication of Ancient Greece 1785-1985*. Vol. 1 of *Black Athena: The Afroasiatic Roots of Classical Civilization*. New Brunswick, NJ: Rutgers University Press, 1987.
Berry, Christopher J. *David Hume*. Major Conservative and Libertarian Thinkers 3. New York: Bloomsbury, 2009.
Blanchard, William H. *Rousseau and the Spirit of Revolt*. Ann Arbor, MI: University of Michigan Press, 1967.
Bloom, Allan. *The Closing of the American Mind*. New York: Simon and Schuster, 1987.
Bonald, Louis de. *On Divorce*. Translated by Nicolas Davidson. New Brunswick, NJ: Transaction, 1992.
Bonar, James. *Philosophy and Political Economy*. New York: George Allen & Unwin, 1967.
Bongie, Laurence L. *David Hume: Prophet of the Counter-Revolution*. Oxford: Clarendon, 1965.
Bork, Robert H. *The Tempting of America*. New York: Simon & Schuster, 1990.
Botwinick, Aryeh. *Ethics. Politics and Epistemology: A Study in the Unity of Hume's Thought*. Washington, DC: University Press of America, 1980.
Bridges, Linda. "Continent Not Cut Off." *National Review* (Aug. 9, 1993) 22–26.
Broiles, R. David. *The Moral Philosophy of David Hume*. The Hague, Neth.: Martinus Nijhoff, 1964.
Brown, Colin. *From the Ancient World to the Age of Enlightenment*. Vol. 1 of *Christianity and Western Thought: A History of Philosophers, Ideas and Movements*. Downers Grove, IL: IVP Academic, 1990.
———. *Philosophy and the Christian Faith*. Downers Grove, IL: IVP Academic, 1963.
Brown, Harold O. J. *The Reconstruction of the Republic*. New Rochelle, NY: Arlington House, 1977.
Brownson, Orestes. "Democracy and Liberty," in *The Wisdom of Conservatism*, edited by Peter Witonski, 2:667–740. Mars Hill, NC: Institute for Western Values, 1981.
Brunner, Emil. *Christianity and Civilization*. New York: Charles Scribner, 1949.
Bulfinch, Thomas. *Bulfinch's Mythology*. Garden City, NY: Doubleday, 1948.
Burke, Edmund. *An Appeal from the New to the Old Whigs*. Reprint, n.p.: Wentworth, n.d.
———. *Reflections on the Revolution in France*. Buffalo, NY: Prometheus, 1987.
Burton, John Hill. *Life and Correspondence of David Hume*. 2 vols. New York: Burt Franklin, 1967.
Cairns, John. *Unbelief in the Eighteenth Century*. New York: Harper & Brothers, 1881.

Canavan, Francis P. *The Political Reason of Edmund Burke*. Durham, NC: Duke University Press, 1960.
Carretta, Vincent. "Who Was Francis Williams?" *Early American Literature* 38, no. 2 (2003), 213–37.
Carter, Stephen L. *The Culture of Disbelief: How American Law and Politics Trivialize Religious Devotion*. New York: Basic, 1993.
Case, Shirley Jackson. *Jesus: A New Biography*. Chicago: University of Chicago Press, 1927.
Cassirer, Ernst. *The Philosophy of the Enlightenment*. Princeton, NJ: Princeton University Press, 1951.
Chappell V. C., ed. *Hume: A Collection of Critical Essays*. Notre Dame, IN: University of Notre Dame Press, 1968.
Chernow, Ron. *Washington: A Life*. New York: Penguin, 2010.
Church, Ralph W. *Hume's Theory of the Understanding*. Hamden, CT.: Archon, 1968.
Cicero. *The Nature of the Gods*. Translated by Horace C. P. McGregor. Middlesex, UK: Penguin, 1972.
Clark, Gordon H. *Christian View of Men and Things*. Grand Rapids: Baker, 1981.
———. *Thales to Dewey: A History of Philosophy*. Jefferson, MD: Trinity Foundation, 1957.
Colson, Charles and Ellen Santilli Vaughn. *Against the Night: Living in the New Dark Ages*. Ann Arbor, MI: Servant, 1989.
Coontz, Stephanie. *The Way We Never Were: American Families and the Nostalgia Trap*. New York: Basic, 1992.
Cooper, James Fenimore. *The American Democrat*. New York: Funk & Wagnalls, 1969.
Copleston, Frederick. *A History of Philosophy*. 9 vols. New York: Doubleday, 1964.
Cornell, George W. "Study Finds TV's Pastor Portrayal Is Not Bad, Not Good." *Yakima Herald Republic*, 28 Aug. 1993.
Cox, Harvey. *Religion in the Secular City: Towards a Post-Modern Theology*. New York: Simon & Schuster, 1985.
———. *The Secular City: Secularization and Urbanization in Theological Perspective*. New York: Macmillan, 1965.
Crawford, Alan. *Thunder on the Right: The "New Right" and the Politics of Resentment*. New York: Pantheon, 1980.
Dallimore, Arnold. *George Whitefield: The Life and Times of the Great Evangelist of the Eighteenth-Century Revival*. 2 vols. London: Banner of Truth, 1980.
Danford, John W. "The Surest Foundation of Morality: The Political Teaching of Hume's Dialogues Concerning Natural Religion." *Western Political Quarterly* 35, no. 2 (Apr. 1982) 137–60.
Dascal, Marcelo and Ora Gruengard, eds. *Knowledge and Politics: Case Studies in the Relationship between Epistemology and Political Philosophy*. Boulder, CO: Westview, 1989.
Dees, Richard H. "Hume and the Context of Politics." *Journal of the History of Philosophy* 30, no. 2 (Apr. 1992) 219–42.
Descartes, René. *The Philosophical Writings of Descartes*. Translated by John Cottingham. 2 vols. New York: Cambridge University Press, 1984.
Dooyeweerd, Herman. *A New Critique of Theoretical Thought: The Necessary Presuppositions of Philosophy*. Translated by David H. Freeman. 4 vols. Grand Rapids: Paideia, 1997.

———. *Roots of Western Culture: Pagan, Secular, and Christian Options*. Edited by Mark Vander Vennen and Bernard Zylstra. Translated by John N. Kraay. Grand Rapids: Paideia, 2012.

Durant, Will. *The Story of Philosophy*. Garden City, NY: Garden City, 1927.

Durkheim, Emile. *The Division of Labor in Society*. Translated by George Simpson. New York: Free Press, 1964.

Edwards, Lee. *The Conservative Revolution*. New York: Free, 1999

Eliot, T. S. *The Literature of Politics*. London: Conservative Political Centre, 1955.

Elkins, Stanley and Eric McKitrick. *The Age of Federalism*. New York: Oxford University Press, 1993.

Ellis, Joseph J. *Passionate Sage: The Character and Legacy of John Adams*. New York: W. W. Norton, 1993.

Farrand, Max, ed. *The Records of the Federal Convention of 1787*. 3 vols. New Haven, CT: Yale University Press, 1966.

Farwell, Byron. *Queen Victoria's Little Wars*. New York: Norton, 1972.

Fawcett, Edmund. *Conservatism: The Fight for a Tradition*. Princeton, NJ: Princeton University Press, 2020.

Ferm, Vergilius, ed. *A History of Philosophical Systems*. New York: Philosophical Library, 1950.

Feuerbach, Ludwig. *The Essence of Christianity*. Translated by George Eliot. Buffalo, NY: Prometheus, 1989.

Flew, Antony. *David Hume. Philosopher of Moral Science*. London: Basil Blackwell, 1986.

———. *An Introduction to Western Philosophy: Ideas and Argument from Plato to Sartre*. London: Thames, 1971.

Forbes, Duncan. *Hume's Philosophical Politics*. Cambridge, UK: Cambridge University Press, 1975.

Frame, John M. *Cornelius Van Til: An Analysis of His Thought*. Phillipsburg, NJ: P & R, 1995.

———. *A History of Western Philosophy and Theology*. Phillipsburg, NJ: P & R, 2015.

———. *Systematic Theology: An Introduction to Christian Belief*. Phillipsburg, NJ: P & R, 2013.

Frohnen, Bruce, et al., eds. *American Conservatism: An Encyclopedia*. Wilmington, DE: ISI, 2006.

Fukuyama, Francis. *The End of History and the Last Man*. New York: Avon, 1992.

Fuller, B. A. G. *A History of Philosophy*. New York: Henry Holt, 1945.

Geisler, Norman L., and Paul D. Feinberg. *Introduction to Philosophy: A Christian Perspective*. Grand Rapids: Baker, 1980.

Giddens, Anthony. *The Consequences of Modernity*. Stanford, CA: Stanford University Press, 1990.

Gilbert, Alan D. *The Making of Post-Christian Britain: A History of the Secularization of Modern Society*. London: Longman, 1980.

Ginzberg, Eli. *The House of Adam Smith*. New York: Octagon, 1964.

Glendon, Mary Ann. *Rights Talk: The Impoverishment of Political Discourse*. New York: Macmillan, 1991.

Gottfried, Paul. *The Conservative Movement*. New York: Twayne, 1993.

Grenz, Stanley J., and Roger E. Olson. *Twentieth Century Theology: God and the World in a Transitional Age*. Downers Grove, IL: InterVarsity, 1992.

Grey, John. "The Left's Last Utopia." *National Review*, July 19, 1993.
Griffin, David Ray. *God and Religion in the Post-Modern World: Essays in Postmodern Theology*. SUNY Series in Constructive Postmodern Thought. Albany, NY: SUNY Press, 1989.
Guinness, Os. *The American Hour: A Time of Reckoning and the Once and Future Role of Faith*. New York: Free Press, 1992
———. *The Dust of Death: A Critique of the Establishment and the Counter Culture and the Proposal for a Third Way*. Downers Grove, IL: InterVarsity, 1973
———. *The Gravedigger File: Papers on the Subversion of the Modern Church*. Downers Grove, IL: InterVarsity, 1983.
Gutiérrez, Gustavo. *A Theology of Liberation: History, Politics, and Salvation*. Rev. ed. Translated by Caridad Inda and John Eagleson. Maryknoll, NY: Orbis, 1988.
Gutjahr, Paul C. *Charles Hodge: Guardian of American Orthodoxy*. Oxford: Oxford University Press, 2011.
Haakonssen, Knud. "The Structure of Hume's Political Theory." In *The Cambridge Companion to Hume*, edited by David Fate Norton and Jacqueline Taylor, 341–80. 2nd ed. Cambridge, UK: Cambridge University Press, 2009.
Hallie, Philip P., ed. *Scepticism, Man and God: Selections from the Major Writings of Sextus Empiricus*. Translated by Sanford G. Etheridge. Middletown, CT: Wesleyan University Press, 1964.
Hamilton, Alexander, et al. *The Federalist Papers*. Edited by Isaac Kramnick. London: Penguin, 1987.
Hamlyn, D. W. *The Penguin History of Western Philosophy*. London: Penguin, 1988.
Hamowy, Ronald. "Scottish Thought and the American Revolution." In *Liberty and American Experience in the Eighteenth Century*, edited by David Womersley, 348–88. Indianapolis: Liberty Fund, 2006.
Hare, Richard Mervyn. *The Language of Morals*. Reprint, Oxford: Oxford University Press, 1991.
———. *Moral Thinking: Its Levels, Method, and Point*. Oxford: Clarendon Press, 1981.
Haring, Bernard. *Faith and Morality in the Secular Age*. New York: Doubleday, 1973.
Harrigan, Anthony. "The Making of American Conservatism: A Personal Account." *The Intercollegiate Review* 29, no. 1 (Fall 1993) 30–37.
Harris, James A. *Hume: An Intellectual Biography*. Cambridge, UK: Cambridge University Press, 2015.
Harrison, Jonathan. *Hume's Moral Epistemology*. Oxford: Clarendon, 1976.
———. *Hume's Theory of Justice*. Oxford: Clarendon, 1981.
Hayek, F. A. "The Legal and Political Philosophy of David Hume." In *Hume: A Collection of Critical Essays*, edited by V. C. Chappell, 335–360. Notre Dame, IN: University of Notre Dame Press, 1968.
Heimbeck, Raeburne S. *Theology and Meaning: A Critique of Metatheological Scepticism*. London: George Allen and Unwin, 1969.
Hendel, Charles W., Jr. *Studies in the Philosophy of David Hume*. New York: Library of Liberal Arts, 1963.
Henrie, Mark C. "Rethinking American Conservatism in the 1990s: The Struggle Against Homogenization." *The Intercollegiate Review* 28, no. 2 (Spring 1993) 17–24.
Henry, Carl F. H. *Twilight of a Great Civilization: The Drift toward Neo-Paganism*. Westchester, IL: Crossway, 1988.

Herberg, Will. *Protestant, Catholic, Jew: An Essay in American Religious Sociology.* Reprint, Chicago: University of Chicago Press, 1983.

Himmelfarb, Gertrude. *Marriage and Morals Among the Victorians.* London: L. B. Tauaris, 1989.

———. *The Roads to Modernity: The British, French, and American Enlightenment.* New York: Vintage, 2005.

Hitchcock, James. *What Is Secular Humanism?: Why Christian Humanism Became Secular and How It Is Changing Our World.* Ann Arbor, MI: Servant, 1982.

Hobbes, Thomas. *Leviathin.* Vol. 23 of *Great Books of the Western World.* Chicago: Encyclopaedia Britannica, 1952.

Hodge, Charles. *Systematic Theology.* 3 vols. Grand Rapids: Eerdmans, 1973.

Hoffecker, W. Andrew, ed. *The Universe, Society, and Ethics.* Vol. 2 of *Building a Christian Worldview.* Philipsburg, NJ: Puritan and Reformed, 1988.

Hogg, Quinton. *A Case for Conservatism.* Harmondsworth, UK: Penguin, 1959.

Hollander, Paul. *Anti-Americanism: Critiques at Home and Abroad, 1965–1990.* New York: Oxford University Press, 1992.

———. *Political Pilgrims: Travels of Western Intellectuals to the Soviet Union, China, and Cuba.* New York: Oxford University Press, 1981.

Hooker, Richard. *Of the Laws of Ecclesiastical Polity.* Edited by Arthur Stephen McGrade. Cambridge Texts in the History of Political Thought. Cambridge, UK: Cambridge University Press, 1989.

Hope, V. M. *Virtue by Consensus: The Moral Philosophy of Hutcheson, Hume, and Adam Smith.* Oxford: Clarendon, 1989.

Horne, George. *A Letter to Adam Smith on the Life, Death, and Philosophy of his Friend David Hume.* N.p.: Kissinger Legacy Reprints, n.d.

Howe, John R., Jr. *The Changing Political Thought of John Adams.* Princeton, NJ: Princeton University Press, 1966.

Hume, David. *Enquiries Concerning Human Understanding, and Concerning the Principles of Morals.* Edited by L. A. Selby-Bigge, revised by P. H. Nidditch. 3rd ed. Oxford: Oxford University Press, 1975.

———. *An Enquiry Concerning Human Understanding.* Buffalo, NY: Prometheus, 1988.

———. *An Enquiry Concerning the Principles of Morals.* Edited by John B. Stewart. La Salle, IL: Open Court, 1966.

———. *Essays: Moral, Political, and Literary.* Edited by T. H. Green and T. H. Grose. Oxford: Clarendon, 1963.

———. *Essays: Moral, Political, and Literary.* Edited by Eugene F. Miller. Indianapolis: Liberty Fund, 1987.

———. *The History of England.* 6 vols. Philadelphia: E. Claxton & Co, 1881.

———. "Letter from a Gentleman to His Friend in Edinburgh." Edited by Ernest Campbell Mossner. Edinburgh: Curwin, 1967.

———. *The Letters of David Hume.* Edited by J. Y. T. Grieg. 2 vols. Oxford: Oxford University Press, 1932.

———. "My Own Life." In *The Life of David Hume*, by Ernest Campbell Mossner, 611–15. Oxford: Clarendon, 1979.

———. *The Philosophic Works.* Edited by Thomas Hill Green and Thomas Hodge Grose. 2 vols. London: Scientia Verlag Aalen, 1964.

———. *A Treatise of Human Nature.* Edited by Ernest C. Mossner. Middlesex, UK: Penguin, 1985.

———. *A Treatise of Human Nature*. Edited by L. A. Selby-Bigge. Oxford: Clarendon, 1955.

———. *Writings on Religion*. Edited by Antony Flew. La Salle, IL: Open Court, 1992.

Hunter, James Davison. *Culture Wars: The Struggle to Define America*. New York: Basic, 1991.

Hutcheson, Francis. *An Essay on the Nature and Conduct of the Passions and Affections*. Indianapolis: Liberty Fund, 2003.

Hutchins, Robert Maynard, ed. *American State Papers; The Federalist; J. S. Mill*. Vol. 43 of *Great Books of the Western World*. Chicago: Encyclopaedia Britannica, 1952.

Immerwahr, John. "Hume's Revised Racism." *Journal of the History of Ideas* 53, no. 2 (Apr.–June 1992) 481–86.

Johnson, William Stacy. "The Reign of God in Theological Perspective." *Interpretation* 47, no. 2 (Apr. 1993) 127–39.

Jones, Peter. *The Gnostic Empire Strikes Back: An Old Heresy for the New Age*. Grand Rapids: Presbyterian and Reformed, 1992.

Jones, W. T. *Hobbes to Hume*. Vol 3 of *A History of Western Philosophy*. New York: Harcourt Brace Jovanovich, 1969.

Kant, Immanuel. *Critique of Pure Reason*. Vol. 42 of *Great Books of the Western World*. Chicago: Encyclopaedia Britannica, 1952.

———. *Prolegomena to Any Future Metaphysics*. Edited by Lewis White Beck. Indianapolis: Bobbs-Merrill, 1950.

Kemp, J. *Ethical Naturalism: Hobbes and Hume*. New Studies in Ethics. London: St. Martin's, 1970.

Kirk, Russell. *The Conservative Mind: From Burke to Eliot*. Chicago: Regnery, 1986.

———. *The Roots of American Order*. Washington: Regnery, 1991.

Koch, Adrienne. *The American Enlightenment: The Shaping of the American Experiment and a Free Society*. New York: George Braziller, 1965.

Kok, John H. *Patterns of the Western Mind: A Reformed Christian Perspective*. Sioux Center, IA: Dordt College Press, 1998.

Kristol, Irving. *Neo-Conservatism: The Autobiography of an Idea; Selected Essays 1949–1995*. New York: Free Press, 1995

Laing, B. M. *David Hume*. New York: Russell and Russell, 1932.

Laird, John. *Hume's Philosophy of Human Nature*. Hamden, CT: Archon, 1967.

Laski, Harold J. *Political Thought in England from Locke to Bentham*. London: Oxford University Press, 1922.

Lavine, Thelma Z. *From Socrates to Sartre: The Philosophic Quest*. New York: Bantam, 1984.

Lindsay, D. Michael. *Faith in the Halls of Power: How Evangelicals Joined the American Elite*. Oxford: Oxford University Press, 2007.

Livingston, Donald W. *Hume's Philosophy of Common Life*. Chicago: University of Chicago Press, 1984.

Livingston, Donald W., and James T. King, eds. *Hume: A Re-Evaluation*. New York: Fordham University Press, 1976.

Locke, John. "Essay Concerning Human Understanding." In *Locke. Berkeley. Hume.*, 93–395. Vol. 35 of *Great Books of the Western World*. Chicago: Encyclopaedia Britannica, 1952.

———. *Second Treatise of Government*. Edited by C. B. Macpherson. Indianapolis: Hackett, 1980.

Lorenz, Konrad. *On Aggression*. Translated by Marjorie K. Wilson. New York: Bantam, 1969.
Lucas, F. L. *The Art of Living: Four Eighteenth-Century Minds; Hume, Horace Walpole, Burke, Benjamin Franklin*. New York: Macmillan, 1961.
Mackie, J. L. *Hume's Moral Theory*. International Library of Philosophy. London: Routledge & Kegan Paul, 1980.
Macintyre, Alasdair. *A Short History of Ethics*. New York: Collier, 1966.
MacNabb, D. G. C. *David Hume: His Theory of Knowledge and Morality*. Hamden, CT: Archon, 1951.
Macpherson, C. B. *The Political Theory of Possessive Individualism: Hobbes to Locke*. London: Oxford Press, 1962.
———. *Burke*. New York: Hill and Wang, 1980.
Mahan, A. T. *The Influence of Seapower upon History*. New York: Hill and Wang, 1957.
Maistre, Joseph Marie, comte de. *On God and Society: Essay on the Generative Principle of Political Constitutions and Other Human Institutions*. Chicago: Henry Regnery, 1967.
Marías, Julián. *History of Philosophy*. Translated by Stanley Appelbaum and Clarence C. Strowbridge, NY: Dover, 1967.
Marshall, Geoffrey. "David Hume and Political Scepticism." *Philosophical Quarterly* 4, no. 16 (July 1954) 247–57.
Matthew, H. C. G. *Gladstone: 1809–1874*. Oxford: Oxford University Press, 1988.
McAuliffe, Joseph R. "Secular Pluralism." *Chalcedon Report* 337 (Aug. 1993). Page range unavailable.
McCullough, David. *John Adams*. New York: Simon & Schuster, 2002.
McDonald, Forrest. *Novus Ordo Seclorum: The Intellectual Origins of the Constitution*. Lawrence, KS: University of Kansas Press, 1985.
———. "The Rhetoric of Alexander Hamilton" In *Modern Age: The First Twenty-Five Years; A Selection*, edited by George A. Panichas, 114–24. Indianapolis: Liberty, 1988.
Meacham, Jon. *American Gospel: God, the Foundimg Fathers, and the Making of a Nation*. New York: Random House, 2006.
Miller, David. *Philosophy and Ideology in Hume's Political Thought*. Oxford: Clarendon, 1981.
Moore, James. "Hume's Political Science and the Classical Republican Tradition." *Canadian Journal of Political Science* 10, no. 4 (Dec. 1977) 809–39.
Mossner, Ernest Campbell. *The Life of David Hume*. Oxford: Clarendon, 1970.
Montaigne, Michel de. *Selections from the Essays*. Edited and translated by Donald M. Frame. Northbrook, IL: AHM, 1973.
Muller, Jerry Z., ed. *Conservatism: An Anthology of Social and Political Thought from David Hume to the Present*. Princeton, NJ: Princeton University Press, 1997.
Murdock, George Peter. *Social Structure*. New York: Macmillan, 1949.
Murray, Charles. *In Pursuit of Happiness and Good Government*. New York: Simon & Schuster, 1988.
Nash, Ronald H. *Faith and Reason: Searching for a Rational Faith*. Grand Rapids: Zondervan, 1988.
Neuhaus, Richard John. *The Naked Public Square: Religion and Democracy in America*. Grand Rapids: Eerdmans, 1984.
———. "A Word on 'The Competition.'" *First Things*, June 1993. https://www.firstthings.com/article/1993/06/a-word-on-the-competition.

Nisbet, Robert. *Conservatism: Dream and Reality*. Minneapolis: University of Minnesota Press, 1986.
Noll, Mark A. *A History of Christianity in the United States and Canada*. Grand Rapids: Eerdmans, 1992.
———. *The Scandal of the Evangelical Mind*. Grand Rapids: Eerdmans, 1994.
Norton, David Fate. *The Cambridge Companion to Hume*. 2nd ed. Cambridge, UK: Cambridge University Press, 2009.
———. *David Hume: Common Sense Moralist*. Princeton, NJ: Princeton University Press, 1982.
Oakeshott, Michael. *Rationalism in Politics and Other Essays*. Indianapolis: Liberty, 1991.
Orr, James. *David Hume and His Influence on Philosophy and Theology*. World Epoch Makers. Edinburgh: T & T Clark, 1903.
Ortega, Jose, y Gasset. *The Revolt of the Masses*. New York: W. W. Norton, 1932.
Orwell, George. *Nineteen Eighty-Four*. London: Penguin, 1949.
O'Sullivan, Noël. *Conservatism*. Modern Ideologies. London: Dent & Sons, 1976.
Phillipson, Nicholas T. *Hume*. New York: St. Martin, 1989.
Plamenatz, John. *The English Utilitarians*. Oxford: Basil Blackwell, 1966.
Plantinga, Alvin and Nicholas Wolterstorff, eds. *Faith and Rationality: Reason and Belief in God*. Notre Dame, IN: University of Notre Dame Press, 1983.
Price, H. H. *Hume's Theory of the External World*. Oxford: Clarendon, 1940.
Putnam, Robert D. *Bowling Alone: The Collapse and Revival of American Community*. New York: Simon & Schuster, 2000.
Quinton, Anthony. *The Politics of Imperfection: The Religious and Secular Traditions of Conservative Thought in England from Hooker to Oakeshott*. London: Faber & Faber, 1978.
Randall, Willard Sterne. *Thomas Jefferson: A Life*. New York: Henry Holt, 1993.
Riley, Naomi Schaefer. *God on the Quad: How Religious Colleges and the Missionary Generation are Changing America*. New York: St. Martin, 2005.
Robertson, John. "A Changed Britain." Review of *Opinion and Reform in Hume's Political Philosophy*, by John B. Stewart. *Times Literary Supplement*, 11 Dec. 1992.
Ross, Ian Simpson. *The Life of Adam Smith*. Oxford: Oxford University Press, 2010.
Rossiter, Clinton. *The Political Thought of the American Revolution*. New York: Harcourt, Brace & World, 1963.
Rotwein, Eugene. *David Hume: Writings on Economics*. Madison: University of Wisconsin Press, 1970.
Rousseau, Jean-Jacques. *Of the Social Contract*. Translated by Charles M. Sherover. New York: Harper & Row, 1984.
Rushdoony, Rousas John. *The One and the Many: Studies in the Philosophy of Order and Ultimacy*. Fairfax, VA: Thoburn, 1978.
Rutherford, Samuel. *Lex, Rex, or the Law and the Prince, a Dispute for the Just Prerogative of King and People*. Harrisburg, PA: Sprinkle, 1982.
Sabine, George H. *A History of Political Theory*. New York: Henry Holt, 1937.
Schaeffer, Francis A. *The Great Evangelical Disaster*. Westchester, IL: Crossway, 1984.
Schama, Simon. *Citizens: A Chronicle of the French Revolution*. New York: Knopf, 1989.
Schlesinger, Arthur M., Jr. *The Disuniting of America: Reflections on a Multicultural Society*. New York: W.W. Norton, 1992.
Schlossberg, Herbert. *Idols for Destruction: Christian Faith and Its Confrontation with American Society*. Nashville: Thomas Nelson, 1983.

Schweitzer, Albert. *The Philosophy of Civilization*. Translated by C. T. Campion. New York: Macmillan, 1960.
Scotchie, Joseph. *The Paleoconservatives: New Voices of the Old Right*. New Brunswick, NJ: Transaction, 1999.
Shearer, Edna Aston. *Hume's Place in Ethics*. Bryn Mawr, PA: Bryn Mawr College Monographs, 1915.
Siebert, Donald T. *The Moral Animus of David Hume*. Newark, DE: University of Delaware Press, 1990.
Skinner, Andrew. "Hume's Principles of Political Economy." *The Cambridge Companion to Hume*. Edited by David Fate Norton and Jacqueline Taylor, 381–413. 2nd ed. Cambridge: Cambridge University Press, 2009.
Smart, J. J. C. "Utilitarianism." In *The Encyclopedia of Philosophy*, edited by Paul Edwards, 8:206–212. New York: Macmillan, 1967.
Smith, Adam. *An Inquiry into the Nature and Causes of the Wealth of Nations*. Vol. 39 of *Great Books of the Western World*. Chicago: Encyclopedia Britannica, 1952.
———. *Essays on Philosophic Subjects*, with a prefix on his life written by Dugald Stewart in 1793. The book is published by Andesite Press with no date and place
Smith, Norman Kemp. *The Philosophy of David Hume*. London: Macmillan, 1960.
Stewart, Dugald. "Account of the Life and Writings of Adam Smith." In *Essays on Philosophic Subjects*, by Adam Smith, ix–lxxxiv. Edinburgh: Cadell/Davies, 1795.
Stewart, John B. *The Moral and Political Philosophy of David Hume*. New York: Columbia University Press, 1963.
Stockton, Constant Noble. "Economics and the Mechanism of Historical Progress in Hume's *History*." In *Hume: A Re-Evaluation*, edited by Donald W. Livingston and James T. King, 296–320. New York: Fordham University Press, 1976.
Stohlman, Martha Lou Lemmon. *John Witherspoon: Parson, Politician, Patriot*. Philadelphia: Westminster, 1976.
Stott, John. *The Letters of John*. Tyndale New Testament Commentaries 19. Downers Grove, IL: IVP Academic, 1988.
Stumpf, Samuel Enoch. *Socrates to Sartre: A History of Philosophy*. New York: McGraw Hill, 1982.
Swinburne, Robert G. "The Argument from Design." *Philosophy* 43, no. 165 (1968) 199–212.
Sykes, Charles J. *A Nation of Victims: The Decay of the American Character*. New York: St. Martin, 1992.
Szulc, Tad. "The Greatest Danger We Face." *Parade* (July 25, 1993) 4–7.
Taylor, Charles. *A Secular Age*. Cambridge, MA: Harvard University Press, 2007.
Thielicke, Helmut. *Nihilism: Its Origin and Nature, with a Christian Answer*. London: Routledge & Kegan Paul, 1962.
Tillich, Paul. *A History of Christian Thought*. New York: Simon & Schuster, 1968.
Tocqueville, Alexis de. *Democracy in America*. Translated by Henry Reeve. 2 vols. New York: Bantam Classic, 2004.
Tsanoff, Radoslav A. *The Great Philosophers*. New York: Harper & Brothers, 1953.
Urmson, J. O. "John Langshaw Austin." In *The Encyclopedia of Philosophy*, edited by Paul Edwards, 1:212–213. New York: Macmillan, 1967.
Van Doren, Carl. *Benjamin Franklin*. New York: Garden City, 1941.
Viguerie, Richard. *The New Right: We're Ready to Lead*. Falls Church, VA: Viguerie, 1981.

Walton, Craig. "Hume and Jefferson on the Uses of History." In *Hume: A Re-Evaluation*, edited by Donald W. Livingston and James T. King, 389–403. New York: Fordham University Press, 1976.

Weaver, Richard M. *The Ethics of Rhetoric*. Davis, CA: Hermagoras, 1985.

Wells, David F. *God in the Wasteland: The Reality of Truth in a World of Fading Dreams*. Grand Rapids: Eerdmans, 1994.

Whelan, Frederick G. *Order and Artifice in Hume's Political Philosophy*. Princeton, NJ: Princeton University Press, 1985.

Will, George F. *The Conservative Sensibility*. New York: Hachette, 2019.

———. *Statecraft as Soulcraft: What Government Does*. New York: Simon & Schuster, 1983.

Wills, Garry. *Explaining America: The Federalists*. New York: Penguin, 1982.

Wilson, James Q. *The Moral Sense*. New York: Free Press, 1993.

Windelband, Wilhelm. *Renaissance, Englightenment, Modern*. Vol. 2 of *A History of Philosophy*. New York: Harper & Brothers, 1901.

Witherspoon, John. *Early American Philosophers. Lectures on Moral Philosophy*. Edited by Varnum Lansing Collins. London: Forgotten, 2012.

Witonski, Peter. *The Wisdom of Conservatism*. 4 vols. Mars Hill, NC: Institute for Western Values, 1971.

Wittgenstein, Ludwig. *Philosophical Investigations*. Translated by G. E. M. Anscombe. New York: Macmillan, 1968.

Wolin, Sheldon. "Hume and Conservatism." In *Hume: A Re-Evaluation,* edited by Donald W. Livingston and James T. King, 239–56. New York: Fordham University Press, 1976.

Womersley, David, ed. *Liberty and American Experience in the Eighteenth Century*. Indianapolis: Liberty Fund, 2006.

Wootton, David. "Liberty, Metaphor, and Mechanism: Checks and Balances and the Origins of Modern Constitutionalism." In *Liberty and American Experience in the Eighteenth Century,* edited by David Womersley, 209–75. Indianapolis: Liberty Fund, 2006.

Index of Scripture

OLD TESTAMENT

Genesis

1	36n88, 71n37, 72n42, 78n77, 118n143
1:26f	35n86, 65n5
1:27	34n77
1:28	123n170
3	87n119
8:22	75n59
9	40
18:16–33	50n57
41:46–49	71n35
47:26	xivn14

Exodus

18	71n35, 141n57
20:5–6	73n50
20:15, 17	88n129
20:17	88n129

Numbers

32:23	73n50

Deuteronomy

19:14	88n129
29:29	76n67
30:19	73n50

1 Samuel

8	117n139, 161n133
8:10–18	17n3
13:11–14	31n63
20:18ff	73n51

2 Kings

6:15–17	68n23

Esther

	xvin25
8:8ff	xivn14

Job

8:8–10	64n2
13:6	57n92
24:19	75n59
28:20–21	76n67
37:16	29n54
38	50n56

Psalms

14	159n124
18:3–4	64n2
19:1	78n77
94:20	xivn14
147:5	29n54

Proverbs

1	73n50
2	73n50
8	73n50
14:23	109n99
16:18	118n145
16:26	88n130
19:15	109n99
26:12	94n14
29:	73n50

Ecclesiastes

1:4–5	75n59
1:9	64n2
3:11	35n86, 65n5
5:5	46n31
8:11–12	73n50

Isaiah

1:18	57n92
40:12–31	50n56
45:1	41n113
48:13	78n77
55:8	30n56
55:8–9	76n67

Jeremiah

	xvin25
6:16	113n113
17:8	75n59
18:15	98n36
25:5–6	83n105
29:4–9	50n57
29:7	31
33:17–21	75n58
33:25	75n59

Ezekiel

22:30	50n57

Daniel

6:3–4	71n35
6:8	xivn14
6:12	xivn14
6:15	xivn14

Amos

6:3–7	73n50

NEW TESTAMENT

Matthew

	32
7:24–27	73n49
12:34	90n141
15:18	90n141
15:19	44n21
16:13	36n93
19:1–11	32n65
25	17n4
25:14–30	46n29

Luke

5:37–39	73n51
8:15	35n83, 68n21
9:22–24	75n64
24:39, 48	119n148
24:48	119n148
24:49	73n51

John

1:3	78n77
1:34	119n148
3:11, 32	119n148
3:32	119n148
6:44	73n49
15:1–9	33n72
16:2–3	75n59
18:39	68n23
20:24–25	44n19
20:29	62n117

# INDEX OF SCRIPTURE

Acts

1:8	119n148
2:44–45	88n128
4:32–35	88n128
7:10	144n67
7:55–56	68n23
10:9–16	68n23
16:37	xivn14
17:2	57n92
17:22–34	159n124
18:4	57n92
18:19	57n92
19:39	xivn14
22:25ff	xivn14
25:11ff	xivn14
28:17	50n53

Romans

1	73n50, 81n96
1:18–19	35n86, 65n5
1:18–23	159n124
1:20	78n77
2	73n50
2:14–16	44n21
3:10–11	29n54
5	87n119
6	73n50
8	73n50
12:4–8	94n13
13:1–4	122n161
13:1–7	31n64, 87n120
15:4	64n2

1 Corinthians

2	66n13
5	122n162
8:2	45
8:7	68n23
10:6	34n74, 35n83
11:1–2	46n33
11:2	35n83, 68n21
11:2, 23	50n53
11:7	65n5
11:16	68n23
11:23	50n53
12:12–27	94n13
13:12	29n54, 45, 62n117
15:1–11	50n53
15:2	35n83, 68n21

2 Corinthians

4:18	62n117
5:7	62n117
10:12	94n14

Galatians

3:26–29	122n165
4:4	30n59
6:7–8	73n50

Philippians

3:12	45
3:14	30n61

Colossians

2:8	30n62, 66n13

2 Thessalonians

2:5	50n53
2:15	30n58, 34n75, 35n83, 46n28, 129n4
3:6	34n75, 35n83, 47n36, 50n53
3:10	109n99

1 Timothy

1:4	62n119
2:1–3	32
2:1–4	50n57
3:7	36n93
4:7	62n119
4:12	34n74, 35n83
5:8	109n99
5:11–13	73n51
5:18	46n30
6:20	66n13

2 Timothy

2:23	62n119

Titus

3:1	31n64
3:9	62n119
3:9–10	48n43

Hebrews

6:15	30n59
8:3	75n61
10:25	30n57
11:2	98n36
13:7	144n67

James

3:9	35n86, 65n5
4:7	73n50

1 Peter

2:13	31

2 Peter

1:3	43n9
1:20–21	46n27

1 John

1:1	119n148
3:2	62n117
4:19–22	94n14

Index of Names

Acton, H. B., 156
Adair, Douglass, 129, 130nn8–9, 130n12, 138, 138n44, 138n45, 160
Adam, 119n150
Adams, Abigail, 106n77
Adams, John, 106, 129n3, 133–134, 133n26, 138n45
Adams, William, 54n82
Addison, Joseph, 10, 131
Agutter, William, 7
Ahlstrom, Sydney, 27n40
Akyol, Mustafa, 151n91
Allen, Diogenes, 8, 8n18
Allestree, Richard, 3
Anderson, James, xivn17
Anderson, John A., xin2
Antaeus, 126, 126n185
Aquinas, Thomas, 16, 16n1
Arnold, Matthew, 28, 28nn49–50
Arnold, Thomas, 28
Atticus, 103
Austin, J. L., 85n111
Ayer, A. J., 1n6, 12n38, 53, 53n72

Bacon, Francis, 76n65
Bahnsen, Greg, 8, 8n17, 9n22
Baillie, Robert, 55n84
Baird, James William, 77n72
Barker, William, xivn15
Bauckman, 119n148
Beattie, James, 55–56, 55n85, 56n86, 56n87, 58
Becker, Carl L., 65n4, 112, 112n111
Bedford, Gunning, 130n12

Beer, Samuel H., 135n32, 143n65
Bellah, Robert, 80n88, 146, 146n76, 150n90
Belloc, Hilaire, 16n1
Bentham, Jeremy, 116
Berger, Peter, 21, 21n14, 27n41
Berkeley, George, 76, 76n65, 114n120, 116n134, 117n134
Berkhof, Louis, 9, 9n21
Bernal, Martin, 13n43
Berry, Christopher, 160
Biden, 16
Blair, Hugh, xii, 11n33, 12n40
Blanchard, William H., 11n34
Bloom, Allan, 155n110
Bonald, Louis de, xvn21, 16, 27, 29, 29n55
Bonar, Andrew, 81n90
Bonar, Horatius, 81n90
Bonar, James, 80, 81n90, 92n4, 97, 97n33, 109, 109n99
Bongie, Laurence L., 127n187
Boorstin, Daniel J., 143
Bork, Robert, 22n19, 23n19
Boswell, James, 5–6
Boufflers, Mme de, 11n33
Breitbart, Andrew, 117, 145
Bridges, Linda, 158n120
Brown, Colin, 10, 10n29, 10n30, 24n25
Brown, Harold O. J., 23n21
Brown, John, 55, 55n84, 55n85, 56
Brownson, Orestes, 32, 32n66
Bruce, Robert, 55n84

Brunner, Emil, xvi, xvin23, 17n1, 25–26, 26n35, 33, 33n71
Buckley, William F., 32n67
Bulfinch, Thomas, 126n185
Bunyan, John, 4
Burke, Edmund, xiv, xv, xvn22, 8n14, 9, 28, 28n47, 30, 30n60, 32, 33, 51, 51n60, 52, 126, 128, 150, 152, 152nn95–96, 152nn99–100, 156, 157
Butler, Joseph, 10n31, 114n120

Cairns, John, 158n122
Calvin, John, 27
Campbell, Colin, 54n82
Campbell, George, 54n82
Canavan, Francis, 52, 52n66
Carlyle, Alexander, 55n85
Carretta, Vincent, 13n43
Carter, Stephen L., 27n42
Cato (African-American servant), 9n20
Caulfeild, James, 5n10
Cecil, Hugh, 17n1
King Charles II, 2n8
Chateaubriand, François-René de, xvn21, 16
Chernow, Ron, 131, 131n13
Chesterfield, Lord, 7
Cheyne, George, 54n78
Cicero, 25, 84n110, 103, 113, 113n114
Clarke, Samuel, 114n120
Cleanthes, 60, 113
Clephane, John, 12n38, 12n40
Colson, Charles, 22n17
Coontz, Stephanie, 154n108
Cooper, James Fenimore, 153, 153n104, 154
Copleston, Fredrick, 40n112, 116n134, 117n134
Cornell, George W., xiin5
Cox, Harvey, 19n7, 24, 24n26, 25
Crocker, John Wilson, 16
Cromwell, Oliver, 11n36
Custis, Mr., 133n26

Dallimore, Arnold, 158n121
Danford, John, 85n111, 86n111

Dante, 150n89
Darwin, Charles, 86
Dascal, Marcelo, 102n57
King David, 75n58
Davidson, Donald, 152n94
Dawson, Christopher, 16n1
De Boufflers, Comtesse, 12n38
De Ruyter, 53, 53n70
Marquis de Sade, 7n14
Dees, Richard H., 128n2
Deffand, Marquise du, 12n38
Demea, xiiin7
Descartes, 4, 34n77, 54n78, 59, 78n73, 156n114
Dickinson, John, 129, 135–136, 138, 143
Diderot, Denis, 112n111
Donne, John, 93n7
Dooyeweerd, Herman, 150n88
Douglas, John, 54n82
Durkheim, Emile, 145, 146n75

Edwards, Jonathan, 130
Eisenhower, Dwight, 29
Eliot, T. S., 17n1, 145, 145n72
Elizabeth I, 115n129
Elkins, Stanley, 131, 132n16, 136, 136n35, 137, 138n42
Elliot, Gilbert, 12n41
Ellis, Joseph, 134, 134nn27–28, 138n45, 139n45
Erskine, Ebenezer, 55n84

Falwell, Jerry, 41
Farrand, Max, 135n31, 135n33, 136, 136n37
Farwell, Byron, 52n68
Fawcett, Edmund, xiiin11, 8n20, 160
Ferguson, Adam, 131
Feuerbach, Ludwig, 53n74
Flew, Antony, 69n29, 84n109, 113n116, 116, 116n132
Frame, John M., 13, 13n45, 19, 19n7, 53n72, 72n41
Franklin, Benjamin, 129, 129n3, 132–133, 132n21
Frey, R. G., 138n44
Friedman, Milton, 9

INDEX OF NAMES 183

Friedman, Thomas, 151n91
Fukuyama, Francis, 53n74, 146–147, 147nn78–81, 159n126

Gabriel, 158n121
Gai, 126n185
Galbraith, Agnes, 54
Gasset, Ortega y, 149, 149n86
Geoffrin, Marie, 133
Gibbon, Edward, 5, 7n14, 8n16, 131
Giddens, Anthony, 24, 24n24
Gilbert, Alan, xiii, xiiin8
Gillespie, George, 55n84
Gladstone, William, 7n14
Glendon, Mary Ann, 149n87
Gottfried, Paul, 41, 41n115
Gould, Stephen Jay, 23
Grant, Ulysses S., 5
Green, Ashbel, 132
Green, T. H., 72n40
Green, Thomas Hill, 1n3
Grenz, Stanley J., 14n47
Griffin, David Ray, 22n18, 23, 23n23
Grose, T. H., 72n40
Gruengard, Ora, 102n57
Guinness, Os, 22n17
Gutiérrez, Gustavo, 19n7
Gutjahr, Paul, 8n20

Haakonssen, Knud, 3n9, 39, 39n107, 94, 94n17
Hallie, Philip P., 60n104
Hamilton, Alexander, 129, 129n3, 136–138, 136n37, 137n39, 142n60, 143, 144, 144n71, 154
Hamilton, William, 1n6
Hamowy, Ronald, 131n15
Hare, R. M., 84, 84n109, 84n110
Haring, Bernard, 27n41
Harrigan, Anthony, 136n33
Harris, James A., 1n1, 6n11, 8n16, xivn13
Harrison, Jonathan, 87n123
Hawking, Stephen, xiiin10
Hayek, F. A., 86n112, 160, 160n129
Heimbeck, Raeburne, 74n52
Helvetius, 12n40
Henderson, Alexander, 55n84

Henrie, Mark, 146, 146n77, 148n84, 151, 151n92
Henrietta (slave), 8n20
Henry, Carl F. H., 14n47, 21, 22n17
Henry, Patrick, 132
Henry VII, 107
Heraclius, 97n35
Herberg, Will, 29, 29n52
Hercules, 127n185
Herder, Johann, 112n111
Herzog, Don, 102, 102n57
Himmelfarb, Gertrude, xin3, xii, xiin4, 20n12, 34n76
Hirsi, Ayaan, 151n91
Hitchcock, James, 20, 21n13
Hobbes, Thomas, 20, 89, 122, 123n176, 124n176
Hodge, Charles, xiiin11, 8, 8n20, 9n20, 132
Hoffecker, Andrew, xivn17, 20n10
Hogg, Quinton, 160
Hollander, Paul, 152n98, 152n101, 153n101
Home, Alexander, 2
Home, George, 3
Home, Henry, 10n31
Home, Joseph, 2
Home, Katherine, 2
Homer, 96
Hooker, Richard, 28, 28n46
Horne, George, 6, 6n12
Howe, John R., Jr., 133n26
Hughes, Philip, 14n47
Hume, David (nephew of Hume), 9
Hunter, James Davison, 14n47, 29, 155
Hurd, Richard, 54n82
Hutcheson, Francis, 3, 7, 18n5, 25, 25n28, 27n43, 83
Hutchins, Robert Maynard, 137nn40–41, 139n48, 140n50, 140n52, 141n54, 141nn56–57, 142n58, 144nn68–69

Immerwahr, John, 56n87

James, 54n78
James II, 2n8

INDEX OF NAMES

Jefferson, Thomas, 129n3, 132, 133n26, 134, 154
Jeremiah, 31
Jesus Christ, 20, 22, 32, 45, 129
John (African-American servant), 9n20
Johnson, Samuel, 5, 7, 153
Johnson, William Stacy, 22, 22n18
Jones, Peter, 22n17
Jude, xi

Kant, Immanuel, 8, 8n15, 68, 69, 69n26
King, James T., 1n6, 130n12
Kirk, Russell, 9, 9n24, 29n53, 130, 130n12, 133n26, 148n83, 153n104, 154, 154n106, 157–158, 157nn119–120
Knox, John, xi, xin3, 55n84
Koch, Adrienne, 129n3
Kojeve, Alexandre, 147
Kristol, Irving, 9n23

Langrishe, Hercules, 126
Laski, Harold J., 116, 116n133, 116n134, 120, 120n154, 156, 156n113
Lavine, Thelma Z., 9, 9n26
Lee, Arthur, 132
Leibnitz, 156n114
Leland, John, 54n82
Lena (slave), 8n20
Lewis, C. S., 19
Livingston, Donald W., 1n6, 47, 47n41, 51, 51n59, 58n95, 58n96, 72n43, 98n40, 130n12, 156, 156nn115–116, 157, 160
Locke, John, 49n50, 68, 76n67, 122, 124, 124n176, 124n177, 125n177, 127n186, 128, 131, 146n76, 147
Lorenz, Konrad, 62n115
King Louis XVI, 7n14
Lucas, F. L., 115, 115n125
Luther, Martin, 27
Lycurgus, 144

Macaulay, 7, 131

Mach, 1n6
Machen, J. Gresham, 132
Macky, John, 2
Macpherson, C. B., 126n179
Madison, James, 6n11, 103, 129, 129n3, 131, 136, 138–146, 138n44, 138n45, 139n45, 139n46, 141n57, 143n65, 144n71
Mahan, A. T., 53n70
Maistre, Joseph de, xvi, 27, 27n44, 28n45, 30
Maritain, Jacques, 16n1
Marshall, Geoffrey, 159, 160n127
Mason, Thomson, 132
Matthew, H. C. G., 7n14, 8n14
McAuliffe, Joseph R., 23n22
McCullough, David, 134n29
McDonald, Forrest, 130n12, 144, 144n70
McKitrick, Eric, 132n16, 136, 136n35, 137, 138n42
Meacham, Jon, 29, 29n51
Melville, Andrew, 55n84
Mill, John Stuart, 116
Miller, Andrew, 11n36
Miller, David, 33n70, 88n124, 160, 160n128
Miller, Eugene F., 9n27, 56n88
Mohler, Albert, 154
Montaigne, Michel de, 53n72
Montesquieu, 139n45
Moses, 32, 141n57
Mossner, Ernest Campbell, xin1, 1nn1–2, 1n5, 6n11, 10n31, 10n32, 11n33, 12n38, 26, 26n39, 53, 53n73, 54, 54nn75–76, 55, 55n82, 55n85, 111n106
Muller, Jerry Z., xvn20, 28, 28nn47–48, 30n57, 160
Murdock, George Peter, 154, 154n107, 155, 155n109
Mure, William, 25n28, 128n1
Murray, Charles, 142, 142n61

Nash, Ronald, 9, 9n25
Neuhaus, Richard John, 19n8, 22n17
Newton, Isaac, 44–45, 44n22, 76n67, 98

INDEX OF NAMES 185

Nicholas, Robert Carter, 132
Nisbet, Robert, 126n180, 145, 145n74, 146, 147, 148, 148n82, 153, 153n103
Noll, Mark, 21, 21n14
Norton, David, 59, 59n98, 60n104

Oakeshott, Michael, 52, 52n69, 111n108, 160
Obama, 16
Olson, Roger E., 14n47
Orde, Nancy, 12n38
Orr, James, xv, xvn19, 7, 7n14, 8n16
Orwell, George, 48n45
O'Sullivan, Noel, 157n120, 158, 158n120, 158n123, 160
Oswald, 56n86

Paine, Thomas, 135, 152
Paley, William, 56n86
Pamphilus, 81n91
Pascal, Blaise, 50
Paul, 32, 78
Phillipson, Nicholas, 105n73
Philo, xiiin7, 60
Pitt, William, 5, 14n46
Plamenatz, John, 80, 80n89, 116n133
Plantinga, Alvin, 56n86
Plutarch, 25
Pope, Alexander, 56
Poseidon, 126n185
Price, Richard, 54n82, 152, 152n97
Priestley, Joseph, 56n86, 112n111
Putnam, Robert, 18, 18n6

Quinton, Anthony, 160

Ramsay, Michael, 54n79
Ramsey, Andrew Michael, 53
Randall, John, Jr., 58n96
Randall, Thomas, 132
Randall, Willard Sterne, 132nn19–20, 133, 133n25, 154n105
Randolph, John, 132
Ransom, John Crowe, 152n94
Reid, Thomas, xiin6, xivn15, 56n86, 72n41
Retz, Cardinal de, 103

Richard III, 115
Ridpath, George, 54n82
Riley, Naomi Schaeffer, 14n47, 29
Robertson, John, 160n130
Robertson, Pat, 41
Robespierre, Maximilien, 112n111
Robinson, James D., xiin5
Rorty, Richard, 23n23
Ross, Ian Simpson, 10n28
Rossiter, Clinton, 138, 138n43
Rotwein, Eugene, 108n95
Rousseau, Jean Jacques, 11, 11n34, 51, 51n61, 54n78, 89, 109n97, 122, 129n3, 147, 152, 160n131
Rumi, Raza, 151n91
Rutherford, Samuel, xi, 50n57, 54n82, 55n84

Sabine, George H., 57, 57n90, 113n115, 125, 125n178, 126, 157, 157n118, 162, 162n1
Samuel, 17
Schaeffer, Francis, 19, 19n8, 20, 20n9
Schama, Simon, 7n14
Schlesinger, Arthur M., Jr., 142n62
Schlossberg, Herbert, 14n47
Schweitzer, Albert, 116n133
Scott, William Robert, xiin6
Seneca, 25, 40n112, 131
Sextus, 60n104
Shakespeare, 67, 67n17
Shakspere, 12n41
Sherman, Roger, 129, 135, 135n31, 143
Siebert, Donald T., 62n120
Skelton, Philip, 54n82
Skill, Thomas, xiin5
Skinner, Andrew, 122, 122n166
Smart, J. J. C., 116n134
Smeaton, Oliphant, xvn19
Smith, Adam, 6, xiin6, 9–10, 9n27, 27n43, 33, 105–106, 105n74, 106n75, 146n76
Smith, Norman Kemp, 25, 25n31, 54n78, 58, 59n99, 70, 70n33
Socrates, 103, 114
Spafford, Horatio Gates, 134, 154
Spence, Joseph, 12n41

Spinoza, 156n114
Steele, Richard, 10
Stewart, Dugald, 106, 106n76
Stewart, J., 39n105, 100n48
Stockton, Constant Noble, 96, 96n25, 108n95, 160
Stott, John, 119, 119n149
Stove, D. C., 58n95
Strahan, William, 9n27, 14n46, 56n86, 105n74, 133
Sykes, Charles J., 142n62
Szulc, Tad, 143n63

Taylor, Charles, 14, 14n47, 24, 24n27, 25
Taylor, John, 133, 133n26
Tennyson, Alfred, 52, 52n68
Terra, 126n185
Tevye, 51
Thielicke, Helmut, 21n15
Thucydides, 32n67
Tillich, Paul, 8, 8n19
Tocqueville, Alexis de, 80n88, 146n76, 146n77, 153n102
Tribe, Laurence, 22, 23n19
Trump, 16
Turgot, Anne-Robert Jacques, 95

Urmson, J. O., 85n111

Van Doren, Carl, 133nn22–24
Van Til, Cornelius, 9, 9n22
Viguerie, Richard, 41n114
Virgil, 150n89
Voltaire, 12n40, 129n3, 131

Wales, Mr., 133n26

Walpole, Robert, 11, 133
Walton, Craig, 129n6
Warburton, William, 54n82, 55, 55n85, 56
Warren, Robert Penn, 152n94
Washington, George, 129, 131, 133n26, 135
Watts, Isaac, 10, 10n32
Weaver, Richard M., 85n111, 86n111, 112n109
Wells, David, 14n47, 19, 19n7
Wesley, John, 7, 10n31
Whelan, Frederick G., 58n97, 118, 118n146, 160, 161n132
Whitefield, George, 158n121
Will, George, xvin29, 1n7, 17, 17n2, 30, 79, 79n80, 145n73, 159, 159n125
Williams, Francis, 13n43
Wills, Garry, xiii, xiiin9, 55n85, 131n14, 136n38
Wilson, James Q., 27n43, 84n111, 85n111, 129, 135, 136, 160
Wishart, George, 55n84, 77n72
Wishart, William, 77, 77n72
Witherspoon, John, 55, 55n85, 56, 131–132, 131n14, 132nn17–18
Witonski, Peter, 32n67
Wittgenstein, Ludwig, 1n6
Wolin, Sheldon, 160
Wolterstorff, Nicholas, 56n86
Womersley, David, 138n44, 141n57
Wood, Gordon, 141n57
Wootton, David, 95n23

Young, Stark, 152n94

www.ingramcontent.com/pod-product-compliance
Lightning Source LLC
Chambersburg PA
CBHW062038220426
43662CB00010B/1548